Edward Cookson

The Registers of St. Nicholas, Ipswich, Co. Suffolk

Baptisms, 1539-1709. Burials, 1551-1710. Marriages, 1539-1710

Edward Cookson

The Registers of St. Nicholas, Ipswich, Co. Suffolk
Baptisms, 1539-1709. Burials, 1551-1710. Marriages, 1539-1710

ISBN/EAN: 9783744779074

Printed in Europe, USA, Canada, Australia, Japan

Cover: Foto ©ninafisch / pixelio.de

More available books at **www.hansebooks.com**

The Registers

OF

t. Nicholas, Ipswich,

CO. SUFFOLK.

Issued By
THE PARISH REGISTER SOCIETY.
(VII.)

The Registers

OF

St. Nicholas, Ipswich,

CO. SUFFOLK.

BAPTISMS	1539—1709.
BURIALS	1551—1710.
MARRIAGES ·	1539—1710.

TRANSCRIBED BY

REV. EDWARD COOKSON, M.A.,

BY THE PERMISSION OF THE VICAR, THE REV. S. GREEN.

CONTENTS.

LONDON :
PRIVATELY PRINTED FOR THE PARISH REGISTER SOCIETY,
1897.

PREFACE.

The Register Books of the Parish of St. Nicholas, Ipswich, are, from their commencement in 1539 to 1812, four in number.

Volume I. contains entries of Marriages from 1539 to 1710, Baptisms from 1539 to 1709, and Burials from 1551 to 1710. It measures $16\frac{3}{4}$ inches long by $6\frac{3}{4}$ inches wide and is of parchment, and at the commencement has the following memorandum,

"This Register book was bought and provided by "Henry Piper and Edward Langley, churchwardens, in "Anno Dni. 1607, for Mariages, Christenings and Burials." It was bought in accordance with the 70th Canon of Convocation of the first year of King James I, wherein it is stated, amongst other particulars relating to Parish Registers and their preservation, that "in every parish church . . . shall be provided one parchment book . . . wherein shall be written the day and year of every christening wedding and burial . . . since the time that the law was first made . . . so far as the ancient books thereof can be procured, but especially since the beginning of the reign of the late Queen." [Elizabeth].

This first book of the Parish Registers forms the present volume, and it is hoped that the succeeding books will make their appearance in similar form.

The following are the particulars of the other registers of the parish previous to 1813 :—

Volume II. is of parchment and measures 13¾ inches by 9½ inches, and contains 23 leaves, with entries of Baptisms, Burials and Marriages from 1710 to 1731.

Volume III. is also of parchment, and measures 15¼ inches by 9½ inches, and contains 43 leaves, with entries of Baptisms from 1732 to 1793, Burials from 1732 to 1792, and Marriages from 1732 to 1754.

Volume IV. is of parchment, and measures 13 inches by 9 inches. It has 27 leaves, and contains entries of Baptisms and Burials only, from 1793 to 1812.

Copies of all the mural inscriptions within the church and those on the grave stones in the churchyard, have been printed in a very valuable monograph on the parish written by B. P. Grimsey, Esq., F.R.Hist. Soc. in 1889, in which will also be found many other interesting details relating to the church and parish of St. Nicholas.

The manuscript from which this Register was printed was verified with the original by E. P. Youell, Esq., J.P.

INCUMBENTS.

Although the Incumbent is known as the Vicar, the living may be better described as a Perpetual Curacy, being in the gift of the Parishioners, the majority determining in case of a poll.

There are no early entries of consecutive institutions to this living to be found in the Bishop's Registry, and St. Nicholas being a donative, little information is derivable even from the Visitation books as to who were the Incumbents; but the following is the most perfect list that can be formed from the above-mentioned sources and from Tanner's MS., and from entries in divers hand-writings on the last sheet in the oldest register-book belonging to the parish.

Tho: Bakuler, cap: par: - -	1555
Simon Wrenche, Curatus - -	1604
John Daye - - -	1612
Jonathan Clarke - - -	1616
Nathaniel Smart, Lic : Cur: -	1617
William Fenner, in the time of Chas. 1st	1625-59
Richard Raymond - -	1633
William Kerrington, Lic: Cur: -	1635
Alexander Reignolds . -	1637
Nathaniel Smart Jun: - -	1642
William Clarke - - -	1646
Roger Young - - -	1653
— Roberts - - -	1664
— Elsden - - -	1666
Thomas Holborough - -	1670
George Raymond - - -	1684
William Reeve - - -	1725
Robert Hudson, Ad: pr: the Parishioners	1755
James Coyte - - -	1785
Mileson Gery Edgar - -	1812
Charles Ward - -	1853
Samuel Green - -	1896

S. Nicholas in Ipswich. { This Register booke was bought & pvided by henry Piper and Edwarde Langley Churche Wardens in Anno Dñii 1607 for Mariages Christenings & burials.

i. Ōf mariages begynynge Ano 1539.

26 May.	Willm Whetkroft to Anna harvye.
21 Juli.	Thoms Calis to Agnes Dowe.
7 Octo.	Rbt Brand to Mget Tompson.
	henry Whitinge to Alice Watson.

1540.

24 Ja.	Willm Bullock to katheryn Swaine.
ii Ap.	Thoms Lambert to Elizabeth h . yward.[1]
2 May.	henry Jenkinson to Marget Parson.
3 May.	John ffare to Rose ffenne.

1541.

6 Octo.	Robte Parrarde to Vrsula Tokelouc.
2 Nov.	Thoms Roper to Marget Vukell.
3 Octo.	Oliver Bunce to Agnes Sowden.
	Rbt hardegue to Beatrixe Wetherbye.

1542.[2]

John Oliver to Alice Man.
John Eton to Marian Johnson.
Willm Andrew to Alice Olyver.
John Johnson to Joan Lawrence.

1543.

Richard Sergeant to Agnes Palline.
Thoms Newton to Anna River.
Richard Johnson to Elinor Giller.
Gilberd Whight to Mget Albright.
John Elis to Agnes fferier.
Willm fforward to Agnes Culpho.

1544.

John Sutton to Alice Allen.
Thoms hampton to Agnes Symond.
John harward to Christian Stone.
John Barnis to Margerye Bardwell.
Richard harkworthe to Agnes Calis.
Ingilbert home to Elizabeth Pasman.

---

[1] Letter gone.
[2] From this year to 1576 inclusive the month and date are, with four exceptions, not given.

B

1545.

henrye Jenkinson to Joan Jepton.
Robte Allye to Amy Stott.
Willm horsbye to Emme Cole.
John Duyne to katheryn Bovrne.
James herst to An Raynborrowe.
John Skyte to Margett Jeffers(?).
Willm Tailkott to Emme Porter.
George hill to Alis Madden.

1546.

John harvie to Alis Luttriche.
John hewetson to Alice Marett.
Thoms. Bell to Elizabeth Cwffye.
John Stevenson to Elizabeth hemsvn.
John [*blank*] to Katheryn Maye.
John hewes to Elizabeth.

Arm frost.

Page 2. Marigges.

Richard Richmond to Agnes ffynkell.
Willm hillary to Annis Allen.
henry Thornton to Elzabeth Balderston.
Willm Watson to Margett Rice.
henry Smyth to Alis Giles.
Robte Selsden to Marg^{r}et Drane,
Allexander Randolph to M^{r}garett Tarver.
Thoms Graye to Mgarett Symond.

1549.

John Onyon to [*blank*].
Adam Blomfeld to M^{r}gett Willett.
Thoms Eliett to Agnes Eires.
Walker Maret to Agnes Morgan.
Dirick Cooke to Josine Quirke.

1551.

Stephen Greenwich to Joane Rayner.
John Knighthe to Anne Tayler.

1552.

Thoms Bragg to [*blank*].
Richard Shepperd to Agnes Catchpoll.
Robte ffosdick to Alis Wellock.
Robte Grains to Margett Johnson.
Thoms holland to Elzabeth Dawndy.
Robt Molson to xpian Wynniff.

1553.

Gawyn Metford to M^{r}garett Cooke.
Robte Dayines to Alis Yonge.
George Cranyn to Margett Tranyie.

John hilder to Katheryn Bullock.
Richard Barker to Alis Gaskine.

Page 3.   1554.

27 Mar.   Christopher Alderman to Joan Mossak.
John Lawrence to Joan Robarte.
Cutbert Mutton to Alice Legge.
Thoms Whissleroft to Joan Stot.
Thoms Rainborroughe to Elzabethe Sanders.
Steven Groce to Agnes Medowe.

1555.
John Tay to Cicelye Canon.
John Bucknam to Agnes Plastone.
Raulphe Colleyne to Katheryne man.

1556.
Peter Persone to Agnes Olive.
Edmond Whitman to Joan Wellems.
13 Sept.   Willm Jeffrey to Katherin Cage.
John River to Margarett Alleyne.

1557.
Willm Rainbye to Alis Rote.
Edward harwoode to Elzabeth Stanley.
Robte Panton Ar. to Madelene Pownse.
Richard Leader to Anne Ramkyn.
John Richemond to Adrie Gener.
John Thordon to Agnes Kempster.
Robte Goodchild to Beatrixe hargrave.

1558.
Thoms Newton to Paskin Carelton.
Phillip Dubble to Ad^rie harvie.
Richard Kinderslie to Dorothie Stooke.
Willm Smith to Elzabeth Baltharsa.
Edmond Bird to Lettis Granger.

1559.
Willm haile to Jane Cage.
Garrard Johnson to Katherine Osborne.
Willm Laye to Katheryn Kitchine.

1560.
Willm Bloise to Alice Nottingham.
Richard Kinderslie to Joan Vale.
Willm Buckenham to Dorothie Pittechar.
John Warren to [*blank*].
Robte Dammeron to Cicelie Elliott.
Willm Todd to Joan fatte.
John hamond to Agnes Reynald.
Thoms hallybread to Alis Bedome.
John Crvnford to Joan Cocke.

Willm̃ Kyllingworth to Joan hawstede.
Thoms harrys to Mawde Richardson.

1561.

Xp̈ifer Rowton to Margarett Roper.
Angell Bonc to Margarett Wellems.
George ffen to Mary Palgrave.
Robte ffosdele to Margett Woode.
Reynald Dowell to Thomasin Gilion.
John Cañon to Elizabeth Osborne.

1562.

Wiłłm harell to An Palmer.
John Johnson to Christian Wood.
George Millen to Joan Adrians.
Allen Clack to Margery hiller.
Willm̃ Alderman to Katherin Nodan.
John Johnson to Anne Waple.

Mariages.

Page 4.   1563.

Willm̃ Sparling to Joan Yonge.
Richard Gullmye to Annes Redlaye.
James Demmock to Alis Estoll.
Richard Gage to Katherin Cage.

1565 (sic).

Rauff Ward to Isabel Michelson.
Cornelis Gilbert to [*blank*] hutwick.
Thoms Stalworthe to Margett hinds.
John Hilton to Elzabeth Berners.
John Camper to Katherin Johnson.
Peter ffokes to Elzabeth Curre.
Thoms Smith to Mary Wetherbye.

1566.

John Belman to Joan Turner.
Thomas Moresull to Elzabeth Johnson.
John Ryvers to Amys Churche
Thoms Thomson to Margett Grenelefe.

1567.

John Remyngale to Katheryne Meashe.
Robte Coleman to Agnes Rayner.

1568.

15 May   Thoms Knappe to Elzabeth Wood.
16 May   John Topliff to Margery Cage.
Robte Brigges to Anne Wourte.
David Goodyere to Joan Sweare.
Edward Tymperlak to Mercce Enfeld.

Robte henson to Elinor Seauell.
Thoms Trenchfeld to Margrett Collinson.
John hewitt to Jone Stannard.

1569.

John Johnson to Elzabeth Petterson.
Leonard Curbie to Alis Game.
John Dammeron to Mawde Dorne.

1570.

Richard harison to Joan Ricards.
Edmond Tayler to Joan Rolfe.
Walter Estoll to Jone Batham.
Willm̃ Archer to Anne Batham.
Thoms hayllybred to Jone Downse.
Richard Ward to Elzabeth Johnson.
Thoñs hockett to Agnes Olbee.
Thoñis Glascock to Mary Porter.
Samuel Estall to Anne Wilkenson.
George Kempe to helen ..

Page 5.   1572.

Jeffrey [*blank*] to Agnes Ward.
Will Jawender to Katherin husne.
Mathew Brand to Rebecka Vberson.
Francis hamelton to Mathee Mossuk.

1573.

Willm̃ Sparrowe to Marget Brovnrig.
Richard Whittle to Martha Berte.
Thoms Cole to Alis Chamber.
John Watson to Margett Sever.
Willm̃ Aggas to Alis Lambert.
Richard Bate to Alis Liste.
Robte Scarlott to Margaret Gage.
Steven Grenewich to Eme Goodeare.
John Moore to Joan Lawrence.
John Ireland to Katherin Johnson.
Edward Lord to Agnes hill.   1574

1574.

John Baker to Sibill Armig^r.
henry Curtes to Joan hart.
Robte Reynald to Jone Somẽr.

1575.

Willm̃ Gleed to Margett Richardson.
Richard Wryght to Cicilie Iue.

1576.

Robte James to Dorethye Redley.
John Vuckle to Elzabeth Sprute.
henry Cage to M^rgaret Page.

Thoms hitchbone to Jone Lyndsele.
Robt Walker to Jone Smyth.

[*No marriage registrations* 1577—1592].

Page 6.   1593.

18 Apr.   Nicholas Crashfeld to Alice Ashley.
             George Whisle to Alice [*blank*].
i Maij   John Grenwiche to Margery [*blank*].
7 Aug.   John Copping to Thomazin Pomisway.

1595.

March 22.   Abraham Grenewiche and Mary [*blank*] his wife.
             Richard Evered and Jone [*blank*] his wife.
22 Mai.   Abraham Osmond to Margarett Trenchfeld.   1598
25 Mai.   John Merrell to Margett pope.
29 June.   Rauff More to Annys Direct.
30 octo.   John Jennynge to Jone Wiseman.
28 Dec.   Daniell Cole to Marion Barnes.
30 Janu.   Willm Aldrich to Anne Beomond.
4 feb.   Rbte hill to Margett Goodaye.

Page 7.   1599.

13 Mai.   Richard Swayne to Edee Quarree.
20 Aug.   John Wilkenson to Dorothie Buckstone.
28 No.   Elias Kempe to Susan Silverside.
4 Sep.   Charles Wines to Prudence Beacon.
22 octo.   John Cooke to Widdowe Sutton.
28 octo.   John Bateman to Alice Wake.
29 octo.   Willm ffeer to Elizabeth Temple.
27 Nov.   henrie Keble to Philip [*sic*] Daines.

1600.

             Willm Deane to Anne Estoll.
             James Phillipson to Elizabeth bower.
27 octo.   Thoms Wainwritt to Anne More.
19 nove.   Robt Snelling to Mary Cutler.
21 Ja.   Thoms Okely to ffrancis Pennigton.

1601.

23 Apr.   Robte hadnham to Abigail Bigges.
17 Feb.   Edward Lewger to Elzabeth hill.
26 Apr.   Richard Ball to Elizabeth Miles.   1602
18 Juli.   Edmund Boule to Katherine Coldune.

1602.

26 Juli.   Peter Bret to Thomasine Estoll.
21 Sept.   John Crane to Katherin Bexter.
7 Decē.   Rauff Salter to Elzabeth Bell.
13 febr.   John Courtall to Thomazin Evered.

1603.

24 Juli.   Umphrey Willie to Elzabeth hill.
8 Sept.   Thomas Salter to Mary Drane.

20 Novē.	Moyses Cleveland to Marget Ticklie.
22 Decē.	Nicholas Watters to x͞pian Petto.
5 feb.	Robte Channon to Alice Paice.
16 Aprl.	James Bowerhowse to Anne Watson. 1604

1604.

28 Apr.	John harvest to Joan Jue.
21 octo.	Thoms Sherrude to Alice Gillit.
3 Nov.	Andrew Tegell to Jone Bret.
10 Decē.	Willm hebden to Mary Gislingham.
7 Mar.	John Johnson to Susan Cage.
29 July	[*blank*] Parkin to Christian Marke.

1605.

14 Apr.	John Lee to Joane Sherwood
20 May.	John Sommers to Alis Channon.
21 July.	Thomas Marritt to Elzabeth Johnson.

[*Entry here erased and illegible*].
Richard Everid to Jone his wife.

1606 [*nil*].
1607 [*nil*].

Page 8.   1608.

Aug. 3.	Edward Cheape to [*blank*] Salmon.
Novem. 19.	John Deale to An piper.
Dece. 21.	John Topliffe to Prudence Johnson.
Dece. 27.	Willm Seersent to Elzabeth Wathwhet.
Aug. 9.	frances Pomfret to Mercy Wright.

Page 9.

Mariages.

St. Nccolas parish in Ipswich.
1609, 1610, 1611, 1612, 1613, 1614, 1615.

february 27.	Michaell Ward to Grissell Scott.
	George Rook to Bridgett hart.
	John Tiler to Anne Bat.
July 30.	henry Wild to Alice Bailie.

1610.

Januar. 14.	John Cooper to Susan Wathwhett.

1611.

May 20.	Richard Edwards to Joane Cleark.
Apri. 7.	Martyn hutchinson to Elzabeth Sted.
Aug. 24.	Robte ffuller to An Johnson.
Octobr 28.	Edmunde Miles to Lidda hawkins.
December ij.	George Downing to Dorcas Bloyse.

1613.

	francis Smith to [*blank*].
	henry ffyn to Elzabeth Cook.
Februarye 1.	Thomas Cowell tooke to wife Marian Daye.
17.	Robert Brightwell tooke to wife Marye White.

Anno Dñi 1614.

June 23.   John ffyrmin tooke to wife Judith Bridge.
July 21.   George Lymbert tooke to wife Elisabeth Smyth.
   24.   Robert Arminger tooke to wife Elisabeth hañiond.
August 16.   Jeremye Raymond tooke to wife Marye hebden.
October 4.   John fforde tooke to wife Brigitt Bate.

Anno Dñi 1615.

Aprill 11.   Simon Thorne tooke to wife Elizabeth Marks.
Maye 29.   George Brett tooke to wife Anne Estye.
August 1.   Simon Youngs tooke to wife Martha Alderman.
September   [*No entry.*]
Desember   Joyse Whely tooke to wife an clarke.
the 12.

Anno 1616.

October 8.   John Sickelmore tooke to wyfe Margaret Bow.
October 10.   Nicholas Smith tooke to wyfe Christian Aplebo͏r.
Octob. 29. { Abraham wathwitt tooke to wyfe Aleche Hill.
            { Robt Allen tooke to wyfe Susan Grenedge.
Decemb͏r17. { Joseph Smith tooke to wyfe Susan Cage.
            { William ffere tooke to wyfe Marie Potter.

Page 10.   1617.

Septemb. 18. M͏r John Lanie tooke to wife M͏rs Elizabeth Bryden wid.
Decemb. 7.   Richard Wade & Bridget Pickis were maried.

Añ Dni 1618 [*nil*].

Año Dni 1619.

March 30.   JohnCouper widower and SusaneAllcin vid were maried.
Aprill 2.   Israel Exton and Marie Mariat were maried.
June 9.   Ferdinando Adavert maried w͏th Rebecca Eardinge.
Septemb͏r 28. Richard Stegall & Sarra Rosse were maryed.

1620.

Januar. 21.   John Hamond vid maried with francis Stone singlewom.
Februar. 12. William Elson single maried with Joane paine widowe.

Año Dñi 1621.

Septem. 20.   John Perkin tooke to wife margaret pickis both single pso.
Novem. 5.   Simon mose singleman tooke to wife Ane Drake widow.
   12.   Nathan Bonifant singleman tooke to wife Elizabeth
              Johnson wid.
Januar. 24.   Thomas Ralphe singleman tooke to wife Alice Coman
              singlewom.
Februar. 2.   Robert Moxton singlem tooke to wife Abigail Bates
              singlew.
   28.   Lewis tooke to wife [*blank*].

Año 1622.

Septemb. 10. Robert pond and Sarah Gravener maried.

Año 1623.

May 1.	Edward [*blank*] tooke to wife Elizabeth Parrish widow.
June 26.	William edgar maried Martha Barnes.
Septeb. 16.	Robert Hawes maried Sara Williams.
Octob. 13.	Richard [*blank*] maried prudence Bell wid.
15.	John Boggs maried Añe Thomas widowe.

Año Dñi 1624.

Aug. 16.	John Wilson maried Susaña Renson.
Septemb. 13.	Daniel Huggins tooke wife to marie Sanders widow.
Septemb^r 23.	Mr John Hodges maried Mrs Abigail Bloys.
Febr. 27.	Robert Fiske maried margaret Deale.

Año Domini 1625.

April 24.	William Blumfield & marie mariot maried.
Septeber 6.	Robert Hamond & Jane Shenning were maried [*last two words inserted*].
Decemb^r 18.	John Nuttall & Elizabeth Wealie maried.
22.	William Wells prisoner & Joane Harvie of Coome maried.

Año 1626.

August 10.	Richard Gardiner tooke to wife Sarah Squire.
23.	Stephen Amys singleman tooke marie Newman.
Octob^r 2.	John Crane tooke to wife Marie Couper.
3.	Thomas Rivers maried Elizabeth Juiene.
7.	John Gyllie maried Edenie Chamberlaine.
Novemb^r 2.	Robert Carnall maried Agnes Kerington.

Año 1627.

April 19.	William Bernard maried Alice Baylis.
Septemb. 25.	{ Samuel Goslinge maried Joane mutley. { John Reynolds maried Katherine Lawrence. { Robert Rushbrooke maried Sara Briant.
October 8.	Nathaniel Pond & Elizabeth Lacie were maried.
Novemb. 23.	John Peacock and Francis Clapton maried.

Año 1628.

Aprill 29.	William Sparrow & Marie Lany were maried.
May 25.	Robert Foxlie and Bettrice Sparks maried.
June 29.	Thomas Cage & Añah Mariot were maried.
Julie 26.	Henrie Herne & Lucie Brett maried.
Septemb. 15.	William Trenam tooke to wife margaret Wright.
Octob^r 26.	Thomas Tunner maried Kimborow Pells.
Novemb^r 9.	William Mosson tooke to wife Elizabeth Rainolds.
Decemb^r 12.	Robert Kings & Alice [*blank*] maried.
Januar.	William Malton & Joane Alderman maried.
Febr. 19.	Gulfrid Talbot maried Elizabeth Brett.

Page 11.   Año Dñi 1629.

Januar. 6.	John Tailor maried marie Starlinge.
21.	Thomas Spouse maried Alice Jackson wid.

Año Dñi 1630.

May 24.	Robert Clarke maried Susaña merchant.
June 22.	Robert Gray wid tooke to wife Añe Archer single Wom.
Julie 27.	Mr William Barker tooke to wife Mrs marie Bridon.
Aug. 30.	John Francis & Rose Creeke were maried.
Septemb. 14.	James Norman maried Francis Sewell.
Novemb. 1.	William Bret sing tooke to wife Susaña Blith wid.

Año 1631.

April 23.	William Atkins maried marie Hollock.
June 23.	John Keeble and marie Salter were married.
Julie 11.	Richard Hurst widowr & martha erman wid maried.
14.	John Leigh wid and Bridgit Fuller were maried.
October 30.	John Luffkin and margaret Wood maried.
Novembr 27.	Richard Larke and Sarah Morgan were maried.
Januarie 17.	John Page & Marie Bert maried.
19.	Christopher Collen & Dorothie Clarke.
Februar. 13.	Tobias Dedham & Dionie Stott were maried.

Año Dñi 1632.

Aprill 22.	John Herne and Susaña Kerington were married.
24.	John moore and Joane Eason were married.
Julie 8.	{ Thomas Fuller & margaret Sansom were maried. William Burrous and Jane Browne.
17.	John fford and marie Akelie were maried.
24.	John marshall and Alice Dringe were maried.
30.	Henrie Keene & martha Draper widow were married.

Anno Domini 1633.

Julye 11.	John Bancocke and Anne Martyne ware marjed.
Sept. 24.	William Morgan and Elizabeth Wells ware marrjed.
Octob. 8.	Samuell Southgate and Elizabeth Brooke ware Marjed.
Nov. 17.	[blank] Bret [blank].
Novemb. 28.	John Roafe and Susan Wood ware marjed.
March 13.	John Belt and mathjw Edgar ware married.

Año Dom. 1634.

Aprill 29.	John Styles and marye Breket ware marrjed.
Maij 25.	Jeffrye Easye and Elizabeth Courtnell ware marrjed.
June 23.	John Wilder and marye Balderstone ware marjed.
Octob. 21.	Robert Blane and Marye Tyler ware married.
Octob. 30.	George Cutbert and Anne Finch ware marrjed.
Januarij 12.	Thomas Sedgewicke and Marye waters ware marrjed.
Jan. 15	Thomas [blank] and Marye Scapye ware marrjed.
Jan. 22.	Thomas Patrich and marye wood ware marrjed.
Feb. 8.	James ffulgue and Susan petto ware marrjed.

Page 12.   [*Undated*].

Septemb. 3.	Robert Hayward and Elizabeth Clerke were marryed.
Octob. 25.	John Belt & Prudence Bell were marryed.
Decemb. 20.	Joseph Palmer & Susan Bowton were marryed.

Februar. 10. Robert Gyrth alias potter & Mary Sparke.
     25. Roger Pettough & Mary Parson.

Marriages.

Anno Domini 1636.

May 9. Nathaniell Blacke & Katharine palmer were marryed.
Maye 28th. George Allers & Marye Moulson weare marryed.
22th of August. John Watson & Anne Palmere marryed.
ffeb. 16th. Thomas Sorrell & Elzabeth Munnige weare marryed.
Edmund Smyth of Shotley and Marye [*blank*] weare married the 24th of Aprill 1637.

1637.

June 4. William Low & Margaret Tis^{d}all were marryed.
June the 18th. Robert haggis and Anne Cotton were marryed.
August 28. Arthure Seigno^r & Dorothy Blomfield.
October 1. Thomas Osborne and Mary Cobb.
October 12. Thomas Matthew & Elizabeth Bennet were marryed.
Novemb. 30. Oliver Barber & Abigall Canham were maryed.
Decemb. 5. henry Trueloue and Sarah Smyth were marryed.
Decemb. 10. Thomas Ottoway and Elizabeth Bowdle were maryed.
Januarythe 21. William Micklefield and Ann hawkins were maryed.
January 30. William Morgan and Anne Brett were marryed.

Marriages.

1638.

March 3. henry Varnesse and ffrances Browne were marryed.
May 20. Robert Woodhouse & Lydia Miles were marryed.
June 15. John Cane and Anne pierr L licencid married.
June 21. John Ward and Rose Cant L licence.
Septemb. 9. John Brown and Margaret Clopton were maryed.
October 2. henry wright and Rose Paynam were marryed.
Octob^r 13. Richard Gray & Elis Sewell were maryed.
January 13. Robert Melford & Elizabeth Yollop, wer maryed.
ffebruary 19. ffrancis harrison and Elizabeth Alderman were maryed.

Marriages.

1639.

Aprill 16. ffrancis Leatherman and Elizabeth Buxton were maryed.
Aprill 21. Richard Clark and Sarah Denny were marryed.
May 3. Rowland Johnson and Sarah Sarson were maryed.
July 2. Robert Gilburne and Mary Stead.
July 13. William Bernard & Elizabeth Goonam were maryed.
August 3. Bazael huit & Mary Wylie were maryed.

Subscribed by Alex^r Rainold Minister of
St. Nicholas parish.
F. Chares. Smith Churchwarden.

Page 13. # Mariages.
1639.

Septemb 24. John Story and Mary hieron were maryed.
Octob. 6. William ffrost & Elizabeth hantly were maryed.
Octob. 28. henry ffidget and Elizabeth Paine were maryed.
Octob. 31. George Bradstreet and Mary Okey were maryed.
January 15. Robt. ffisk & Marin Wiseman were maryed.
January 29. Alex[r] Rainold and Susan Risby were maryed.
ffeb. 13. Thomas pounsett & Elizabeth Sicklemore were maryed.
ffeb. 18. Jeremy Colman & Katherin Dryver maryed.
ffeb. 19. Daniel Grigson & Elizabeth woodgate maryed.

Mariages.
1640.

Aprill 7. Samuel Raffe and Susan Savadge were maryed.
Aprill 7. Nathanael Raffe and Anne Campell maryed.
May 3. Thomas Palmer[1] & Mary Brett[2] were maryed.
May 25. John Semicroft & Susan Collyson were maryed.
August 11. Stevin hall & Elizabeth Johnson were maryed.
August 18. henry Smyth & Anne philipps were marryed.
Septemb. 24 William Nun and Elizabeth hardie were married.
January 22. Simon Smyth & Susan Marshall.
ffeb. 9. Abraham Smy and Marie Chapman were maryed.
  Henry Brame & Avis Arminger weare marryed the 18th of ffeb. 1640.

1641.

William and marget Cagew . . .

1642.

January gorge Bockenham & Rebeckca Notingham was maryed
29 day in 1645.

1646.

Junuery. Isaac Albrey & Margrate Longly both single psons maried.

1647.

Robert Hardwicke & Abigaile Clarke both single psons were married July 14th 1647.
Aug. 12. Michel Palmer & Kimburrow Haward were marryed.
Oct. 13. Hammond Doughty & Susan Gooding both single psons.

1648.

July 30. Thomas [*written over*] Dooer & Susan Havis were married.
Sept. 14. M[r] John Daines & M[rs] Briget Dade were maried.
Nov. 30. Elias Thurston & Sarah wonwright were maried.
Dec. 22. [*blank*] Browne & Elizabeth [*blank*] were Maried.

---

[1] Brett erased, Palmer written over.
[2] Palmer erased, Brett written over.

Octob. 16.   John Paskal & Mary Cuckow were maried.

1652.

Sept. 30.   Richard Coe & Margery Colson were Maried.

Octob 19.   Nathanael Smart & Kath Clarke were maried by Mr Waite at the Key Church.

1653.

May 16.   Thomas Byshope of Tachbrook in Warwickshire & Sarah Judd were married.

Page 14.

Decemb. 18th beinge saboth day as also upon twoe Saboth daies following a contract of Marrage was published wthin the pish Church of St Nicholas in Ipswh in the county of Suff : between Henery Buckinham singleman of Halsworth in the county of Suff Doctor in Phizick one the one pte And Elizabeth Nichollson singlewoman one of the Daughters of ffrancis Nichollson of the pish abovesaid Esquire one the other pte were maried.

Junvary 3.   henery Buckenham & Elizabeth Nickholsone.

Decem. 25.   michaell Thurtell & Rose freeman were published & 2 lordes dayes folowing.

Janv. 10.   William Moodey & mara waker were maried.

Janv. 13.   Michael Thurtell & Rose freman were maryed.

Janv. 1.   william lake & lyda hall were published & 2 lordes dayes fowlowing.

Janv. 1.   John browne & Ealse Marten were published & 2 lordes fowlowing & were maried Janvary the 24.

Janv. 26.   William Lake & Lidea hall were maried.

Janv. 15.   John wedes & Susan Edwardes were published & 2 lordes dayes following & were maried the 31 of the same month.

Janv. 15.   John Goslen & em ong were published & 2 lordes dayes following & weare maried february the 7.

Janv. 15.   John Buckenham & Susan Rofe were published! & 2 lords days following & weare maried february the 9.

Janv. 22.   George paskall & frances peaneall weare published & 2 lords dayes following & weare maried february the 6.

febr. 23.   Robert may & mara Jesvp were maried.

febr. 4.   Edward watters & Elizabeth Jackesonn were p. & 2 lordes following & weare maryed the 25 of the same month.

feb. 12.   Robert frost & Anna Shettellborrow were p. & 2 lordes following & weare maryed the 28 of the same month.

mar. 5.   Christopher Langle & Sara Morgen wear published & 2 lords dayes following & weare the 19 of the same month.

Marriages.
Año 1654.

Aprill xiijth.	John Samon & Elizabeth frost Were Married.
May 19.	Anthony lewes & Elizabeth web weare maried.
June 19.	John minter & mathew Cooke were maried.
June 29.	Thomas warwicke & Elizabeth horsman were maried.
July 20.	william Chiniry & Rebecke hine were maried.
Octob. 29.	John Keene & margarit Crose was maried.
novē 23.	Joseph hodeson & margrit Debbedge was maried.
Dese. 12.	John Billite and Jvdey Stote was maried.
Jan. 10.	William Brookoose & Ann Midleton was maried.
Jañ. 15.	Jacob Wathwit and Ann Waller were maried.
Jañ. 16.	Tobias Lewis and Mary Wilson were maried.
ffeb. the 8th.	robart leachick and An ruickman maried.
ffeb. 22th.	Edward Oates & Prudence haggis Maried.
marhth 9.	Edward clea And An Toke mared.

Page 15.

Marriages.
1655.

Aprill 10th.	Philip Gray and Ann Day were married.
Aprill 24th.	Robert heady and Martha Juon married.
May 1th.	John Day and Rodius Blaxhall Married.
Sep^t 18th.	Richard Wilder and Mary Osborne Married.
Sep^b 19th.	Luke Coates & Elizabeth Wharner Married.
Octob. 16th.	James Pare and Mary Goymer married.
Nov. 5th.	John Rivers and Mary Cullum married.
Nov. 15th.	John Osborne & hester Copping wid maried.
Nov. 19th.	Tobias Barker and Rachel Luffkin maried.
Nov. 20th.	Beniamin Alefounder & Katherin Suñer m.
ffeb. 5¹.	Jeremy Tye & Susan Alderman were maried.

Marriages.
1656.

10 Aprill.	Roger Younges Clerke & Susen Lebon were married.
June 3d.	Charles Winds & Mary Browne Married.
July 22th.	Thomas Brand & [blank].
July 29th.	John Browne and ffaith Barker married.
Aug. 19th.	Edmond Jenings & Amy Spalding mar.
Aug. 29th.	Joseph Lockwood & ffrances Adams. mard.
Octob. 1^t.	Tobias Legg Clerke & Elizabeth Styles, ma.
June 27th.	Jeremy Jermyn & Martha Browne mard.

Marriages.
1657.

Aprill 9th.	Edward Shinglehoud and Lidia Lay married.
Septemb. 19.	Robbart Turtle and Mary Gasste married.
Octob. 13.	John Lauender and Mary Thurston married.
Decem. 29.	John Rednall and Mary whelly married.

Decem. 29. John Podd and Susan Nun married.
January 29. Thomas Copper and Mary Bacon married.

1658.

Aprell 22. John maynaril and Sarah Juefes married.
January 6th. Arnold Tilleson & Susan Shles married.
Deceṁb.31th. John Studd & Thomazin Pilgrim married.
March 15th. Jeames hornigold & Alice hardy married.

Marriages.

1659.

ffebruary 5th. henry Page and Mary Browne Marryed.

1660.

Aprill 3th. John Pake and Bridggitt Troudgitt married.

Marriages

1661.

January 9th. Andrew ffolke & Elizabeth Buckenham were married.
Jan. 14th. Henry Wilkinson and Susan Tilson were married.

Page 16.   ## Marriages.

1662.

Aprill 25th. Robte Ratsey and Mary Gage were married.
July 10th. Lawrence Knights and Anne Carter were married.
Noveṁb. 30. Tho Billamore Widdower Thomazin Rose Widd married.
Deceṁb. 3d. Ambrose Thurston and Mary Brand married.
March 2° Thomas Rowe singleman & Susan Baker wid married.
March 13° John Barnes widdower & Elizbeth Parkhurst married.
March 19° Mathew Simpson and Phnye Vnderwood married.

Anno 1663.

July 2° Henry Wade and Grace Shiman Widd. married.
August 9° Thomas Golding and Mary Wyth were married.
January 14. Sa [*blank*] and Sarah Browne married.
January 14° Thomas Reader and Sarah ffrost married.
Deceṁb. 31° ffrs Turner and Mary Ottaway widd maried.
January 31° George Thistlewood and Mary Lewes married.
ffebuary 4° William Neave and Sarah Mudd were married.

Anno 1664.

Decem. 22. William Boycut & Sarah Sweet married.
     25. Roger Lugar & Sarah Bemmont married.
ffeb. 6th. Georg Augur & Mary Smyth married.

1671 [*sic*].

Desember 14th.Roger fox and sari barker mareid.

Page 17.   1667 [*sic*].

ffrancis laughter & Sarah Glanfeild single persons were marryed the
    28th of May 1667.
Henry Hummocke & Susan Larke single persons were marryed the
    29th of May 1667.

Peter Lee & Judeth Coocke Single persons were marryed the 6th day of June 1667.

Mathew Rose widower & Martha booth singlewoman were marryed . the 11th day of June 1667.

Thomas May Singleman & Mary Sicklemore widow were marryed the 13th day of June 1667.

Edward Webster & Margarett Mills Single persons were marryed the 23th of July 1667.

John Pascall & Sarah Horneby were marryed the 12th of ffebruary 1667.

Samuell James & Abigail more were marryed the 19th of March 1667.

Robert Grauenoll & Elizabeth younge were marryed the 24 of March 1667.

[1668].

William Munt & Jane Reynolds were marryed the 1st day of September 1668.

Edward Martin & Sarah Garwood wid maryed at St Mathews Sept. 17th 1668.

[1669].

Thomas Browne and Rosoman burroughs were marryed the 8th day of June 1669.

Robert Alderton Solut & Mary Aldham Vid were married 10th Aug. 1669.

John Wilson and Thomasin Mempris were Marryed the 23th day of Nouember 1669.

Daniell Walton and Elizabeth Elionett were marryed the 25th day of Nouember 1669.

[1670].

Andrew Reader & Martha euerard were marryed the 11th of September 1670.

Novem. 9th 1670. Edward Cooke & Ann Cowper wid. were marryed.

[1672].

John Coocke & Mary Upcher were marryed the first day of Aprill 1672.

John Bates & Isabel Robinson were marryed the 29th of June 1672.

Robert Rush & Mary Hayre were marryed the 12th of September 1672.

Nicolas ffarebrowne & Hannah Edgar were marryed the sixt of October 1672.

Nicolas Carnaby & Sarah Thurston were marryed the 28th of Nouember 1672.

Joseph Cocke & Roase whiting was mareyed January the twenty-eight 1672.

Samuell mody and hany gill was mared Aprell the 10th 1671 [*sic*].

[1673].

John Russell and Anne Spalding was marryed Aprill 16 167$\frac{2}{3}$.

Thomas Pascall and Mary Carniby was Married October the 30 1673.

William Hubbard and Sary Trulufe was Married December the 30 1673.
William Steuenes and Mary Lyilles was Married ffebruary the 3 1673.
Richard Mayhew and ffrancis Turner was married ffebruary the 9
1674 [*sic*].

Page 18.   Marragis.

1674.

ffeb. 16th.   Steven Sersson & ffrances Mannester were Married.

[1675].

May the 20.   John hasellwood and Elezebeth Wright was married in
yᵗ yeare 1675.
Junethe4day. John byum & Elezebeth Clopton was married in the
yeare 1675.
Jun ᵗʰ 23.   John Smaleman & marey thorne was marrid 1675.
August 1 day. marting Shrius & briggett foster marrid.
Septemb.
    14 day.   Gorge haye & beartx finsim.
Septemb. 14. John Grinwood & Ann Ship marrid 1675.
Octob. 14.   thomas Cusinge & margrett Skafe marrid 1675.

Marriages.

Anno 1676.

April 25th.   John Woolverton and Mary Cussens.
May 26th.   Thomas Lee and Allis Woodards.
Septemb.26th.William Whittle and Mary Rafe.
October 12th. William Nash and Ann fflowerdin.
October 18th. Henry Coussens and Tamasin Smyth.

Maraiges in the yeare 1677.

Aprill 16.   John youngs and Margret Last were maried.
May 15.   John Denton and Martha Newcomen were maried.
June The 28. John mixter And Elizabeth manser ware maried.
November8th.Robart Jacob and Grase Kempe was mared.

Marregs in the yeare 1678.

May 14th.   Henry Sparow and Margret wright was marred.
May 21.   Thomas Estrawe and Elizabeth Raymer was marred.
November 21. Martan Robinson and Ann Hasted was marred.
November 27. William Green & hanna Raymer marred.

Marriages.

Anno 1679.

April 15.   James Pattet and Elizabet shukford was marred.
October 16.   John Barnes & hanna Green was marred.

[1680].

Thomas Smith and Judith Searls were maried the tenth
of Nouember 1680.
John Offwood & Mary Trueloue single persons were marryed the
29th of December 1680.

C

Marriages.

Año Dñi 1680.

ffeb^y 10th { Ephraim Daldy & Mary Barnes }
1680.   {   all Single p^{r}sons } marryed.
           { John Cullum & Mary Jannings }

Page 19.   **Marriges.**

1681.

Mr Thomas Aldis was married to Ann Clopton the twenty ninth of may.

Robt Reder And Elizebeth ffedham Singell persons wear Marryed. Aprill ye 5th At Aknaham by Mr Thomas holborouge minister of S^t nickoles.

Mr Robert Copping vid)
          &   } marryed Oct. 13 1681
Mrs Mary Osborne vid)

Benjamin Wade   )
          &   } vid marryed May 31 1682.
Elizabeth Pattison   )

July ye 27th 1682.
Mr John Blumfeild   )
                 Sol. } marryed by Caue Becke Clark.
Mrs Margret Soriell   )

Henries Fonway (a Dutchman) sol.) marryed Aug. 17 1682.
Elizabeth Stebbing of St Pet^{r}s vid }

December the 22th 1682. Richard Bowett & Sarah peack) At S^t
     Booth Single psons wear marryed   } Nickolas.

John Ashfeld and mary Cooke wid. wear mareyed.

William harper and Sarah Coe wear mareyed nouember the 4 1684.

Danill Buge and Elizbeth Beaks wear mareyed September the 13 1685.

Thomas Billimor and Elizabeth Whiting both singel persons wear mared October the 25 1685.

frances gilderslue and Elizbeth King wear mared december the 6 1685.

Roger Sands and Amy Shindhel wear mared december the 20 1685.

Richard hayles To Susan Cole Nov. ye 12th 1686.

Joseph gullifer gentl^d & mary Butcher wear maried Jan. y^e 17th 1686 Singell persons.

Samvell hardy & Mary Legwas wear maried Jan. y^e 20th 1686 singell persons.

John Leas And Bridget Pake wear maried Janvery the 30th 1686 sol.

                                                 Geo. Raymond.

Page 20.   **Marages for 168$\frac{6}{7}$.**

Samvell Lewis Widower and Lidia Lewis Singell Woman wear Maried feb. y^e 20th 1686.

Ambross Jifer Singell man and Jane ffreeman singell weoman wear Maried August y^e 8th at y^e pish of S^t. Nicholas In Ipswich.

Mr Joseph Fisk of Ratlesden & Mrs Lydia Groome of Stratford maried by license novemb. 10th 1687.

1683.

William Rogers & Sarah Crake were married the 25 Aprill both Single Persons.

James Sallet & Hannah more both Single Persons were married by Licence the Eight Day of may 1688.

Thomas Web widdower & Prudence Lulpey Singlewoman were married the 21 of August 1688.

Robert Allin widdower & Elizabeth Ling widdow were married the sixteenth of September 1688.

Henry Studd of Cleydon sol. & Mary diggins of Watsfeild singlew. licence first had were married from the Goale the twentieth of October 1688.

Joseph Cattin and Auise Palmer both single Persons were married the twentieth of October 1688.

John Greene of Norwich was married to Martha Breen of St Lawrance Parish in Ipswich by Licence the ninteen of Nouemb.

Christopher Turner was married to Abigaill Sweetman the ninth Day of December 1688 both Single Persons both of St Climance Parish.

John Harison was married to Ann Payn by Licence the twenty three of December both Single Persons 1688.

Robert Harison widdower & Rose Banbridge Single woman And Christopher Wilson was married to Elizabeth Banbridge both single persons the twelf Day of february 1688 both by Licence.

Thos. Coop.

1689.

Mr Tho. Harvoy Sing^m & Mrs Mary Garnham Sing^{le} was married by License the forth day of Aprill 1689.

1689.

Mr Joseph Coleman widdower & Mrs Debory Ward single was married by Licence the ninth of September 1689.

Octob. 3th.	John Bagley of Emsett & Ledia Bird of Bramford was married by Licence the third of October 1689.
Nouemb. ye 10.	Mr Willm Bak^{er} of Munckcely Clerke & Susan Sparrow daught. of Rob Sparrow Gent. of Ipswich.
Jan. 16.	Matha [sic] Goodwing and Sarah Bigebe both of Ipswich.

1690.

Ap. 27.	Thomas Bret and Judith Poull Both Single Persons were maried.
Jun. 15.	John Baker and Alic Wills were maried both Single Persons.
Sept. ye 16.	Thomas Gouldsbury widdower & Ann Petts single wo. were married.
Octob. y 9th.	Robert Linsey widdower & Mary Lauender Single woman were married. Geo. Raymond.

Page 21.   Marriages in 1690.

Octob. ye 19th. Michall Daniell and Elizabeth Salter were married.

Decemb. ye 23. James Steuens widdower and Susan [blank] widdow were married by lisence.

C^2

[Decemb.] y⁰ 26.	John Cushing widdower and Mary Parkis widdow were married by licence the 26 of December.
Jan yᵉ 13.	Bazzell Huit Junier Widdower and Margret Death single woman were married the thirteen of January
yᵉ 18.	Philip Parker and Rose Deney Both Single persons were married the Eighteenth of January.

1691.

June yᵉ 1th.	Mʳ Truth Norris wid. Mʳˢ Sarah Roberson wid. } by Licenc.
June 1:.	⎰ Thomas Selsby & Susan Tetterson } Wid. ⎱ both of Sᵗ Petters pish Johnathan Reylye widʳ dwelling in Sᵗ Mary Ellms pish, & Ann Patterson of this Pish wido.
July 10.	Nicholas Osbond of Debingham & Eliz. Barker of yᵉ same Towne both single.
August 30th.	Abraham Bleshingham & Mary Skeet both Single.
Oct. 6th.	Tho. Hewett widoʳ and Matha Bayly of Sᵗ Petters wido.
Nouemᵇ 15.	Jacob Kee & Mary Sadeller both Singˡ.
No. 17.	Jeremiah Beets & Eliz. Browne both Singˡ.

1692.

May 26. 1692.	Jeamˢ Whekley & Eliz. Harson both Widʳ.
July 28. 1692.	Nathaniel Pickess widʳ } by Lince. Keziah. Pickess wido.
Aug. 9.	Edward Hubart widoʳ } by Lin. Elizabeth Skefener wido.
Janᵒ 5th 169⅔.	Tho. Bacon widd. and Eliżb.Welham Single were married by License.
feb. 7 169⅔.	John May & Dorkas Houell alls Smyth both Single where maried by Licence.
feb. 23 169⅔.	Auther Roper wid. and } maried. Dorcas Bowe Single where
feb. 27 169⅔.	John Price Soulger and Eliżb. Skeet where maried.
March 2 169⅔.	Vster Peacocke & Sarah Osborne were maried.

1693.

Aprill 23th 1693.	John Blisingham & Mary Hackwell both single.
June 18.	Ben Skeet & Sarah Hulke both Single.
June 22th.	Charles Michall & Hanah Laurance both Single.
June 27th 1693.	Nathan Turner widower of Woluerston & Ann Blaine singlew of Ipswich where maried June 27th 1693.

Geo. Raymond.

Page 22.
1693

Marages for 1693.

July 20th.	Stephen de Bourget of Ipswᶜʰ: a frenchman & Ann Haruey of Whitton were married by Licence.

Octob. 23.	Thomas Radlee & Grace Beacham both single.
Decm^b 28th.	Abijah Manser & Eliz. Burning both single.
feb. 4.	Anthony Lanester & Margrett Sindersen both of Tudingham were maried.
feb. ye 13th.	John ffrainces & Susan Turner both wido.

1694.

Apr̃ ii.	Mr John Peek & Mrs Sarah Wade were Married.
July 8.	ffranĩ Southwell wid^r & Marg^t Quinton Wido. both of St Mathews pish were married.
Augt 21th.	Samuell Denton & Sarah Wade were Married.
Sep^t 2.	William Beille^r & Mary Nuton (vid.) were Married.
Octob. first.	Tho. Tokely sing^l & Eliz. Soutwell sing^l both of St Mathies pish of this Towne maried.
Second.	Robert Pennall & Sarah Purkis both sing.
Nouemb. 15th.	Mr Samuell Hutson of Stutton & Mrs Eliz. Smart of this pish both single were Marri^d.
Decemb. y^e 2 1694.	John Haywood widower of St Peters & Briget Munings singlewoman were Maried.
Decem^r 20.	Richard Cole single & Matha ffurman both Single both of St Clements were married.
23.	James Beatts & Eliz. Dañering of St Marykee both Single were Married.
169$\frac{4}{5}$.	John Randell sing^{lm} of Hadledg and Mary Pettifer wido were married Jan^o y^e 9th 169$\frac{4}{5}$.

1695.

Mar. y^e 25 1695.	Mr John Parsons of hadleigh sing^l and Mathae Mullinder. sing^l daug^t of Mr Lare Mullyner by Lince.
M^r 28.	John Huntyball & Anna Cooper both sing^l.
May 5th.	William Trusson Wi^d & Mary Goward Sing.
May 18.	Robt. Feild of Bealings pav. sing. & Sussanna Bobbitt de Tuddenham wid.
July 14 1695.	William osborn & Alice Norris both sing. of St Nicholas pish were maried July 14.

Page 23.

Geo. Raymond.

Octob. 3d.	Thomas Garwood Wid. And Dinah Goffe wid. of St Nicolas parish mar. by Banns.
Octob. 24.	Henry Augur sol. & Thomasin Chenery sol. of St Nicolas mar. by Banns.
Nouemb. 14.	James Newton of Wherstead sol. & Debora Stott of Ipswich mar. by License.
Febr. 2d.	John Salmon & Elizabeth Whiting of St Mary at ye Elms were mar. by banns.
Febr. 9th.	Benjamin Hall & Mary Sweetman.

1696.

April 12th.	Thomas Siddenham of Chattham & Margaret Siklemore of Ipswich mar. by license.
April 23.	John Manning of St Mathews & Mary Lawrence of St Nicholas were mar. by Banns.

May 1st.	Willm Waller of Briset Widd. & Esther Bacon of Willersome singlewom. mar. by License.
June 23.	Edward Man of Woodbridge & Ann Sutton of Ipsw. mar. by License.
Novemb. 12.	William Green & Sara Symonds of Ipsw. married by License.
January 12.	Robert Rowse of Dennington & Margaret Church of Hoxne married by License.
March 16.	George Bowle of Battisford & Elizabeth Elliot of Ipsw. wer^e Married by License.

1697.

April 13.	Henry Francis & Sarah Brand mar. by Bāns.
April 14.	William Brett & Ann Lynes mar. by Banns.
May 7th.	Samuel Truelove & Ann Debenham of Ipsw. married by license.
Jan. 24.	Jonathan Elmer of Shotsham & Hannah Seumare of Ipsw. Married by Banns.
July 30th.	John Carew of Freston Cler & Esther Trunbull of Ipsw. sol. married by license.
August 3^d.	Samuel Hich & Elizabeth Siclemore were married by Banns.
August 24.	Daniel Hornsby & Lydia Strogin of Ipsw. were married by Banns.
Sept. 12.	John Smith & Elizabeth Bretton by banns.
Octob. 7th.	Thomas Beams & Sarah Slye were married by banns.

Geo. Raymond.

Page 24.   Marriages.
1697.

Nouemb. 25.	Thomas May & Bridget Ashely were married by Banns.
Decemb. 2^d.	Robt Cook wid. & Elizabeth Manning sol. married by license.
Decemb. 31.	William Goster of Walton & Hannah Revell of Felixstow were married by licēse.
Feb. 13.	Thomas White & Rose Moulson were married by Banns.
March 1st.	Thomas Burlace & Ann Hopper married by License.

1698.

May 1st.	Joseph Hudson & Dorothy Nevil maried by Banns.
May 3^d.	Joseph Dew & Ann Barber married by Banns.
January 1.5.	William Rogers wid. & Jane Cooper sol. by Banns.
Jan. 25.	Francis Bowl of Nedging to Deborah Gislinghm of Ipsw. married by Bans & certificate.
Feb. 4.	James Frost of Badly sol. & Ann Mirton of Occold sol. married by License.

1699.

Mar. 26.	Robert Parradine of Colchester wid. & Dorothy Jobson of Ipsw. sol. married by License.

Octob. 10th.   John Ward of Ipswich sol. & Martha Pickus of y° same sol. married by License.

Octob. 24.   William Crehny sol. & Elizabeth Trulove sol. both of Ipswich were married by License.

Decembʳ 11th.   John Fuller sol. & Lydia Turner widd. both of Ipswich were marryed by License.

Jan. 7th.   John Jobson widd. & Ann Caston widd. both of Ipswich were marryed by License.

feb. 13.   John Manser of Ipsw. widd. & Frances Salter of Ipsw. widd. were married by License.

feb. 27.   Jeremiah Folkhard sol. & Susan Ham sol. both of Ipswich were marryed by License.

1700.

Mar. 25.   John Bates Widd. & Mary pippin wid. both of Ipswich were married by license.

May 26.   George Mayer of South Elmham sol. & Elizabeth Ward of Ipsw. sol. were married by License.

June 5th.   Robt Farrer of Campsy Ash sol. & Abigail Aylwork of Wickam market wid. were married by License.

Geo. Raymond.

Page 25.   # Marrages.

1700.

August 7th.   Thomas Lilly of Woodbridge sol. & Elizabeth Sallowes of ye same sol. were married by License.

Febr. 25.   Jeremiah Goddard sol. & Ann Pickas sol. both of Ipswich were married by License.

Mar. 1st.   James Raymond sol. & Sara Heard sol. of Ipswich were married by license.

Mar. 24.   William Wright sol. & Margaret Wright sol. both of Ipsw. were marryed by License.

1701.

Apr. 22.   John Taylor sol. of Charsfeild & Elizabeth Bond wid. of the same were married by License.

July 20th.   William Bull sol. & Mary Hudson sol. were marryed by Banns.

July 27.   Otho Lockwood sol. & Anna Vpson sol. were married by Banns.

Septemb. 4th.   Thomas Youngs wid. & Susan Hall sol. both of Ipswich were marryed by License.

Septʳ 30.   Samuel Cobern of Cobdock & Mary Luff of Ipswich (both single) were Maryed by Banns.

Novʳ 11th.   William Lovis of Falkenham sol. & Rose Cullum of Sᵗ Nichs sol. were marryed by Banns.

Decʳ 10th.   Lawrence Ollson sol. & Sarah Lettis sol. both of Ipswich were married by License.

1703.

Mar. 28.   Joseph Cook sol. & Jane Brooke sol. both of Ipswich were married by License.

April 1st.	Richard Hearson a soldier & Ann Casby of Ipswich were married by License.
June 8th.	Benjamin Crocker & Anne Rowning both of Ipsw. were married by License.
July 13.	Zachariah Bennet of Codenham & Frances Hearson of St Lavr Ipsw. were married by Banns.
Aug. 29.	William Coleman widd. & Hannah Sayer Sol. were married by Banns.
Septr 7th.	Joseph Coggeshall of Bramford & Elizabeth Gildersleeve of Westerfeild were married by License.
Octob. 8th.	Willm Davy of Alleburgh in Norf. widd. & Martha Goodwin of Ipswich sol. were married by License.

Geo. Raymond.

Page 26. ## Marriages.

1703.

Octob. 28.	John Smith of Harwich sol. & Elizabeth Smith of Ipsw. widd. were Marryed by License.
Febr. 2^d.	William Chamberlain of St Stephens widd. & Sarah Worledge wid. of Ipsw. were maryed by License.
Febr. 8th.	Peter Sharp Widd^r & Anne Paschal sol. were marryed by Banns.
Febr. 13.	William Cook of St Nicolas sol. & Mary Holborough of St Lawr. sol. were marryed by License.
Feb. 28.	John Luggate of Ofton widd. and Hannah Wynn of Ofton sol. were married by license.

1704.	1704.
Apr. 27.	John Allen of St Nicolas sol. & Frances Keeble of the same sol. were Marryed by Banns.
Aug̃ 8.	Thomas Good of Earl Stonham sol. & Mary Bates of St Nicholas widd. were married by License.
Septr 16.	William Cracknel of St Clements Ipswich widd^r & Frances Davis sol. were marryed by License.
Septr 27.	Francis Glanfeild of St Nicholas sol. & Mary More sol. were Marryed by Banns.
Decr 28.	James Seaman of Woodbridge Widd. & Elizabeth Waith of Ipsw. sol. were married by License.
Feb. 18th.	John Girling of St Mary at Elms & Sarah Courtnall were married by License.

1705.	
May 6.	Levi Dardy of St Clements sol. & Sara Wright of St Nicolas were married by License.
May 9.	Robert Gildersleev of St Nicholas & Mary Shipman were Married by License.
May 29.	Robert Lewis of St Lawrence sol. & Mary Foulser were Marryed by License.
July 24.	John Gilder of Bealings Magn & Elizabeth Rose of Ipsw. were Marryed after publication of Banns ducly certified.

Octob. 16.   Cornelius Palmer of St Clements widd. & Sarah Bacon sol. were Marryed by License.

Novr 18.   John Starling of St Lawrence & Frances Catchpoll sol. were Marryed by License.

Febr. 14.   Thomas Gray of Harwich & Anne Jolly of Ipswich sol. were married by License.

Geo Raymond.

Page 27.   Marriages.

1706.   1706.

April 5th.   John Jolly of St Stephens in Ipswich Widd. and Susan Fairchild sol. were Marryed by License.

July 4th.   John Wright Barrister at Law & Rachel Fuller sol. were married by License.

July 25.   James Harlwin of Needham Market widd^r & Sarah Blichenden of St Nicholas singlewoman were marryed by Banns.

Novr 7th.   Plampin Brabrook of Shelly & Susan Glanfeild of Rayden sol. were Marryed by License.

Decr 24.   William Fowghst sol. & Susan Woods sol. of Ipsw. were marryed by License.

Jan. 13.   Thomas Croswell & Christian Brown were married by Banns.

Jan. 14.   Vri Topley sol. & Margaret Syer vid. were Marryed by Banns.

1707.   1707.

May 18.   John Stewart widd. & Susan Trudget sol. from St Mary Tower were Maryyed by License.

September 14 Willm Woolnough Widd^r & Bridget Thredkill Widd. were married by Banns.

Septr 19.   Charles Rayner of Harwich sol. & Anne Blackborn widd. of ye same were Maried by a License.

Decr 31.   Willm Bixby of Tattingston & Elizabeth Martyn of Bently were Maried by License.

Jan. 2^d.   John Church of Aldham wid^r & Bridgett Steggal of Somersham wid. were Maried by license.

March 2.   Maxy Wall of Royden & Mary Brawbrook of ye same were Maried by License.

1708.

April 1.   John Minter sol. & Anne Burrage sol. were maried by license.

May 23.   John Perkins wid. & Anne Chinery wid. of Ipsw. were married by license.

June 8.   John Baddison & Sarah Baker of Ipsw. sol. were Married by License.

June 11.   James Mansur & Elizabeth Cook of Ipsw. both single were Married by License.

Aug. 8.   Willm Scarlet & Elizabeth Aldridge both of Ipsw. sol. married by Banns.

Page 28.

Aug. 24.   John Marlow sol. & Elizabeth Cole sol. both of Ipswich
                were Marryed by License.

Octob. 26.   John Johnson sol. & Elizabeth Pickas sol. both of Ipsw.
                were married by License.

Decemb. 17.   James Vllson sol. & Susan Cawdy sol. both of Ipswich
                were married by Licẽse.

Jan. 6.   Samuel Blomfeild sol. & Jane Cook sol. both of Ipswich
                were Married by License.

Febr. 5.   James Southgate widd[r] & Mary Turner sol. both of
                Ipswich were Marryed by License.

1709.

May 23.   Francis Coleman widd[r] & Elizabeth Phillips sol. both of
                Ipsw. were maryed by License.

Aug. 7.   Robert Smyth of Hintlesham & Hannah Beaumont of
                Ofton were marryed by license.

Sept[r] 5.   Daniel Fullard a soldier & Elizabeth Mills widd. were
                Marryed their Banns having been thrice published.

Sept[r] 18.   John Day of S[t] Lawrence sol. & Abigail Creting of S[t]
                Nich. sol. were Married by Banns.

Sept[r] 22.   Richard Sadd sol. & Priscilla Allen sol. were Marryed
                by Banns.

Octob. 3[d].   Stephen Brook of S[t] Mary Tower sol. & Abigail More
                of S[t] Nicholey sol. were marryed by Bannes.

Octob. 11th.   William Woods of Woodbridge sol. & Anne Grimes
                of Ipswich sol. were marryed by License.

Novemb. 3[d].   John Betts & Elizabeth Barfutt both single were married
                by Bannes.

Novemb. 3[d].   John King of Cleydon and Sarah Calbin of S[t] Nicholas
                both sing. were Maryed by Bannes.

Decemb. 20.   Richard Child of Lavenham sol. & Sarah Quicksly of
                y[e] same sol. were maryed by License.

Jan. 16.   George Dodds & Mary Parkis both single were married
                by Bannes.

1710.

April 18.   John How & Sarah Backhouse both of Ipswich & both
                single were marryed by License.

                                              Geo. Raymond.

Page 29.   Christenings beginning An° 1539.

25 Mar.	[*blank*] Traves.
13 Apr.	Lawrence Courtnall.
12 Juli.	Alice Castleman.
29 Juli.	Xpian Thonge.
6 Aug.	Agnes Rydnes.
ii Aug.	helen Stevens.
6 Sept.	Margery Lambert.
10 octo.	John Kitriche.
16 No.	helin Martin.

1540.

i Jan.	Thoms Sherwoode.
10 Ja.	Roger Beckett.
2i Ja.	Richard Beomond.
30 Ja.	James Miller.
23 feb.	Elizabeth Rainborouge.
1 March.	Joan Smith.
3 Apri.	Anne Bottrick.
8 Apri.	Elzabeth Calis.
7 Mai.	Elzabeth Pitchard.
22 Juli.	Elzabeth Brand.
24 Juli.	Margerie Swaine.
7 Sep.	Willm Cranthorne.
10 Sep.	Willm Thrower.

1541.

Aug.	John Bume sonne of Oliver.
Apri.	Rose Travis dawght[r] of John.
Apri.	Dionis London daug[r] of John.
Sept[r]	Elzabeth osborne Daug. of Xpõfer
Sept[r]	Anne Thrower Daug of Willm.
Octb.	John Grenewich son of John.
March.	Adam Peterson son of John.

1542.

7 Mai.	Susan Lillie daug. of John.
Apri.	Walter Smith son of Edmond.
June.	Joan Roper daug. of Thoms.
Juli.	Richard Cleveland son of Willm.
Juli.	Thoms hollond son of Thoms.
Decem.	Anne Bobbet daug[r] of Thoms.
Janu.	Agnes homebie daug[r] of Willm.
Mar.	Anne Colis daug[r] of John.
Mar.	Peter Peterson son of John.

1543.

Apri.	Thoms Oliver son of John.
Apri.	Sebastian Cage son of John.
Mai	Margery Becket daug. of Thoms.
June	ffrancis Rainsborroughe son of Thoms.

Juli	Alice Williamson daug[r] of Dirick.
Aug.	Richard ffosdick son to John.
Aug.	John Wilkin son to Katherin fornica.
Aug.	Willm Eirich son to Rote.
Sept[r]	Willm Caline son to Thoms.
Sept[r]	Walt[r] Robertson son to Richard.
Octo.	Joan harryson daug[r] to Robte.
Octo.	Charles Beomond son to Willm.
novem.	Agnes Witherbie daug[r] to Adam.
Decem.	Joan Davie daug[r] to Margett.
Janu.	Margery Bobett daug[r] to Thoms.
Janu.	Mathew Thrower son to Willm.
Janu.	Robte Colman son to Robte.
feb.	Robte Blackamore son to Roger.
march.	Margerye Osborne daugr to Xpōfer.

Page 30. ## Christenings.

1544.

March.	Joan Witherby daugr to Mary a fornica.
June.	Willm Mussock son to Walter.
Juli.	John Johnson son to Arnold.
Juli.	Walter Powell son to Robte.
Juli.	Rose ffaneed Daugh[r] to John.
Juli.	Thomazin Smyth Daug[r] to Edmond.
Juli.	Jeffrey Travis son to John.
Aug.	James Newton son to Thoms.
Aug.	Beatrix daughter to John Oliver.
Aug.	Agnes daug[r] to Willm fforward.
Aug.	Elzabeth daug[r] to Thomas Rainbroughe.
Sept[r]	Josua son to John Tyler.
octo.	Alice Cleveland daug[r] to Willm̄.
octo.	John son to John Peterson.
novem.	Willm̄ son to Jeffrey Cawche, Baker.
novem.	Margrett daug[r] to George Norfolk.
Janu.	Alice holland dawg[r] to Thoms.
Janu.	Agnes dawg[r] to Alice Willm̄s a fornac.
Janu.	John son to John lyllye.
feb.	John son to James Michell.
feb.	Robte son to Robte Cage laborer.

1545.

Apri.	Alice dawg[r] to Xp̄ofer Osborne.
Apri.	John son to James Turner.
Apri.	Alice dawg[r] to John Pitcher.
Mai.	Robte son to John Garnett.
Mai.	Sebastian son to Dirick willms.
June	Walter son to Willm̄ ffrinan.
octo.	Willm̄ son to John ffosdick.
octo.	Susan daug[r] to Thoms Bobet.
Nove.	Elzabeth dawg[r] to Willm Throware.

dece.	Adam son to henry Johnson.
feb.	mary dawgʳ to Thoms Jeley.
feb.	John son to Robte Packare.
feb.	John hamont son to [*blank*].
feb.	Allexander son to Adam Witherby.
feb.	Margett dawgʳ to henry howes.
marc.	Willm̄ son to John Cooke.

1546.

1546.

Mar.	Thomazin Dawgʳ to Arnold Johnson.
Apri.	Elzabeth Dawgʳ to John Baules.
Mai.	John son to Willm Marret.
June.	Thoms son to Edmond Smith.
June.	Jone Dawgʳ to John Quante.
Aug.	John son to George Bushe.
Aug.	Anne Dawgʳ to Roger Blackamore.
Aug.	henrye son to John Blomfeld.
Sept.	Agnes Dawgʳ to John Abbott.
Sept.	Alice Peterson daughʳ to John.
Octo.	Marget Daugʳ to Thoms Nunne.
novem.	Thomazin Daugʳ to Thoms Bobett.
novem.	Dionis Daught to Walter Mvssock.
Janua.	Dionis Daughtʳ to John Lanson.
Janua.	Anne Daughʳ to Robt Kittrige.
march.	Anne Daughʳ to Steven Greneleff.
	Jone Daugtʳ to Robte king.
	James hastis child was xp̄ined.
	henry hawis child was xp̄ined.

1547.

Page 31.

Christenings.

1547.

23 Aug.	Robte son to Roger Lawrence.
Aug.	Peter & Susan children to John Allen.
Aug.	Ezechias son to Wᵐ Champivn.
Septʳ	Margery Daughʳ to John Cage.
	Mary Daughʳ to Peter Martin.

1548.

Apri.	Thoms son to henry Jankinson.
Mai.	Thoms son to Willm Bucknam.
June.	Margett Daughʳ to John Williamson.

1549.

1550.

1551.

9 Juli.	Susan Daughʳ to Xp̄ofer osburne.
Juli.	Margett Daughʳ to John Baule.
Juli.	Jone Daughʳ to Edmond Smyth.
Aug.	Robt & Margett children to Wᵐ Norham.

Aug.	Jone Daught^r to W^m hunt.
Sept.	James son to Wiłłm Nottingham.
Sept.	Margery Daught^r to George Bushe.
Sept.	Anne Daught^r to John Daines.
Sept.	Xpian Daught^r to Edmond Smith.
Octo.	Jone Daugh^r to Walter Mossock.
Novem.	Alis. Daught^r to Robte Cutler.
nove^r	John son to Thoms Smyth.
nove^r	Richard son to Richard Quant.

1552.

marc.	Susan Daugh^r to John Cooke.
Apri.	[*blank*] Daugh^r to Thoms Ranson.
Apri.	Gidfry son to Jeffrye Cauche.
Apri.	Sebastian son to James Peñierton.
Marc.	Jone daugh^r to Roger lawrence.
Julie.	Michaell son to Thoms Skynner.
Sept.	Edmond son to Thoms Bobett.
Sept.	Jone daugh^r to Edward Batham.
octo.	Richard son to Thoms Selsdon.
octo.	Jone daugh^r to henry Roberson.
octo.	Susan daugh^r to Edmond Ranger.
nove.	James son to Thoms Walter.
nove^r	Cornelius son to John Peterson.
dece^r	Robt son to John Dayns.
Dece^r	Edmond son to John Lyllye.
march.	henry son to Thoms Boyer.

1553.

28 Mar.	Mirable daugh^r to John Stringer.
June.	Sara daugh^r to Wiłłm Bucknam.
	Jone Martin [*blank*].

1554.

Julie.	Thoms Batham son to Edward.
Juli.	Xpofer son to Robt Molson.
Aug.	Rebecca daugh^r to Willm hunte.
Sept.	Jane daugh^r to henry Röbsvn.

Page 32.   # Christnings.

1556.

5 octo.	Margarett the daugh^r to John Estoll.
	⎧ Richard son to Xpofer Osborne.
nove.	⎨ Marie daugh^r to Thoms Bobet.
	⎩ Margery daugh^r to George Balls.
24 novem.	Jone daugh^r to Richard Bell.
4 dec^r	Robte son to Robt Daines.
9 dec^r	Wiłłm son to John Peterson.

1 Janua.

1557.

17 Ja.	Jone daugh. to Willm Buckenham.
24 Ja.	Anne daugh^r to Thoms Woode.
4 feb.	Jone daugh^r to Robte Cutler.
11 feb.	Emme daugh^r to John Quant.
13 Mar.	Katherin daugh^r to Peter Parson.
4 Apri.	Thoms son to Robte Peynson.
	Margarett daug^r to John Ryver.
15 Jun.	Thoms son to Robte Lane.
9 Aug.	John son to Thoms Davis.
1 Sept.	Jone daugh^r to Robte ffosdick.
3 Sept.	Alice daugh^r to Richard ffoxe.
16 Sep.	Thoms son to David Belis.
1 Nove.	Anne daught^r to Jeffery Archer.
23 Nov.	Jone daugh^r to John hart.
5 Dec.	Daniell son to Roger Lawrence.
Dec.	John son to Edmond Goodwin.
24 Ja.	homes [*sic*] Lennaker daugh^r to Edward.
29 Ja.	Xpofer son to Edward Batham.
16 feb.	Mary daugh^r to Rbte Selsden.
21 feb.	Jone daugh^r to Richard Barker.
8 Mar.	Rbte son to Mary Goltie fornica.
27 Mar.	John son to John donne.
13 Apri.	Rbte son to Thomas aWoode.
17 Apri.	George son to George Balls.
10 Mai.	Thoms son to Nicholas Panton.
3 June.	Margrett daugh^r to Nicholas Edwards.
15 June.	Jone daugh^r to Jone Baker fornica.
9 Aug.	Margrett daugh^r to Peter Peterson.
10 Aug.	Anne daugh^r to Willm Smyth.
	Alis daugh^r to Robte daynes.
2 Octo.	Margret daugh^r to Thoms Davis.
13 Octo.	Willm Son to Ravff Gardener.
17 Octo.	Margrett daugh^r to Rbte Richardson.

1558.

20 Octo.	John the son to Garrad Vinson.
23 Octo.	Robte son to John Peterson.
octo.	John son to henry Peterson.
2 novē	John son to Arthur Bower.
10 novē	Elenor daugh^r to Thoms Balie.
12 novē	Mary & Charatie children to Richrd Johnsvn.
27 novē	Vrsula daugh^r to John River.

1559.   1° Janua.

29 Janu.	Elzabeth daugh^r to Thoms Madock.
9 feb.	Alice daugh^r to Robte ffosdick.
5 feb.	Elzabeth daugh^r to Robte Cutler.
7 feb.	Willm son to John Skelton.
23 feb.	Richard son to larrence Clubbe.

10 May.	James the sonne of John Leman.
20 Aug.	John son to Rbte Pynswyne.
5 Sep.	Thoms son to Nicholas Panton.
8 Sep.	Jone Daught^r to Nicholas Regate.
27 Sep.	Jone & Jone twinnes to Robte lane.
9 Nove^r	Anne Daug^r to Robte Daynes.
26 nove.	Marion Daugh^r to Xp̄ofer Alderman.

1560.

21 Jan.	Magdalen daugh^r to Philippe Duble.
12 feb.	Lambert son to Richard foxe.
1 Mar.	Margarett daugh^r to John Abbot.
31 Mar.	Jone daugh^r to Edward Batham.
2 Apri.	John son to Willm Laye.
4 Apri.	Jone daugh^r to John Baker.
8 Apri.	Margarett daug^r to John Gardner.
23 Apr.	John son to Richard Man.
29 Apr.	Valentyn son to John Sweare.
5 May.	Samuell son to Steven Grenwiche.

1561.

21 octo.	Jeffrey Alderman son to Xp̄ofer Ald^rman.
30 No.	Mary ffosdel [*sic*] daug^r to Robt ffosdet [*sic*].
4 Ja.	Jone Duble daug^r to Philip Duble.
22 Ja.	Willm kete son to Ione [*sic*] kete.

1562.

5 Apri.	Beatrix Algate daug^r to Robt. Algat.
7 June.	Thoms Luk son to Lawrence.
7 June.	Willm Cutler son to Robte & Parnell.
23 Juli.	Margery hallebread daugh^r of Thoms.
27 Sep.	Michell Pinson son of Robt.
29 No.	Richard Abbot son of John.
15 No.	Willm Bloise son of Willm & Alice.
22 No.	John Dickesvn son of Thoms.
18 Ja.	Willm Daye son of John.
18 Ja.	Mary Marser daug^r of Willm.
25 Feb.	John Emner son of Nicholas & Jone.

1563.

4 Apri.	Willm Beckett son of John.
9 May.	Rose ffosdick daugh^r to Robte.
14 June.	Philip daug^r to Robte Daynes.
16 June.	Jone the daug^r of John Crayford.
14 Sept.	Willm the son of Willm hailes.
14 Octo.	Xp̄ofer the son of Georg Bales.
14 Octo.	{ hubard the son of John Rendry. { John the son of Richard ffoux.
2 Dece.	Margarett the Daughter of xpofer Ald^rman.
3 Dece.	Beniamy the son of Robt Cutler.

19 Dec.	{ Margery the Daughter of John Cannon. { Mary the Daughter of Allan Smith.
25 De.	{ John the son of Richard Lakelonne. { Margarett the Daughter of John Leman.
30 De.	Grisell the Daughter of Thoms huwat.
3 Janu.	Robte the son of Thoms Madock.
12 Ja.	Elzabeth the Daughter of John oxle. Mary the Daughter of George ffen.
14 Mar.	Willm the son of ffrancis Aldam.

1564.

9 Aprl.	Barnaby the son of John Beckett.
1 May.	Jane the Daughter of John Lane.
17 June.	{ Margery the Daughter of Davy Beles. { Charitie the Daughter of Michell Manhood.

Page 34.

23 Jun.	Elzabeth the Daughter of Robte ffosdick.
30 July.	Mary the Daughter of Robart Bridges.
8 Aug.	Thoms the son of John Grene.
31 Sep.	Roger the son of Thoms hallybred.
28 Sep.	Willm the son of Willm Brabye.

1565.

25 June.	Alice the Daughter of Willm Bloise.
29 June.	Giles the son of Thoms Michell.
7 July.	Willm the son of John Beckett.
26 July.	Samuell the son of Robte Cutler.
19 Sep.	Willm the son of Willm Midnall.
21 Sep.	Jone the Daughtr of Willm hailes.
24 Sep.	{ Alice the Daughter of Willm Ramsby. { George the son of Robte Daines.
2 Octo.	Margarett the Daughter of Robte ffosdick.
6 Nove.	Margaret the Daughter of John Crowford.
2 Dece.	Alice the Daughter of Willm Beniamyn.
17 Dece.	ffrancis the son of John hewin.
22 Jan.	Rose the Daught of Anthony Brarston.
6 Ja.	Steven the son of Allen Smyth.
26 feb.	Edward the son of John Cooke.
3 Mar.	Elzabeth the Daughter of ffrancis owdren.
14 Mar.	{ Richard the son of Robt Daynes. { John the son of John Ryvers.

1566.

6 Apl.	{ Jone the Daughter of Thoms hallybred. { Richard the son of Robt Collyns.
10 May.	John the son of Richard Collyn.
16 June.	Elzabeth the Daughter of Peter Pape.
11 July.	Emme the Daughter of Robte Cason.
15 Aug.	Joseph the son of Robt Cutler.
8 Sep.	Abraham the son of Thoms Stalworth.

D

6 octo.	Robte the son of James Denny.
9 octo.	Katheryn the Daughter of Wiłłm Mercer.
2 Nove.	Elzabeth the Daughter of Wiłłm Bucknam.
19 Jan.	Margarett the Daughter of Anthony fflotham.

1567.

1 Aprill.	George hills the son of Richard.
6 Ap^{ll}.	Robte the son of Robte ffosdick.
7 Ap^{ll}.	Robte the son of Lawrence Clubb.
20 Ap^{ll}.	Betherus the son of henry Sever.
17 Aug.	{ hercules Lane son of Robte Lane. { John Garne son of Thoms Garne.
1 Sept.	Anna the Daughter of John Belman.
18 octo.	John the son of John Garrard.
15 octo.	Richard the son of Richard Bradson.
30 No.	Abraham the son of ffrancis Cooe.
1 Dec^e.	Robte the son of Wiłłm Midnall.
17 Jan.	Mary the Daughter of Robte Cutler.
10 febr.	Mary the Daughter of Rafe Stone.
2 Mar.	John the son of Allen Smyth.
10 Mar.	Thoms the son of Wiłłm Benjamyn.

Page 35.

21 Mar.	Cicilie Trves the Daughter of Richard.
	Alice the Daughter of Richard lakeland.

1568.

28 Mar.	Anne the Daughter of Xpofer Ald^{r}man.
30 Mar.	Thoms the son of Wiłłm hailes.
11 June.	Robte the sonne of Willm Bloise.
16 Julie.	Mary the Daughter of James Denny.
8 Aug.	Jone the Daughter of John Ryver.
18 Aug.	Robte the son of Robte ffosdick.
23 octo.	Wiłłm the son of Robte Lane.
30 octo.	Edward the son of Robte Reumn.
4 Nove.	Judith the Daughter of Richard Stowe.
7 Nove.	John the son of John Wheler.
18 Jan.	Roger the son of Robte Cutler.
21 febr.	Annis the Daughter of Wiłłm fferes.
	Thoms the sonne of Thoms Evered.

1569.

22 Ap^r.	Xpiam the Daughter of Edward Timplak.
19 June.	Robte the sonne of Allen Smith.
17 July.	John the sonne of John Smith.
25 July.	James the sonne of John River.
11 Sept.	Agnes the Daughter of Thoms Ive.
2 octo.	Jozine the Daughter of Willm̃ Bucknam.
7 octo.	Sarah the Daughter of Willm̃ Belman.
7 octo.	Richard Cooke the sonne John Cook.
17 octo.	John the sonne of John Cannon.

1 Novem.	Anne the daughter of xpofer Parkhurst.
8 Decem.	Samuell the sonne of Lawrence Clubbe.
13 Decem.	Mary the Daughter of Philip Cressye.
8 Janua.	Alis the Daughter of John Palton.
11 Janua.	ffrancis the Daughter of Wm Barnarton.
15 Janua.	Thoms the sonne of Nicholas clewen.
26 Janua.	John the sonne of Robte Renam.
8 Feb.	Margarett the Daughter of W^m hailes.
17 febru.	Willm the sonne of Willm hall.
24 feb.	Rebecca the Daughter of henry Sever.
28 febr.	Steven the sonne of ffrancis Coe.
11 Mar.	Susan the daughter of Richard Stowe.
19 Mar.	Elizabeth the daughter of Wm Beniamyn.

1570. 1135689

	Samuel the sonne of Richard hill.
29 Mar.	Margery the Daughter of Edward Templak.
6 Aprill.	Margarett the Daughter of John Johnsvn.
23 Apr.	Elzabeth the Daughter of Thoms hitchbone.
27 Apri.	John the sonne of Jeffrey Archer.
4 May.	Anne the Daughter of Robte ffosdick.
21 May.	Susan the Daughter of John Garnett.
30 May.	Rebecca the Daughter of John Bellemal.
6 June.	Willm the sonne of Thoms Trenchfeld.
19 July.	Daniell the sonne of George Wingh.
8 Aug.	Richard the sonne of James Deanen.
27 Aug.	Mary the Daughter of Robte Cheape.
5 octo.	Nathaniell the sonne of John Tynnighell.
29 Aug.	Susan the Daught^r of Andrew harrison.
30 octo.	Abraham the sonne of Wm Cleaveland.
26 nově.	John sonne of John Dammeron.

Page 36.

4 Janu.	Willm son of Richard hill.
7 Janu.	Anne Davghter of John Belcham.
13 Jan.	Robte son of Robte Briggs.
31 Jan.	Robt son of xp̄ofer Alderman.
20 febr.	An Daughter of Thoms Podd.

1571.

26 Mar.	Thomasine Daughter of Thoms Evered.
1 Apri.	Dorcas Daughter of John Atkyn.
2 Apri.	Daniell son of Richard Stowe.
3 May.	humfrey son of Thoms Gillisha.
5 May.	James son of [blank] ffreze.
10 May.	Rebecca Daughter of John Belleman.
15 July.	Martha Daughter of Ruben Goodgine.
18 July.	ffrancis son of George Ball.
16 Sept.	Willm son of Adam Greene.
23 Sept.	Michaell son of Edward Templane.
27 Sept.	Richard son of John Gardner.

D 2

14 Octo.	John son of Walter Estall.
28 octo.	Serson son of Michael Paneel.
5 Nove.	Margaret Daughter of Thos. Trenchfeld.
8 Dece.	Katheryn Daughter of John Johnson.
19 Jan.	Suzan Daughter of Richard Collins.
27 Jan.	Peter son of Thoms hallybred.
4 febr.	Thoms son of henry Jolly.
	Suzan Daught^r of Alen Smithe.
6 febr.	Allexander son of Willm Clearke.
	Martha Daughter of John Dutson.
9 Mar.	Sibill Daughter of John Adam.
10 Mar.	John the son of Richard Boughton.

1572.

14 Apri.	Judith Daughter of Richard Stowe.
19	John son of Richard Jaques.
22	Edward son of Robte Cutler.
30 Aug.	Thoms son of Thoms hockett.
30 Aug.	John son of Willm Cope.
31	Thoms son of Nicholas Plevyn.
13 Sep.	Margarett Daughter of Willm hale.
16	ffrancis son of Doctor ffrancis.
28	George son of George Light.
	Abigail Daughter of Richard Ward.
8 Decem.	Thoms son of James Coe.
18	An hailes.
12 Janu.	Willm Beniamyn.
15 febr.	Elzabeth hill Daughter of Richard.
7	Mary Daughter of Thoms Glede.
1 Mar.	Anne Estall.
21 Mar.	John Kennigall.
23 Mar.	James Lawrence.
	Mary hichebone.

1573.

8 Apri.	Richard Steed.
10 May.	Lawrence Clubb^e.
12 July.	W^m son of Thoms Evered.
24 Aug.	Daniel son of Thoms Christmas.

Page 37.

10 Septe.	Lester Daughter of Richard Cleveland.
13 Sep.	Anne Daughter to John Johnson.
18 octo.	Mary Daughter of Thoms Trenchfeld.
20 Decem.	John son of John Belcham.
10 Decem.	Barbara Daughter of George Wiggen.
10 Janu.	Richard sone of Richard Wade.
31 Janu.	Andrew son of Peter Mormont.
13 febr.	Elizabeth Daughter of Allen Smithe.
24 febr.	Mary Daughter of Willm Cope.
	Robte Estowe son of Samuell Estowe.
25 Mar.	Elizabeth Daughter of Thoms Battell.

14 Apr.	Mary Maye Daughter of John Maye.
15 May.	Josua Keningale.
27 May.	Mary Daughter of Rauff Scrivener.
25 June.	{ John son of John Wattson. { Anne Daughter of Thoms Gynson.
4 July.	{ Thoms son of Thoms Gleed. { John son of John Grenewich. { Willm son of Wᵐ Wignoll.
7 July.	Abigail Daughter of Jeffrey Todd.
20 July.	Jethro son of Richard Bate.
9 Aug.	John son of John Rivers.
15 Aug.	Dorothie Daughter of ffrancis Tokele.
22 Sept.	Alice Daughter of Wᵐ Aggus.
17 octo.	James son of John Dodson.
18 octo.	Walter son of Walter Estall.
20 octo.	Steven son of Robte Stowe.
13 Nove.	John Daughter [sic] of Willm Lyne.
28 Nove.	Thoms sonne of Thoms Cole.
23 Dece.	Willm sonne off Adam Greene.
27 Dece.	Christian Daughter of Robte Lane.
23 Janu.	Mary the Daughter of Thoms Cowlby.
13 febr.	Elizabeth Daughter of John Dawbney.

13 Apri.	{ John sonne of Richard Beniamyn. { John sonne of Richard Glyde.
25 Apri.	Margarett Daughter of George harrison.
5 July.	John sonne of John hockson.
11 July.	Sara Daughter of Thoms Martyn.
17 July.	Agnes Daughter of John Annys.
19 July.	Samuell son of Samuell Smith.
18 octo.	Eunica Daughter of John Dunston.
31 octo.	John sonne of Thoms Trenchefeld.
28 Dece.	Agnes Daughter of John lynes.
3 Jan.	Edward sonne of Walter Estoll.
6 Jan.	Thomazin Daughter of Wᵐ Cowden.
16 Mar.	Willm sonne of John Watson.

13 Apri.	Lucy Daughter of Jeffrey Everell.
18 Apri.	Samuell son of Thoms Gleed.
21 Apri.	Ann Daughter of Jeffry Todd.
24 Apri.	Mathew son of Mathew Brand.
29 Apri.	Willm son of Willm Cope.

Page 38.

22 June.	Sara Daughter of Jhon Kynnigale.
29 July.	Edward sonne of Edward Lord.
5 Aug.	Abigail Daughter of John Adams.
7 Aug.	Luke sonne of Thoms hockett.

19 Aug.	{ Elzabeth Daughter of Richard Writt. { Margarett Daughter of John Smith.
29 Aug.	John son of Wiłłm hart.
11 Sep.	Ambros sonne of Thoms Everett.
14 Sep.	Sibill Daughter of Thoms Burman.
15 Sep.	John sonne of henry Cage.
18 octo.	James sonne of Richard Stowe.
22 octo.	John sonne of John so Johnson [*sic*].
19 Dece.	{ Bridgett Daughter of Rbte Dawbney. { Thoms. sonne of John Belcham.
24 Jan.	Dorothie Daughter of Wm Beniamyn.
24 feb.	Robte son of Nelkyn Glid.
17 Mar.	Jane Daughter of Thoms hitchbone.

1577.

14 Apri.	Anthony sonne of Wiłłm Boycatt.
23 Apri.	John sonne of John Vomtwist.
25 Apri.	Mary Daughter of Thoms Cole.
1 May.	Anne Daughter of Aime Ryvers.
13 June.	Suzan Daughter of Wiłłm Bloye.
30 June.	Elizabeth Daughter of Walter Estoll.
18 July.	ffrancis Daughter of John Johnsvn.
21 July.	Thomazin Daughter of John Annys.
22 July.	John sonne of John Dunston.
4 Aug.	Wiłłm sonne of Ruby Goodwich.
9 Aug.	W^m sonne of Wiłłm persevant.
25 Aug.	(Mary Daughter of Edward Lord. { Susan Daughter of John Smyth. (John sonne of John holme.
1 Sept.	Susan Daughter of Robte Patten.
16 Sept.	Lettis Daughter of Thoms Evered.
19 Sept.	Suzan Daughter of Richard Cleveland.
29 Sept.	Bastian sonne of Symond fflower.
17 octo.	Suzan Daughter of Thoms Trenchfeld.
17 Nove.	Wiłłm sonne of Thoms Gleed.
24 Nove.	Jone Daughter of Thoms Burman.
6 Dece.	Jone Daughter of John Greene.
2 Jan.	Steven son of Adam Greene.
20 Jan.	Sara Daughter of of John Kyningale.
30 Jan.	John son of Samuell Smithe.
20 Mar.	Angill Daughter of Wiłłm hart.

1578.

1 Apri.	Elzabeth Daughter of Peter Trew.
4 May.	{ David son of Thoms hitchbone. { Annis Daughter of John Adam.
11 May.	Elzabeth Daughter of John Ireland.
22 May.	Annys Daughter of Robte hall.
25 May.	Jone Daughter of Nicholas Wainwritt.
Page 39.	
8 June.	Anne Daughter of Thoms Martyn.

29 June.	Jone Daughter of Richard Glede.
9 July.	John son of Jeffrey Todd.
4 octo.	Willm son of Willm̃ Boycatt.
8 octo.	Richard son of Richard Beomvnd.
1 nove.	Richard son of John Daines.
2 nove.	Mary Daughtor of Robte Stare.
7 nove.	Thoms son of Robte Cutler.
17 nove.	Katherin Daughter of John Skydmore.
22 nove.	Susan Daughter of Wulfren Roos.
6 Dece.	Jane Daughter of John More.
20 nove.	Susan Daughter of George Downinge.
13 Dece.	Elzabeth Daughter of Thomas Topline.
5 Jan.	Robte sonne of Thomas Burman.
7 Jan.	Mary Daughter of Edward hunting.
7 febr.	John the son of John Smyth.
15 febr.	Elzabeth Daughter of John Johnson.
17 febr.	Sara Daughter of John Smith.
21 febr.	⎰ John son of Thoms Cole. ⎱ Abigaill Daughter of Nelken Glede.
24 febr.	Jone Daughter of John Kinge.
6 mar.	Christian Daughter of Richard Stowe.
12 mar.	An Daughter of Robt hall.

1579.

13 Apri.	Mary Daughter of Walter Estall.
1 May.	John son of John Keningall.

1580.

3 mai.	John and Mathew Scrivener the sonnes of Rauff Scrivener.
18 May.	Anne the Daughter of John Cage.
29 mai.	Anthony son of Thoms Everett.
22 June.	Thoms son of Thoms Bloberd.
3 July.	Mary Daughter of Thoms hill.
13 July.	Robte son of Robte Greene.
24 July.	ffrancis son of ffrancis Ashelye.
30 July.	Arthur son of Mathew ffokes.
	Thomasin Daughter of Samuell Estall.
20 nove.	Elizabeth Gleed Daughter of Richard.
13 Dec.	Richard son of Richard Mynter.
15 Dec.	Elzabeth Daughter of John Kynge.
21 Dec.	Robte son of Thoms Glede.
22 Jan.	Robte son of Beniamyn Cook.
26 Jan.	Robte son of Robte Pettall.
12 febr.	Henry son of Thoms Cuff.
6 mar.	Samuell son of Adam Greéne.

1581.

7 may.	Elzabeth Daughter of Willm̃ Gilbert.
10 may.	John son of Nicholas Crashfeld.
21 may.	Susan Daughter of John Bus.

1 June.	Abraham son of John Wilkenson.
18 June.	Suzan hunting Daughter of Edward.
23 July.	Samuell son of Walter Estall.
6 Aug.	John son of Thoms Lawrense.
10 Aug.	Elizabeth Daughter of Godf^ry Ostler.
	John son of Wiłłm Beniamyn.
17 Sept.	Mary [son, *ruled out*] Daughter of Richard Beomvnd.
15 octo.	Thoms son of Robt Starre.
22 octo.	John son of John Alderman.
3 Dece.	Mary Daught^r of Thoms Toplif.
27 Dece.	Wiłłm son of Richard Osburne.
6 Jan.	Alice Daught^r of John Cooke.
13 Jan.	Anne Daughter of ffrancis Ashelye.
4 Feb.	Jone Daught^r of John Daines.
6 Feb.	Willm̃ sonne of Willm̃ Aggus.
6 Feb.	John son of Robte Greene.
5 Mar.	Theophilus son of John keningall.
14 Mar.	Anthony son of Anthony Barcock.
19 Mar.	Sara Daught^r of Thoms Gleed.

1582.

1 Apri.	{ Robt and Alice son & Daugh of Anthony Annger. { John the sonne of henry kyrne.
8 Apri.	Mary Daughter of John Johnson.
15 Apri.	John son of John Cage.
29 Apri.	Robt son of Nicholas Palmer.
6 May.	{ Judith Daughter of John Lany. { Willm son of John Sturgen.
15 May.	John son of Willm Carow.
17 May.	John son of Edward Gooding.
15 June.	Thoms son of Naboth hueilt.
24 June	{ Abraham son of Richard Gleed. { John sonne of Wiłłm Boycatt.
29 July.	Anne Daughter of Robte Garrett.
2 Sept.	{ Edward son of [*blank*] Michaell. { Willm̃ son of Richard Mynter.
16 Sept.	Alice Daughter of Thoms Burman.
1 octo.	xp̄ofer son of Thoms Evered.
15 nove.	Anne Daughter of Valentyn Bate.
18 nove.	Thoms sonne of [*blank*] Braseye.
3 Dece.	John son of Jeffrey Man.
4 Dece.	Edward sonne of Edward hunting.
8 Dece.	Thomasine Daughter of John Cowper.
4 febr.	Nicholas son of Rauff Scrivener.
22 Mar.	Robte son of Steven Barcock.

1583.

14 Apri.	{ Mary Daughter of [*blank*] Tibbald. { Anne Daughter of Wm Beniamyn.

16 Apr.	Alice the Daughter of Robte Cutler.
5 May.	Katherin & Martha Daughte[rs] of John lanye.
8 May.	John the son of John keniñgale.
2 June.	Beatris Daughter of Thoms Lawrence.
9 June.	Elzabeth Daughter of John Duckett.
5 Aug.	Judith Daughter of Richard Beomond.
10 Aug.	Abigail Daughter of John Sturgeon.
29 Aug.	Martyn son of Robte Garrett.
22 Sept.	John huggens the son of John.
26 Sept.	Parnell the Daughter of Robte Pettall.

Page 41.

30 Sep.	Christian Daughter of Richard Osborne.
20 octo.	{ Wiłłm sonne of Robt Seersent. { Annis Daughtr of Thoms Jemson.
10 Nove.	Gabrell sonne of Robte Wak.
5 Dece.	henry sonne of henry Cage.
8 Dece.	Abigall Daughter of Walter Estoll.
23 Jan.	John the sonne of Edward Cage.
5 febr.	Wiłłm sonne of Wiłłm Gilbert.
17 febr.	{ John sonne of John Cruxall. { Alice Daughter of Robte Grimson.
20 feb.	Josvph sonne of Thoms Grimwood.
22 feb.	Elzabeth Daughter of John hart.
8 Mar.	Alice Daughter of Edie Cruxall.

1584.

28 Mar.	henry sonne of John Patten.
10 Apri.	John son of John Blaxall.
19 Apri.	John son of John Thurston.
26 Apri.	{ Edmond son of John Johnson. { Suzan Daughter of Cnarles Luffe.
30 Apri.	Jone Daughter of xpõfer Ald[r]man.

1585.

20 June.	{ Custann Daughter of W[m] Aggis. { Katherine Daughter of henry kyme.
8 July.	Mary Daughter of Robt Cutler.
13 July.	John sone of John Cook.
18 July.	Madlen Daughter of Thoms Burman.
5 Aug.	Margarett Daughter of John Garrad.
8 Aug.	Abigall Daughter of Ewyn Gilpyn.
5 Sept.	Edward son of Edward Martyn.
17 Sept.	Jeffrey son of Jeffrey Tod.
7 octo.	Elzabeth Daughter of Walter Estoll.
30 octo.	harver son of John Cruxall.
2 nove.	{ Symond son of Symon Wilkyn. { Christian Pettall Daughter of Robte Pettall.
19 Dec.	{ John son of Richard Mynter. { Alice Barcoke baptised the 14 of november. { Thoms son of Thoms Wiseman.

16 Jan.	Mary Daughter of John Huggin.
25 Jan.	John son of Richard Osborne.
30 Jan.	{ Robt son of Robt Cheape. { Samuell son of Samuell Estoll.
9 feb.	Willm son of John Garrad.
7 Mar.	Abraham son of John Johnson.
20 Mar.	Xpofer son of Esdras Sherwood.

1586.

4 Apri.	Willm̃ son of Willm Gleed.
17 Apri.	John son of John Whitting.
19 Apri.	Xpofer son of Gilbert Crane.
13 June.	{ Thomasin Daughter of John Towson. { Margarett Daughter of John More.
30 June.	Steven son of Nicholas Crashfeld.
3 July.	Willm son of John Black.
15 July.	Alis Daughter of henry Cage.
30 July.	{ Elzabeth Daughter of Robte Cutler. { Bridgett Daughter of Valentyn Bate.

Page 42.

21 Aug.	Willm son of Will Christmas.
28 Aug.	Anne Daughter Willm Loost.
1 Sept.	Thomazine Daughter of Mathew Cordett.
4 Sept.	{ James son of Lawrence hulinge. { Robt son of Robte Andrewes.
22 Sept.	Robt son of xpofer Alderman.
27 Sept.	Elzabeth Daughter of Rauff Scrivener.
13 octo.	Anna Daught of Willm Bate.
13 octo.	Thoms son of John Daynes.
23 octo.	Xpofer son of Thoms Trenchfeld.
8 Jan.	Xpofer son of John Alderman.
22 Jan.	Alis Daughter of John Wincvll.
11 feb.	Rose Daughter of Edmond Luckas.
12 Mar.	Willm son of Micheos (*or* Micheas ? Michael) Sympson.
24 Mar.	{ Nicholas son of Willm Boycatt. { Elzabeth Daughters of Thoms Wood.

1587.

29 Mar.	Margery Daughter of Edward Cage.
23 July	Margett harus Daughter of John haras.
27 June.	Alis Daughter of Robte Cutler.
7 Sept.	Richard son of Richard osborne.
10 Sept.	Elzabeth Daughter of John Parson.
17 Sept.	{ Sara Daughtʳ of George ffunell. { Mary Daughter of Bartholomew Sallowes.

1588.

25 Apri.	{ Edward son of Robte Cheape. { Robte the son of Robte Cheape.
11 May.	John the son of Edmond Estoll.
23 June.	Anne Daughter of Mathew Cordett.

26 June.	John sonne of xpofer Alderman.
7 July.	Dorckas Daughter of Esdras Sherwood.
10 July.	{ Michobell harrold Daughter of [*blank*]. { Jone Daughter of Richard Leathes.
25 Aug.	Steven son of John Blage.
20 octo.	John son of John Winckoll.
29 Decem.	Giles son of Willm Stidman.
2 Jan.	Steven son of Isack Grenewich.
5 Jan.	Steven son of Steven Talmage.
22 Jan.	John son of Thoms Daye.
2 febr.	Edmond son of John Bantock.
6 febr.	John son of Richard Quant.
10 Nove.	{ Robte son of Robte Cutler. { Thoms son of Robte Greve.
8 Decem.	{ Thomazin Daughter of John Johnson. { Grace Daughter of Willm Boycatt.
15 Decem.	Richard son of Wm Ayres.
22 Decem.	Thoms son of Thoms hawkins.
19 Jan.	Martha Daughter of Thoms Carew.
23 feb.	{ Tobyas son of Tobias Browne. { John son of Willm Cleveland.
6 Mar.	John son of John Cruxall.
20 Mar.	Margery Daughter of John huggen.
30 Mar.	Thomas son of Edmond Luckas.

1589.

12 Apri.	Thoms & xpofer sons of Valentyne Bate.
ii May.	Willm son of Edward haile.
29 May.	John son of John harris.
5 June.	Mary Daughter of Richard Osborne.
15 June.	Thoms son of Willm Aggas.
22 June.	Xpofer son of Thoms Batham.

Page 43.

13 July.	Lawrence son of John Vanne.
Aug.	Elzabeth Daughter of John Sturgen.
17 Aug.	Bridgett Daughter of Thoms Palmer.
8 Sep.	John son of henry Veale.
21 Sep.	John son of John Parson.
17 feb.	Samuell sson of Robte Cutler.
17	Bridgett Daughter of John Lost.

1590.

31 Mrch.	{ Mary Daughter of Xpofer Aldrman. { Nicholas son of John Glenne. { Elzabeth Daughter of Miles Riggs.
19 May.	Jane & Anne Daught^rs of Nicholas Crashfeld.
24 May.	John son of Michael Sympson.
31 May.	Beniamyn, son of Thoms Wiseman.
19 July.	{ Elzabeth the Daughter of Richard Marks. { John son of Willm Bate.
23 July.	Elzabeth Daughter of Marcke long.

27 Aug.	Judith Daughter of Richard lord.
30 Aug.	Debora Daughter of Willm̃ Stidman.
5 octo.	Abigail Daughter of Arthur Croxall.
18 octo.	Thoms son of Rauff more.
25 octo.	Anne Daughter of Wiłtm Cole.
28 octo.	James son of John Johnson.
10 Nov.	Edmond son of James herold.
7 No.	Jone Daughter of Willm̃ Prick.
2 Dec.	Robart son of Steven Talmage.
10 Ja.	Prudence Daughter of Robte Pettall.
14 Ja.	Allyn son of Allin Cove.
17 Ja.	Robte son of Robt Greve.
22 Ja.	Katheryn Daughter of Edmond Luccas.
31 Ja.	Thoms Salter son of Thoms Salter.
17 Ap.	Thoms son of Thoms Warnes.

1591

1591.

27 Ap.	Katheryn Daughter of John Allyn.
2 May.	Wiłtm son of Robte Cutler.
3 octo.	Mary Daughter of Thoms Batham.
24 no.	John son of John Goffe.
28 no.	Susan Daughter of Philip Eton.
20 De.	Elzabeth Daughter of Isack Greue.
21 De.	{ Valentyne son of Valentyne Bate. Margery Daughter of Valentyne Bate. Elzabeth Daughter of John hall.
6 Jan.	Thoms son of Thoms hayward. John son of John Walter.
16 Ja.	{ Grace Daughter of John Sherman. ffrancis Daughter of Thoms Robtson.
17 Ja.	Mary Daughter of Willm̃ Ayres.
6 Feb.	{ James son of Allen Cobe. Martha Daughter of John Burges.
23 Mar.	Samuell son of Isack Grenewich.

1592.

2 Apr.	Elzabeth Daughter of Robte Chepe.
9 Apr.	Dorithie Daughter of Robte Pettall.
i May	Margarett Daughter of Michaell kinge.
24 June	John son of Thomas List.
2 July	Jone Daughter of John Winckoll.
24 Aug.	Susan Daughter of Mark lvny.
3 Sep.	Dorcas Daughter of Wiłtm Bloyse.

Page 44.

2 Sep.	Dorcas Bloyes Daughter of Wiłtm Bloise [*repetition with altered date*].
24 Sep.	Martha Alderman Daughter of Xpofer.
19 Sep.	Elizabeth Daughter of Willm haires.
i octo.	Richard son of Paull Peterson.
2 octo.	Beniamyn Cutler son of Robte Cutler.
5 nov.	Grace Daughter of Richard hasiell.

14 Nov.	Jone Daughter of Rauff Collin.
8 feb.	Elizabeth Salter Daughter of Thoms Salter.

1593.

Apr. 24.	{ Anne Luccas Daughter of Edmond. { Willm sonne of [*blank*] Barber.
	Anne Daughter of Allin Cone.
	Elzabeth Worslett.
	Richard Marke.
	Mary Prick.
	Alice Aldam.
15 July.	Robte son of Robte Bert.
	Richard Bastard son to Widdow ffurnell.
13 Ja.	Anne Daughter of [*blank*] Wittingham.
6 Ja.	Thoms son of Isack Grenwiche.
15 Ja.	{ Willm son of Willm Boicatt. { Willm son of Edward harrold.
11 feb.	Peter son of Willm Perhonn.

1594.

5 May.	Thoms sonne of Thoms List.
9 May	{ Abigaille Daughter of Valentyne Bate. { John Buxton. { George Robinson.
28 July.	{ Joane Duk und Thoms Watters son of John Watt^rs. { 14 July
4 Aug.	Robte Aggas.
20 octo.	An Daughter of Steven hart.

1594.

10 Dec.	Thoms son of xpofer Ald^rman.	
6 Apr.	John Cook son of John Cook.	1595
6 July.	John son of John Wilson.	1595
11 July.	Jone Daughter of Allen Cove.	
4 Dece.	Elzabeth Cook Daught^r of John Cook.	
2 Ja.	Willm Prick & Elizabeth Tassell.	
6 febr.	xpofer hart the sonne of Stephen.	1596
13 febr.	Willm Allison & George Cuspe.	
	George Cobball the 27 Aprill.	

1596.

5 May.	Blanche Salter daughter of Tho. Salter.
27 febr.	{ Anne Mixture. John Wilson 6 July. { Olive Poppes. Elzabeth Cook 2 January. { Anne Alderman. xpofer hart.
6 Mar.	{ Robt Briswood. 12 May Willm Perrŏm. { John Pall the sonne of paul Peterson.
	Alice Bloyes the Daught^r of Willm Bloyes.

1597.

15 Apr.	John son of Michael king.
29 Apr.	Richard son of Anthony Colby.

12 May.	Jacvb son of Abraham Wathwith.
	Rauff son of David Goodene.
28 May.	Samuell Watters the son of John Watters.

Page 45. 1599. 1599

25 Mar.	Robte the son of John Wilson.
9 Apr.	{ Anne Daughter of Thoms Davy.
	{ Isack son of Richard Poppes.
20 May.	Susan Daughter of Nicholas Bias.
24 Jun.	Barnabas son of Robte Gosse.
8 July.	Robt son of Robte Moulson.
6 Aug.	Robt son of Thoms Page.
8 Aug.	Elzabeth Daught of Isack Grenewiche.
12 Aug.	Wiłłm sonne of Wiłłm Clyat.
26 Aug.	Rose Daughter of Margaret harryson base.
4 Nove.	Thoms sonne of Thoms Robteson.
ii nove.	{ Mathew son of Thoms Bennett.
	{ Elzabeth Daugher of Thoms hart.
2 Dec.	Susan Daughter of Thoms Stevenson.
9 Dec.	Anne Daughter of Willm Sudbury.
17 Jan.	Katherin Daughter of Willm Tilletson.
26 Jan.	Elzabeth Daughter of Steven hart.
28 Jan.	Robt son of Angell Nightingale.
3 feb.	Mary the Daughter of Edward [*sic*].
10 feb.	Jone Daughter of Richard Churche.
24 feb.	Elzabeth Daught^r of Wiłłm Philppe.
2 Mar.	Bethea Daughter of George Bevill.
9 Mar.	Edward son of Thoms Bashpoll.
23 Mar.	Robte son of Wiłłm Attlebrige.

1600.

3 May	Edward son of Robte Cutler.
13 Ap.	Nicholas son of Richard Osborne.
27 Ap.	{ hughe son of Robte Kinghtall.
	{ Alis Daughter of Katheryn Golding.
12 May.	{ Alis. Daughter of John Posford.
	{ Isack son of Thoms Burnishe.
18 May	Charles son of Charles Wines.
6 July	Margarett Daughter of John Stepven.
27 June	Dorithye Daughter of John Wilkenson.
15 July	Wiłłm sonne of Wiłłm Bloise.
20 July.	ffrancis Daughter of Elzabeth Riggs base.
27 July.	John the sonne of Richard Poppes.
24 Aug.	Ambrose sonne of Samuell Cleveland.
14 Sep.	{ Elzabeth Daughter of Richard fforder.
	{ Anne Daughter of Wiłłm ffeerye.
5 octo.	Jone Daughter of Wiłłm Powline.
26 octo.	Thoms son of John Garrad.
9 Nove.	Elzabeth Daughter of John Bateman.
30 Nov.	Dorethie Daughter Rauff Bane.
14 Dece.	Mary Daughter of Abraham Grenewich

i febr.	Margery Daughter of Nycholas Bias.
12 febr.	henry sonne of henry Piper.
15 febr.	prissilla Daughter of Tho. Keningalle.
22 febr.	Willm̄ sonne of hughe Edward.
6 mar.	John sonne of John Lynes.
22 mar.	Elzabeth Daughter of Rauff Buckton.

1601.

26 Apr.	Thoms son of Thoms Buller.
18 May.	Sara Daughter of Davy Goodene.
20 July.	Paul son of Paul Peterson.
July.	Robt sonne of Thoms Stevenson.
	Elzabeth Daughter of [blank] Barrell.

Chistinnys.

1602.

2 Aug.	John the sonne of Willm̄ Clyatt.
23 Aug.	Elzabeth Daughter of Thoms Page.
22 Sep.	Samuell son of Samuell Cutler.
29 Nov.	Thoms son of John Peryman.
20 Dece.	Peter son of Richard cleark.
14 feb.	Barnabas son of Charles Wines.
25 feb.	Willm son of Philipp fforde.
12 Mar.	John son of Abraham Wathwith.
8 Apri.	Thoms son of hughe Edwards.
25 Ja.	Steven son of Steven hart.
30 Ja.	{ Allexander son of James Gravener.
	{ Anne Daughter of Thoms hart.
15 feb.	Margaret Daughter of henry Veale.
	Thoms son of Richard Poppes.
7 mar.	Ezechiell son of Roger Cutler.

1603.

16 Apr.	Thoms son of Willm̄ Philippes.
18 Apr.	Robt son of Willm Panton.
3 July.	John son of hughe Edwards.
17 July.	James son of Paul Peterson.
17 Aug.	Thoms son of Thoms Keningall.
28 Aug.	George son of George Gipson.
4 Sep.	Alis Daughter of Willm Powling.
9 octo.	Robte son of Willm Clyatt.
14 octo.	Margaret Daughter of John Berry.
23 Octo.	Mary Daughter of Simeon Wrinche.
18 Nove.	Mary Daughter of Willm Attlebrig.
4 Dece.	Christian Daughter of Willm fferry.
28 Ja.	Steven son of henry Veale.
26 feb.	{ Isack son of Moyses Cleveland.
	{ Anne Daughter of John ffrost.
5 mar.	Mary Daughter of Steven hart.
24 mar.	Robte son of John Pofford.

i Apri.   ffrancis son of John Archer.
i2 May.   { humfrey Welye.
            { Margarett harris.
27 May.   { Willm̃ son of Willm̃ Bell.
            { Willm son of Willm Panton.
i June   Rebecca Daughter of Mary Briant base.
15 July   Thomasin Daughter of John Debdyn.
12 Aug.   Barbara Daughter of Nicholas Bias.
26 Aug.   Robt sonne of Richard Poppes.
10 Sep.   John son of Charles Wines.
13 Sep.   ffrancis son of Willm̃ Bloise.
14 octo.   John son of Will Phillips.
20 octo.   Edward son of Nathaniel hubaucks.
28 octo.   Abigaile Daughter of John Paul.
4 nove.   Pricilla & Barbara Daughters of John Bateman.
13 no.   Steven son of Willm Stanly.

    Page 47.   1605.
21 May   Joseph. sonne of Roger Cutler.
16 June   Mary Daughter of John Palmer.
30 June   Mary Daughter of Thoms Moulson.
7 July   John son of John Berry.
14 July   Jone Daughter of Roger Raynam.
25 June   Jane Daughter of Thoms hailes
17 Nove.   Robte son of Thoms Cutler.
14 Apr.   Steven son of hugh Edwards.
21 Apr.   Sara Daughter of Willm Gravener.
28 Apr.   { Richard sone of Steven hart.
            { Beniamyn son of John Cressall.
26 De.   Thoms son of Edmund Miller.   1604
3 feb.   Robte son of Robt Gosse.   1604
15 mar.   Elzabeth Daughter of Eward harrrold.
26 Aug.   Mary the Daughter of Edward langley.   1605
9 feb.   hanna Cook Daughter of Nathaniell Cook.
18 feb.   Abigaile Bloise Daughter of Willm Bloise.
23 feb.   ffrancis son of [*blank*] hill.
23 Mar.   Martha Daughter of Willm̃ Elliett.

            1606.
    John Wilder the son of Richard Wilder baptized the
        $\frac{27}{29}$th June.

    Page 48.   1607.
28 March.   Edward the sonne of Edward Langley.
            Joan the Daughter of Thoms Steven.
Julie 25.   Richard the sonne of Richard Watters.

            1608.
6 Julye.   Elizabeth the Daughter of Edward Langley.
Juliee 13. Walter Simons baptisd.
4 Septembr. Nathaniell the sonne ef Nathaniell Cooke.

1609.

Augu.	13.	ffrancis the sonne of ffrancis Nailor.
Sept.	3.	Anne Bane.
octo.	15.	Elza Daine.
Novem.	12.	Lidda Hebden daughtr of Wm Hebden.
No.	25.	James Osmond & Samuell Welie.
Dece.	17.	John Acton sonne of Daniel Action & Mary the Daughter of Willm Stopher.
Janua.	7.	Elzabeth Daugh. of Thoms hobbes.
	18.	Susan Daugh. of Edward Cheape.
	21.	Susan Dolton.
	27.	John Irish.
febru.	25.	Thoms hawkins. ffrancis Langley sonne of Edward Langly. ffrancis Potter and Thomasine hellmet.
februa.	2.	Jonathan the sonne of Willm Mounsey sen.
	26.	Anne Starkey daughter of [*blank*] Stark.
Mar.	12.	Dorcas Molson [*blank*] Richard Wilder & Mary Empson.
	26.	*Robte Neauell.* 1610
April	30.	Martha Daughter of John Cole.
May	2 i.	Sarah Popps.
June	28.	hanna Burrowe.
		John Ward sonne of Michaell Ward.
		John the sonne of Thoms Jarvice.
April	i.	Mary Durrant.
	22.	John the sonne of Thoms Man.
June	3.	Robte the sonne of John Bateman.
July	2.	Marye the Daught. of Mr Willm Bloise.
	8.	Richard the sonne of Richard Daynes.
	29.	Joseph the sonne of James hobbes.
Aug.	5.	Symeon Bennett.
Sepr	24.	henry Wilder.
	26.	Priscilla Brett.

Page 49. 1610.

Septemr	30.	Thoms Savage.
Octo.	14.	[*blank*] of Daniell Barker.
Decemr	9.	Symeon the sonne of Simeon Poynter.
	30.	John the sonne of John Aldrman.
Janua.	i.	Wynefred Daught. of Roger Cutler.
	20.	Samuell the sonne of Willm hebden.
februa.	3.	Salter the sonne of Richard Watters.
March	7.	Anne Daughtr of Beniamyn Brand.
		[*blank*] of Edward Dolton.
Nov. ye	13th.	Mary ye Daughtr of george bret.

1611.

March	25.	Elizabeth Daughtr of John Paddy.
	3 i.	[*blank*] of Richard Swaine.

Apri.	14.	Priscilla Daught^r of James Osmond.
	2 i.	[*blank*] and [*blank*] sonne & Daugh^tr of Ja. Graven.
	28.	[*blank*] of [*blank*] Blunte.
May	5.	Thoms CresWell & Elzabeth Stork.
	26.	Mercy Daught. of ffrancis Pownsett.
June	6.	Thoms the sonne of Thoms CresWell.
	16.	John the sonne of Wiħm Stopher.
Aug.	4.	Samuell Panton & [*blank*] Daught^r of Jeremy Siclemore.
Sept.	i.	John the sonne of [*blank*] Elmett.
	24.	Arthur sonne of Edward langley.
Octob^r	20.	Alice Daugh^r of James hills.
Novem^r	11.	Anne Daught^r of Daniell Barker.
	24.	Anna Daught^r of Daniell Acton.
Decem^r	1.	Margaret Daught^r of [*blank*] hutchingson.
Januarj	1.	Avis Daughter of Michell Ward.
	4.	John sonne of Willm Bloise Portman.
	5.	Jane Daught^r of Israell Williams.
februarij	9.	{ Hester Daught^r of Milsey Monsie. / Thomas sonne [*blank*] Tuttle.
	23.	{ Josuah sonne of Joseph hawkins.
februa	23.	{ Judith Daughter of Thoms Woodgate.
March	9.	{ Alice Daughter to James Bate. / Debora Daughter to Wm Hebden deceased. / Rebecca Daught^r to Wiħm Evered. } Baptd all in one Daie.

1612.

Apriel	26.	Joan Daughter of John Alderman Jun.
Maij	17.	{ Katherine Daughter to John Alderman sen. / Thomas Sonne to Abraham Smithe. / Christian Daughter to Nicholas Watters. } Baptd all in one Daie.
May	24.	Elizabeth Daughter to Edward Cheape.
Julie	19.	{ Peter the sonne of Peter Brett. / Isaake the sonne of [*blank*] Cleaveland. / Elizabeth the Daughter of Richard Daines. } baptd all in one Daie.
Julie	26.	Robte the sonne of Edmunde Daulton.
	28.	henrie the sonne of John Veale.
August	8.	Marie the Daughter of [*blank*] Morgan.
Sept^r	6.	Alice the Daughter of henrie Gale.
	13.	{ Jeremie the sonne of Jeremie Durrant. / John the sonne of [*blank*] Topcliff. } bapt.
	20.	{ Thoms sonne of Thoms Creswell. / Thoms sonne of [*blank*] / Thoms sonne of [*blank*] / Richard sonne of Richard Swaine. } baptd all in one Daie.
October	4.	{ Edward sonne of [*blank*] Lambe. / Mary Daughter of [*blank*] Colman. }

[October]   8. | Susan Daught^r of ffrancis Nailor.   ⎫
             31. ⎩ Marian Daught^r of John Cornelius. ⎭
Decem^r 13. Edwarde sonne of Thomas Martyn baptised.
Januarij   17. Thomas sonne of [*blank*] Burrowes.
             31. Jane Daught^r of Clem^t Alsoph.
febra.   2. Anne Daughter of [*blank*] Jarvice.

    Page 50.

St Nicholas parish
  in Ipswich.   Christings.   1612, 1613, 1614.

ffebruarij   14. Susanne the Daughter of John Jentilman.   Baptiz.
                  [*blank*] the sonne of [*blank*].
March   7. John the sonne of John Barker.   ⎫
             14. Willm the sonne of Willm Stofer   ⎬ Baptized.
             24. ⎰ Edmund the sonne of Edmonde Clerke   ⎭
                 ⎱ Joan the Daughter of James Osborne
                        1613.
Aprill   19. Thomasine Daught^r of Edward langley.
             25. Steven the sonne of Steven Crashfeld.
August   8. henry sonne of Wittm fferye [*or* ffrrye].
             22. Elzabeth Daught^r of George °//° More.
J.T. Maye 23.   Gilbert the sonne of Richard & Mary Waters was
                    baptized.
Marion the Daughter of Alexander and Agnes Marret was baptized
    October 10.
Rebekah ye Daughter of James and Judith Gravener was baptized
    October 24.
November 14. Alice the Daughter of Thomas & Alice Parker was
    baptized.
             21. Elizabeth ye daughter of Robert & Elizabeth Pascall
                    was baptized.
December   5. Elizabeth ye daughter of John & Martha Reade was
                    baptized.
             20. John ye sonne of Mr John Smith & of Elisabeth
                    his wife was baptized.
             23. Anna ye daughter of Thomas & Esther Johnson
                    was baptized.
January   27. Marye the daughter of Robert & Anne Browne was
                    baptized.
February   6. Richard ye sonne of Nicolas & Christian Watters
                    was baptized.
             16. Richard ye sonne of Richard & ffrancis Darlye was
                    baptized.
             20. Elisabeth ye daughter of Robert & Elisabeth Darnell
                    was baptized.
                    Anno Dñi 1614°.
Aprill   10. Moses ye sonne of William & ffrancis Stempson
                    was baptized.
             24. Abigaill ye daughter of Robert & Margaret Potter
                    was baptized.

    E ^{2}

Maye   1.   Hester ye daughter of Thomas & Joane Storke was baptized.

      15.   Lydia ye daughter of Edmund & Lydia Miles was. baptized.

June   5.   { Alexander ye sonne of Alexander & Agnes Thomas / Marye ye daughter of ffrancis & Anne Smith ʄʄ } were baptized.

      19.   Thomas ye sonne of Thomas & Letice helmett was baptized.

July   17.   Robert ye sonne of Tobias & Marye Potter was baptized.

      24.   { John ye sonne of John & Alice Alderman was baptized. / Simon ye base borne childe of Margarett Edwards widdow was baptized. }

      31.   Margerye ye daughter of John & Alice Alderman was baptized.

August   21.   Sarah ye daughter of Richard & Marye Smyth was baptized.

      28.   John ye sonne of John & Katharine ffuse was baptized.

September   4.   Alice ye daughter of John & Prudence Topliffe was baptized.

      11.   { Abigaill ye daughter of John & Brigitt Waters ʄʄ / Susan the daughter of Edmund & Susanne Dalton / Anne the daughter of Martine & Elisabeth hutchinson } were baptized.

      25.   Abigail the daughter of Abraham & Susanne Andrews was baptized.

      27.   John ye base sonne of John hobbs & Elisabeth Mockted was baptized.

October   9.   Beniamin ye sonne of William & Hannah Panton was baptized.

      28.   John ye sonne of Thomas & Anne Waple was baptized.

      30.   Susan ye daughter of William & Katharine Morgan was baptized.

November   6.   Henry the sonne of henry & Hannah Gale was baptized.

December   6.   Jonathan ye sonne of William & Elisabeth Stopher was baptized.

January   1.   John ye sonne of Peter & Thomasin Brett was baptized.

      15.   Elisabeth ye daughter of William & Elisabeth Briden was baptized.

      22.   John the sonne of Charles & Marye Dennye was baptized.

February 4. Thomas } the children of Thomas & Elisabeth
Martha } Woodgate were baptized.

5. Thomas yᵉ sonne of Robert & Marye Steddye was baptized.

12. { Timothye yᵉ sonne of Richard & Marye Homes
Robert yᵉ sonne of Edmund & Abigail Clarks } were baptized.

Page 51. Subscribed by { John Daye minister of the parish of Sᵗ Nicolas in Ipswich.
Nathˡ Warde.

Sᵗ Nicholas parish in Ipswich.

Christings. 1614, 1615.

February 19. Eunice yᵉ daughter of Richard & Margaret Bennet was baptized.

March 3. William yᵉ sonne of ffrancis & Katherine Annisse was baptized.

12. Abigail yᵉ daughter of John & Elizabeth Browne was baptized.

19. John yᵉ sonne of Robert and Elisabeth Pascall was baptized.

Anno Dm̃ 1615.

26. { Henry yᵉ sonne of Henry & Thomasin Buckenham
William the sonne of Walter & Bathsheba Gilbert } were baptised.

Aprill 2. { Susan the daughter of John & Anne Deale
Thomas yᵉ sonne of Marmaduke & Mary Tillson } were baptized.

6. Marye yᵉ base childe of Joan Scott widdowe was baptised.

10. George yᵉ sonne of John and Marye Depden was baptized.

16. Marye the daughter of John & Martha Reeve was baptized.

23. Thomas yᵉ sonne of Thomas Sanders & Joan Mendham was baptised.

Maye 7. { Isaak yᵉ sonne of George & Emme Moore ff
Sarah yᵉ daughter of Henry & Sarah Clerk } were baptised.

14. { Nathaniel yᵒ sonne of Nathaniel & Anne Church
Sarah yᵉ daughter of Robert & Rachel Yellupp ff } were baptized.

28. William yᵉ sonne of George & Elisabeth Daynes was baptized.

June	4.	Robert y° base childe of Robert Bacon & Alice Sparrowe was baptized.
	18.	Thomas ye sonne of Thomas & Elizabeth Martyn was baptized.
July	23.	⎧Katharine yᵉ daughter of Richard & Katharine Osburne⎫ were baptised. Elisabeth yᵉ daughter of Thomas & Susan Man
	30.	Alice yᵉ daughter of John Alderman yᵉ yonger & of Alice his wife was baptized.
August	6.	John yᵉ sonne of Thomas & Alice Parker was baptized.
	27.	Mary yᵉ daughter of Richard & Mary Smith was baptized.
September	10.	Henry yᵉ sonne of Henry & Elizabeth ffinne was baptised.
October	8.	⎧George yᵉ sonne of George & Elisabeth Lymbert⎫ were baptised. Susan yᵉ daughter of Robert & Elisabeth Darnell
	15.	John yᵉ sonne of Edward & Hellen Langley was baptized.
	22.	Dorothee yᵉ daughter of Thomas & Elizabeth Rendall was baptized.
	29.	Samuel yᵉ sonne of Nathaniel and Elizabeth Ward was baptised.
November	5.	⎧Simon yᵉ sonne of George & Brigit Rooke⎫ were baptised. Mary the daughter of Walter & Christian Attlebrig
	12.	Beniamin the sonne of James & Priscilla Osburne was baptized.
December the	10.	letes fuse the dauter of John and Marget fuse was baptised.
Decem.	21.	Samuell the sonne of Charles & Dorathy Bourne.
March	30.	Elizabeth the daughter of Jeremy & Elizabeth Sicklemore.

1616.

August	25.	Isacke yᵉ sonne of James Gravner was baptised.
Sep.	14.	Edward Smith the sonn of John Smith baptised.
Octo.	27.	John Crashfeild the sonⁿ of Steven Crashfeld baptised.
November	23.	Thomas Darly the sonn of Richard Darly was baptised.
Decemb.	1.	Sarah Bennett the daughter of Richard Benitt baptized.
	14.	Robt Cutler the sonn of Robt Cutler Jun baptized.
	29.	John ffinn the sonn of Henery ffinn baptized.

Septemb.   7.   Marie Swaine the daught^r of Richard Swaine was baptized. [*Repeated on page 52*].

Page 52.   S. Nicholas pish.   1617.

Septemb.   7.   Marie the daughter of Richard Swaine was baptised.

Septemb.   21.   { Anna Estall the daughter of John Estall and Marie was baptizd.
Susaña Smith ye daughter of Joseph and Susana Smith was baptizd.

            29.   Nathaniell the sone of Charles & Dorothie Bourne was baptizd.

Octob.   5.   Isaak Wathwhite the sone Abraham and Ales Wathwhite was baptizd.

            12.   Isaak Gravner the sone of James and Judah Gravener was baptizd.

Novemb.   2.   { Marie Gaie the daughter of Thomas and Marie Gaie was baptizd.
Priscilla Pouncet the daughter of Frauncis and Marie Pouncet was baptizd.

            9.   Triffena Osburne The daughter of James and Priscilla Osburne was baptizd.

            30.   { Susaña Huske the daughter of Richard & Susaña Huske was baptizd.
Dorcas Manhod the daughter of John Manhod and Dorcas was baptizd.

Decemb.   8.   Abigaile Clarke was baptised.

            22.   Samuel Thomas the sone of Alexander Thomas was baptisd.

Januar.   11.   Jacob Moulson the sone of Thomas Moulson was baptizd.

            18.   Bridgit Garvis was baptisd.

Febru.   21.   James Creasall the sone of Thomas Creasall was baptizd.

March   1.   Elizabeth Sicklemore the daughter of Jeremie Sicklemore was baptizd.

            22.   Añe Alderman the daughter of John Alderman was baptizd.

Año Dñi 1618.

Aprill   5.   Marie Weelie the daughter of Humfrey Weelie was baptzd.

1618.

Julie   26.   John Deale the sone of John Deale was baptized.

August   2.   { Nathaniel the sone of Nathaniel Smart was baptised.
Winifred Panton the daughter of William Panton was baptized.

Octob.   25.   Thomas Parker the sone of Thomas & Alice Parker was bap.

Octob.   25. {
Anne Wade the daughter of Richard Wade was baptizd.
Nathaniel Balder the sone of William Balder was baptized.
Deborah yᵉ daughter [*blank*] [the daughter of Richard Gudberd *(erased)*].
}

Novemb.   15. Benjamin the sone of Benjamin Cutler was baptised.

Decemb.   6. {
John the sone of John Benet was baptised.
Benjamin the sone of [*blank*] Suggate was baptised.
}

March   20. John the sone of Mʳ John Lanie was baptisd.

Año Dñi 1619.

1619.   1619.

Apriell   25. Elizabeth Coppinge the daughter of Richard Copping and Elizabeth Copinge his wiffe was baptised the 25th of Apriell 1619.

Mãy   .. John Smith the sone of Richard Smith was baptisd.

Septemb. 19. Thomas Paschall the sone of [*blank*] Paschall was baptisd.

Octob.   24. Peter Chamberlaine the sone of [*blank*] Chamberlaine baptisd.

October   27. Francis the daughter of Richard Puplet was baptisd.

Decemb.   5. marie Kennington was baptisd.

Decemb.   12. Elizabeth Manwood the daughter of John manwood baptisd.

Decemb.   26. Elizabeth martin the daughter of mathias martin baptizd.

Janu.   16. William Nobell the sone of William Noble Baptised.
John Randall the sone of [*blank*] Randall was baptised.

          30. John Church the sone of [*blank*] Church baptisd.

februar. 11. {
marie Exton the daughter of Israell Exton was baptisd.
marie Beamont the daughter of Benjamin Beamont baptisd.
}

          13. Susaña Cooper the daughter of John Cooper baptisd.

March   5. Jeremie Barber the sone of Jeremie barber was baptisd.

          12. {
Valentine Bates the sone of Valentine Bates was baptisd.
Susaña Harse was baptisd.
}

          19. Edmund Brett the sone of Peter Brett was bapttissd.

Año Dñi 1620.

March   26. Ane wilbore the daughter of Nicholas wilbore was baptisd. [*This entry erased in toto.*]

          31. John Panton the sone of william Panton was baptisd.

Aprill   2. Rebecca Adams the daughter of ferdinando Adams was baptisd.

July   15. Elizabeth Davie the daughter of Henrie Davie baptisd.

July	23.	Samuel Fine the sone of Henrie Fine was baptisd.
August	19.	Elizabeth Stoper the daughter of William Stoper was baptisd.
	27.	Abigail Beñet the daughter of John Benet was baptisd.
Septemb.	3.	Hañah Deale the daughter of John Deale was baptisd.
	05.	Ezeckeel the sone of Nathaniel & Hañah Smart was baptisd.
Octob.	24.	Alice the daughter of John and Alice Alderman baptisd.
Novemb.	12.	{ Jude Paine the sone of Robert paine was baptisd. Elizabeth Johnson the daughter of Edward Johnson was baptisd.
	13.	[blank] of George Brett.
	19.	John Brame the sone of [blank] Brame was baptisd.
Decemb.	17.	Francis the daughter of Christopher wilkinson was baptisd.
Januar.		Sarah.
		marie the daughter of Saunder mariot was baptisd.
		Deborah the daughter of William Lakish was baptisd.
		[blank] of Lord was baptisd.
		Subscribed by { Nathaniel Smart minister of the pish of St Nicholas.

Page 53.

1620.

Christenings.

Januar.	29.	Richard the sone of Richard Puplet was baptisd.
Februar.	2.	Margaret the daughter of Richard Wade was baptisd.
	25.	Edmund the sone of Edmund miles was baptised.
March	21.	Margaret the daughter of Michael Ward was baptizd.

Año Dñi 1621.

Aprill	2.	Abigail Sicklemore the daughter of Jeremie Sicklemore was bap.
	19.	Susaña the daughter of John Hill was baptisd.
	22.	{ Sarah the daughter of Izaak Damarin baptisd. Thomas the sone of Richard Norton baptizd.
May	29.	Joseph Savage baptisd.
Jul.	21.	{ John the son of James Osburne was baptisd. And George the sone of Robert Paschall.
Aug.	2.	[blank] of Bordman baptisd.
	15.	[blank] of Thomas Onge baptisd.
	20.	[blank] of Thomas Creswell Baptisd.
Sept.	2.	John the sone of Wittam Brett was baptizd.
	23.	Hañah the daughter of Vali Bates baptisd.
Octobr	7.	Nicholas the sone of John Stanifer was baptisd.
	14.	Margery daughter of Christophr Harris was baptisd.
	28.	[blank] of John Glasse.

Novem.	4.	Daniel the sone of Thomas Randoll baptisd.
	„	Peter Lambe the sone of William Lambe baptisd.
Decemb.	16.	{ Silus Eaton the sone of Anthonie Eaton was baptisd.
		{ Abigail Stover the daughter of William Stover.
	21.	marie eadger the daughter of Robert eadger.
	26.	the child of Thomas Nun.
	27.	{ Alice Martin the daughter of matthias martin was baptisd.
		{ Susañ Bucknam daughter of John Buckman.
Januar.	20.	marie Hamond the daughter of John Hamond bap.
	31.	Eme Wilbore the daughter of Nicholas Wilbore bap.
Feb.	7.	Samuel moulson the sone of Thomas moulson was bap.
	17.	marie Burton the daughter of John Burton was bap.
March	1.	Abigail Cope the daughter of Samuel Cope was baptisd.
	10.	Joseph Suggate the sone of Bartholomew Suggate was bap.

Año Domini 1622.

March	25.	Thomas Cutler the sone of Benjamin Cutler baptisd.
May	1.	William Smith the sone of [*blank*] Smith baptisd.
	6.	Thomas Holliway the sone of John Holliway baptisd.
	14.	Thomas Raphe the sone of Thomas Raphe baptisd.
June	15.	{ William Ladhish the sone of Willm Ladhish bap.
		{ marie morgan the daughter of Willm morgan baptisd.
Aug.	18.	Christopher mose the sone of Christopher mose bap.
	19.	Henry Brame the sone of Henrie Brame was baptisd.
	25.	William Darnell the sone of Robert Darnell baptisd.
Septemb.	22.	martha Reeve the daughter of John Reeve bap.
Octob^r	11.	marie Hañer.
	13.	Hañah Beñet the daughter of Richard Beñet baptisd.
Novemb^r	1.	Thomas Blosse the sone of Mr Thomas Blosse baptisd.
	24.	marie Hawkins the daughter of Joseph Hawkins was bap.
	29.	John Scott the sone of John Scott was baptisd.
Decemb^r	17.	Robert Neale the sone of Henrie Neale was baptisd.
	29.	{ Thomas Browne the sone of [*blank*] Browne bap.
		{ marie Tilson the daughter of marmaduke Tilson was bap.
		{ marie Church the daughter of [*blank*] Church bap.
Februar.	2.	Edmund Puplet the sone of Mr Richard pupplet bap.
	18.	Samuel Smart the sone of Nathaniel Smart was bap.

Año Dñi 1623.

Aprill	5.	John mudd the sone of John mudd baptisd.
May	11.	Martha Whitbie the daughter of [*blank*] Whitbie bap.

[May]	27.	Ane Harris the daughter of Christopher Harris baptisd.
June	5.	Robert Wade the sone of Richard Wade baptisd.
Aug.	3.	John Steggall the sone of Richard Steggall bap.
	17.	Samuel manhood the sone of John manhood baptisd.
Septemb.	5.	{ Margaret Blumfield the daughter of Wiłłm Blumfield Bap. Edward Hulin the sone of Edward Hulin baptisd.
Novemb.	16.	Ane Sansom the daughter of William Sansome bap.
	26.	Damaris mumford the daughter of Robert momford bap.
Januar.	6.	Thomas Lany the sone of Mr John Lanye baptisd.
Februar.	4.	{ William Wilbore the sone of Nicholas Wilbore baptisd. Ane Raphe the daughter of Thomas Raphe baptisd.
	7.	{ Thomas Coppin the sone of [blank] Coppin baptisd. Sarah Cope the daughter of Samuell Cope baptisd.
March	7.	Matthias martin the sone of matthias martin baptisd.

Año Domini 1624.

Aprill	7.	Hanah Male the daughter of Wiłłm male baptisd.
	11.	{ Ane Brett the daughter of Peter Brett baptisd. Esther Norris the daughter of Richard Norris baptisd.
May	25.	marie Glasse the daughter of John Glasse baptisd.
	26.	marie Blosse the daughter of Mr Thomas Blosse was baptisd.
June	20.	Samuel Thirston the sone of William Thirston baptisd.
	27.	{ Elizabeth Wilkinson the daughter of Christopher Wilkinson bap. Richard Beedom the sone of Richard Bedom.
August	8.	{ Nathan the sone of Nathan Bonifant was Bap. Christian Deeringe the Daughter of John Deeringe.
	14.	Elizabeth Hill the daughter of John Hill was baptisd.
Septem^r	26.	marie Bordman the daughter of Robert Bordman baptisd.
	28.	Christian the daughter of Nicholas Smith was baptisd.
	29.	Alice Berrie the daughter [blank].
October	7.	{ Anthonie Eaton [blank]. John Wilson [blank].
Novemb.	9.	Thomas puplet the sone of Richard puplet was baptisd.
	14.	Izaak Arberie the sone of [blank] Arberie.
Decemb^r	5.	Mary Lakeland the daughter of Theophilus Lakeland baptisd.
Februar	21.	{ Christopher Alderman baptisd. James [blank].
March	6.	Sarah List the daughter of Thomas List bap.

Subscribed by { Nathaniel Smart minister
S. Nicholas in Ipswich.

Page 54.   Christenings Año Dñi 1625.

Mar.	27.	John Steggoll the sone of Richard Steggoll bap.
Apr.	3.	Marie Huggins the daughter of Daniel Huggins bap.
	25.	Thomas piercen the sone of Thomas piercen was baptisd.
June	2.	Lidia Lines the daughter of Arthur Lines.
		Aug. 14. David locke.
Septemb.	27.	Samuel Backler the sone of Edmund Bockler bap.
	29.	Añe Cutler the daughter of Mr Benjamin Cutler.
	25.	Henrie Neale the sone of Henrie Neale.
	30.	Nathaniel puplet the sone of Mr Richard puplet.
October	2.	John Hulin the sone of Edward Hulin.
	16.	Thomas Babbe the sone of Thomas Babbe was baptisd.
	30.	Lidia Wicke.
October	9.	[*blank*] Church.
November	6.	Elizabeth Berrie the daughter of [*blank*] Berrie.
	20.	Elizabeth Bordman the daughter of Robert Bordman.
December	4.	Sarah Brame the daughter of Henrie Brame.
	30.	Jane Lany the daughter of Mr John Lany was bap.
Februar.	12.	Thomas Rice the sone of Thomas Rice was baptisd.
	19.	Thomas Wilshire the sone of Thomas Wilshire.
	26.	Ane Smith daughter of Nicholas Smith was bap.
	27.	Marie Wade the daughter of Richard Wade.
	28.	John Wilbie.
March	3.	Christopher Wilkinson the sone of Christopher Wilkinson.
	18.	Loys Dearinge the daughter of John Dearing bap.

Ano 1626.

Mar.	25.	Robert Ladhish the sone of [*blank*] Ladhish bap.
Apr.	8.	Daniel Mudd the sone of John mudd bap.
April	10.	Samuel Smart the sone of Nathaniel Smart ministr baptisd.
	30.	Marie Bates the daughter of Valentine Bates.
May	10.	Isaac Osburne the sone of James Osburne was bap.
	12.	Robert Sounds the sone of [*blank*] Sounds.
Julie	20.	{ John Lakeland the sone of Theophilus Lakeland bap. { Christian Smith daughter of Nicholas Smith.
	16.	John Waters baptisd.
Aug.	23.	marie the daughter of Mathias Martin bap.
Octob.	1.	Martha Hawkins the daughter of Joseph Hawkins was bap.
	8.	John Bucknam the sone of John Bucknam was bap.
Januar.	28.	William Bordman the sone of Robert Bordman bap.
	30.	Sarah Bishop daughter of Helen Bp. prisoner.
Febr.	16.	mathew Catchpole the sone of Mr Catchpole proctor.

Ano 1627.

April	1.	George Cutbert the son of Richard Cutbert was baptised.

April	7.	Hañah Thirston the daughter of Wiłłm Thirston baptisd.
	19.	Rose Akelie the daughter of william Akelie was baptisd.
June	10.	⎧ Marie Blumfeild the daughter of William Blumfeild bap. ⎩ John Wilkinson the sone of Christopher Wilkinson.
Aug.	5.	Benjamin moulson the sone of Thomas moulson was baptisd.
	9.	Benjamin Baker sone of Thomas Baker was baptisd.
	19.	Abraham Arberie the sone of Abraham Arberie was baptisd.
September	13.	James Blith sone of James Blith was baptisd.
	16.	Abigail Bates daughter of Valentine Bates was baptisd.
	23.	Abigail Wicks was baptisd.
	30.	Agnes Church daughter of John Church was baptisd.
Novemb.	4.	John Church the son of John Church was bap.
	11.	⎰ marie mudd daughter of John mud was baptisd. ⎱ Judith Haffin was bap.
	25.	Marie & Martha daughters of William Leke were baptisd.
	26.	Abigail & Hañah daughters of Nathaniel Smart were baptisd.
	28.	Elizabeth base child of yᵉ wid Hills was bap.
Decembᵣ	19.	Edmund Wilbeye son of Nicholas Wilbey was bap.
Januar.	13.	Chrian Loe was bap.
	20.	⎰ Joseph Backler sone of Edmund Backler was bap. ⎱ Henrie Bucknam sone of John Bucknam was bap.
Februar.	20.	Bridget Lanie daughter of Mʳ John Lanye baptisd.
March	16.	martha moore daughter of William moore was baptisd.
	19.	Abigail Beamond daughter of Benjamin Beamond

Anno Dni 1628.

March	30.	⎧ Thomas Allen the sone of Thomas Allen baptised. ⎨ Abigail Lakeland the Daughter of Theophilus Lake- ⎩ land was bap.
April	13.	Samuel Makarie the sone of William Makarie bap.
	15.	Alice daughter of Jacob Wathwait was baptisd.
May	4.	⎰ John Alderman the sone of Christopher Alderman was baptisd. ⎱ Elizabeth Osburne & Elizabeth Cotton were baptisd.
June	3.	John Downinge the sone of John Downinge bapt.
July	2.	Marie Ainsworth daughter of Henrie Ainsworth was baptisd.
	13.	Elizabeth harris baptd.
Aug.	3.	Thomas Paschall sone of Robert Paschall was baptisd.

[Aug.]   10. Marie Neale the daughter of Henrie Neale was baptisd.

17. Alice Norris the Daughter of Richard Norris was baptisd.

24. Isaac Darnell the sone of Robert Darnell was baptised.

Septemb^r   Alice Clarke was bap.

Novemb.   John the sone of John Elson was baptisd.

William Bates the sone of Valentine Bates was baptisd.

Margaret Beamond daughter of Benjamin Beamond bap.

Richard Thursbie the sone of Simon Thursbie was baptisd.

Henrie Catchpole sone of Gabriel Catchpole was baptisd.

Elizabeth Cutler the daughter of Mr Benjamin Cutler baptd.

John Dearinge the sone of John Dearinge was bap.

John Church the sone of John Church was [*blank*].

William Boicat the sone of William Boicat was baptisd.

[*undecipherable*] the sone of [*undecipherable*].

[*blank*] daughter of Simon Webber baptisd.

Subscribed by { Nathaniel Smart minister
              { of the pish of S. Nic.

Page 55.

Christeings Año Dñi 1629.

April   15. William & } Skeet bap.
              Richard   }

Edmund Wilkinson the sone of Christopher Wilkinson was bap.

francis Mud the soñe of John mud was baptisd.

Julie   5. { Mathias martin the soñe of Mathias martin was baptisd.
             { Christopher Akelie the soñe of William Akelie.
             { Margaret Warne daughter of Robert Warne was bap.

16. Ithiel Smart the sone of Nathaniel Smart minist^r was bap.

August   2. marie Johnson the daughter of Steven Johnson was bap.

9. Susana Lakeland daughter of Theophilus Lakeland bap.

September 25. Thomas the sone of William De la Hay bap.

Octob^r   11. Susana Akberie daughter of Abraham Akberie was bap.

18. Elizabeth Bentum.

25. Abigail Brame the daughter of Henrie Brame bap.

Novemb.	8.	Rose Fiske daughter of [*blank*] Fiske bap.
	29.	John Rivers the sone [*blank*].
Decemb.	20.	Matthew moulson the sone of Thomas moulson was bap.
Januar.	1.	John Allein the sone of [*blank*] Allen was bap.
	3.	William Arnold sone of John Arnold was bap.
	17.	Ane Firmin the daughter of John Firmin was baptisd.
	22.	Sarah Blumfield daughter of William Blumfield baptisd.
	31.	Robert Harris the sone of Christopher Harris was bap.
Februar.	7.	Marie English the daughter of [*blank*] English was bap.
	14.	Susana Rich.
	20.	Oliver and Elizabeth Barber the children of Oliver Barb[r] bap.
	28.	Samuel Cope the sone of Samuel Cope was bap.
March	1.	marie Ferriman the daughter of Willm Ferriman was bap.
	7.	William Backler the sone of Edmund Buckler bap.

Ano Dni 1630.

Mar.	21.	Francis Bowle daughter of John Bowle was baptisd.
	25.	James Catchpole sone of m[r] Gabriel Catchpole was baptisd.
April	9.	[*blank*] Hardie.
	25.	William Boicat sone of Willm Boicat was baptisd.
	22.	John Buckenham sone of John Bucknam baptisd.
May	9.	John Clarke sone of Edmund Clarke was baptisd.
	16.	Ane Cage daughter of Thomas Cage was baptisd.
June	27.	Ane Pulford daughter of John pulford was baptizd.
Julie	18.	Edmund Garwood sone of Edmund Garwood bap.
	20.	John Burnish sone of John Burnish baptisd.
Septemb[r]	7.	Peter Hardie the sone of Peter Hardie baptisd.
Novemb.	5.	William Hemson the sone of William Hempson bap.
	28.	Sara Berrie was baptisd.
Decemb.	11.	Henrie Norman the sone of Henrie Norman bap.
Januar.	4.	Robert Warne sone of Robert Warne was baptised.
	10.	{ Ane daughter of Richard Norris was baptisd. { Daniel Brane son of Thomas Bran.
	26.	Thomas Blosse sone of Thomas Blosse was baptised.
	30.	{ Thomas Wilkinson sone of Christoph[r] baptisd at { ye Tow. pish.[1] { Susana [*blank*].
March	1.	Elizabeth Alderman daughter of Christopher was bap.
	11.	marie Rivers daughter of John Rivers was baptised.

[1] (S. M. Le Tower, Ipswich.)

Año Dñi 1631.

Mar.	27.	Thomas Mud sone of John mud was baptisd.
April	10.	Dorcas Fiske daughter of Robert Fiske baptizd at St Peters.
	24.	Priscilla Arnold daughter of John Arnold was bap.
May	1.	Alice Malton daughter of William malton was baptisd.
	11.	Marie Tailor daughter of John Tailor was baptisd.
June	2 i.	William Catchpoole sonn of Gabriel Catchpole.
Julie	31.	Robert Paschall sone of Robert Paschall baptisd.
August	7.	John Burmish was baptisd.
	9.	William Barker the sone of m^r Willm Barker baptisd.
Novemb.	20.	John Foxelie was baptisd.
Decemb^r	30.	Armiger Withered baptisd & borne within 4 daies after their mariage.
Januar.	29.	Charles Wilshire was baptisd.
Februar.	5.	Elizabeth & Alice Lewin daughters of Francis Lewin were [*blank*].
	22.	John Crosie was baptisd.
March	1.	Martha Blomfield daughter of Thomas Blomfield baptisd.
	5.	Abigail Francis daughter of John Francis.
	11.	{Nathaniell Blosse of Thomas Blosse baptizd. and marie Salmon.
March	15th.	Peter Rivers sonn of John Rivers was baptized.

Ano Dni. 1632.

April	15.	{Elizabeth Hardie daughter of Peter Hardie was baptizd. John Harris sone of Josup Harris baptisd.
May	20.	William Wilkinson son of Christopher Wilkinson was baptisd.
May	31.	Daniell Smart ye sone of Nathaniell Smart was baptisd.
June	8.	{Margerie Bates daughters of Valentine Bates bap. Abigail.
Jul.	20.	Samuel Church sone of John Church baptisd.
	29.	John Tailor sone of John Tailor baptisd.
Octob^r	28.	[*blank*] Tileson.
Novemb^r	4.	Hañah Boicat daughter of William Boicat bap.
Deceb^r	19.	Susaña daughter of Ane Gardiner prisoner bap.
	23.	Nicholas Harris sone of Christopher Harris bap.

Page 56. Subscribed by Nathaniel Smart menest^r.

St Nicholas Ipswich.

Cristenings. 1632.

March	17.	Susan ye daughter of [*blank*] Brundish.
	17.	Martin ye sone of nicholas Wildbore.
		Lidia Daughter of Henery norman was Baptized Aprill ye 27th 1632.

| Aprill | 10. | Anne Smithier the daughter of John Smithyer baptised. |

Thomas Lambe.

William Barrow.

Aprill	25.	Richard Raymond the son of Rich Raymond minister and Anne his wife baptized.
June	27.	Edward Catchpole sonn of Gabriel Catchpole & Elizabeth his wife.
Aug.	—	Rebeckah Payne the daughter of John and Scholastica Payne baptized.
Aug.	14.	William Cross the son of John Cross baptised.
Aug.	25.	Marye Christmas daughter of Thomas Christmas of S. Peters parish baptised.
Sept.	6.	Marye Blomefeild the daughʳ of Tho. Blomfeild baptized.
Septemb.	22.	{ William { Thomas Bate son of Valentine Bate baptized.
Oct.	10.	Ruben Eaton spurius baptizatus fuit.
Octob.	18.	Anna Foster daughter of Richard foster Anna hys wif Baptized.
Nov.	3.	Seazi Albrough dafter of Abram Albrough.
Nov.	21.	Steven Cresall the son of Tho. Cressall baptized.
Nov.	24.	Elizabeth Wilkin the daughter of Thomas Wilkin baptized.
Nov.	30.	Sarah Smith daughter of John and Katherine Smith baptized.
Decemb.	i.	Samuel [blank].
Jan.	12.	[blank] Backler.
Feb.	4.	[blank] Price.
Feb.	16.	Mary Allen.
Feb.	23.	Hannah [blank].

Anno 1634.

| feb. | 24. | William Boicock son of Will Boicock & Anis his wif. baptised. |
| Aprill | 8. | Thomas Hardye the son of Peter Hardye & Elizabeth baptized. |

Thomas Wilkinson son of Christopher Wilkinson baptized.

| Aprill | 20. | Bridget Smithyer the daughtʳ of John Smithyer and Anne baptised. |

Susan Cooper the daughtʳ of thomas Cooper & Susan baptized.

Aprill	21.	Dinah Dedham daughter of Tobjas and Dinah Dedham baptised.
October	19.	Bettres Syer daughter of henry Syer baptised. 1634.
May	4.	John Bantocke the son of John and Anne baptised.
May	20.	Samuell Sugget the son of Samuell Sugget baptised.

F

Maj	23.	Dorothye Brooke daught^r of Mr William Brooke and the Ladye Ireton baptised.

Maj   23.   Dorothye Brooke daught^r of Mr William Brooke and
                    the Ladye Ireton baptised.

Maj   25.   John Russell son of Alexander Russels.

June   8.   Jane garet daughter of Edmund and Jane garet
                    baptised.

June   Elizabeth Frauncis daught^r of John and Rose baptise.

Aug.   1.   Willjd Foxe the sone of Robert and Bitteresse Foxe
                    baptized.

Aug.   4.   Elizabeth Bucknam daughter of John & Kathren
                    baptised.

Sep.   John Burrow son of Willjam and Jane Burrow
                    baptised.

                    [*blank*] son of John Taylor baptizd Sep^t 14.

Sep.   15. { John wixe and Abigaile wixe } twines of John and margery wixe baptised.

Oct.   4.   John birt son of John and Anne birt baptised.

Octob.   1.   Marye Waters ye daughter of Rich. and Marye
                    waters of S. Laur baptised.

                    Prudence ffiske daughter of Rob. and dorcas baptised.

Page 57.   Subscribed by me { Richard Raymonde minister of St Nicholas.

Novemb.   16.   Rebecka Ward daught. of Thomas ward baptised.
1635.   Anno Domini 1635.

June   24.   William the sonne of John Rivers & of Katherine
                    his wife was baptised.

July   5.   Mary the daughter of John Church was baptized.

       19.   Elizabeth ye daughter of Mihells Leuchas was
                    baptized.

August   9.   Henry the sonne of Adam Marret was baptized.

       16.   William the sonne of Robert Blaines was baptized.

       23.   Abigail the daughter of Richard Cole.

       23.   Anne the daughter of Robert Scrafford.

       30.   Elizabeth ye daughter of John Smith.

Septemb.   6.   James ye sonne of James Stone.

       13.   Susan ye daughter of Francis Goodin.

Octob.   17.   Joane y^c daughter of Henry Norman was baptized.

       28.   Thomas ye sonne of Thomas Sudgeviche & of mary
                    his wife was baptiz.

Nouemb.   1.   John ye sonne of Jacob wathwhet & of Susan his
                    wife was baptizd.

       30.   William ye sonne of William oakes & of Bridget
                    his wife was baptizd.

Decemb.   13.   William ye sonne of Thomas Cooper & of Susan
                    his wife. Also

                    Mary ye daughter of Richard Tilletsonne.

       20.   Thomas ye sonne of William & Jane Burrow.

       27.   Mary daughter of Robert Wilchin & of Anne his
                    wife.

January	15.	Anne daughter of Nicholas Loft & of Anne his wife.
	31.	John sonne of Thomas Allen & of Elizabeth his wife.
Februar.	3.	Allen sonne of m^r Gabriell Catchpole & of Elizabeth his wife.
	14.	Elizabeth daughter of Robert yellop.
	22.	Margaret daughter of m^r John Crosse & of Anne his wife.
March	3.	Josepth ye sonne of Henry Brame & of Parnell his wife.
	8.	Anne ye daughter of Rainold Manship & of Alice his wife.
	13.	John the sonne of Christopher Harris & of Elizabeth his wife.

Subscribed by { William Kerrington minister of St Nicholas.
William Boicock Churchwardenne.
Henry Syer Churchwarden.

Page 58. Anno Domini 1636.

Aprill	3.	Henry the sonne of m^r John Smithier & of Elizabeth his wife.
	10.	Thomas the sonne of John Bantocke. Also James the sonne of Isacke Busse & of Grace his wife.
May	8.	Alice ye daughter of Edward Veale & Margaret his wife. also Margaret the daughter of Joshua Harris & Margaret his wife. also Abigail daughter of John Coale & of Anne his wife of St Peters pish.
May	10.	John ye sonne of Mr Beniamin Cutler & of Joane his wife.
June	12.	Alice the daughter of Thomas & Margeret Pounset bap.
July	16.	John the sonn of John wix & Margere his wyf. bap.
	23.	Elizabeth the Daughter of William & Ann Bret his wyf.
	24.	William & Edward twins the sons of Edmund Garrett and Jane his wyfe.
Augst	2.	Jeames the sonn of Peter heardy & of Elizabeth his wyfe.
	24.	Thomas the sonn of John Tayler & of mary his wyfe.
	21.	Elizabeth Sharpe the daughter of Thomas & Judeth sharp of ye tower pish was baptised in St Nickholas.
Sept.	25.	Jeames ye sonne of Jeames hulin & of Susan his wyfe.

F^2

[Sept.]   29.   John the sonn of william huchin & of Judy his wyf. Willm [*blank*].

1636.   ## Christnings 1636.

Jennary   15. { Martha Daugh. of mathias martin & Margery his wife baptized at S^nt 'Steuens pish.

Jennary   21.   William sone of John Erman and Elisabeth his wife.

March the 19.   henry ffiggett the Son of henry ffidget & Alice his wife wch Son was borne in St Nicholas but christened the said day in St Peters church by reason of the want of a Minister at St Nicholas.

ffeb.   2.   Susan daugh. of georg. Allyn and mary his wife.

ffeb.   9.   John the sonn of John Woodye and Alis his wife Baptd.

March   20.   John sone of John Classe and Abikel his wife.

25th of Aprill { ffrancis Black sonn of Nathaniel Blacke & Katherin
1637.   {   his wife was baptized.

Robart howe Churchwarden.

Christnings 1637.

Bridget Cryspe the daughter of Christopher Cryspe and Mary his wife was baptized the 14th of May 1637.

Simon the sonne of william Shaw & Mary his wife was baptized the 18th day of May 1637.

Susan Wilshin the daughter of Thomas Wilshen and of Auice his wife was baptized the 22th day of May 1637.

John the sonne of John hardy and Rebecca his wife was Baptized May the 29 1637.

June the 18th 1637. henry the sonne of Michael Palmer and Martha his wife was baptized

Anne Serocold the daughter of Ralfe Serocold and Martha his wife was baptized June the 26 1637.

July 23 1637.   Elizabeth the daughter of Tobias Browne & Sarah his wife.

July 24 1637.   Thomas Smyth the son of Mr Robt Smyth & Cathrin his wife was baptized.

Subscribed by { Alex^r Rainold minister of S^t
              {   Nicholas
              { frauncis Smyth Churchwarden.

Page 59.

1637.   ## Christnings.

Agust   8.   Tobias the son of Tobias Deadham & Dinah his wife.

Agust   9.   John the sonne of John Ede & Anne his wife.

Agust   13.   Thomas the son of Ranoulds Manshippe & Alice his wife.

August   15.   James the sonne of Nicholas Bishop & ffrances his wife.

August   17.   John the sonne of John Pascall & Marget his wife,

Septemb.	3.	Elizabeth the daughter of William Malton & Joane his wife. [*Entry erased*].
Septemb.	24.	Marie Addington the daughter of Robert Addington and Eme his wife.
September	29.	Robert Smithier the sonne of John Smithier and Elizabeth his wife.
October	8.	Jane the daughter of Robt ffisk & Dorcas his wife.
Octob.	8.	William the son of John Watson & Amie his wife.
October	22.	Elizabeth the dawghter of Samuel Sugget & Elizabeth his wife.
October	22.	Bridget the daughter of John Creswell & Bridget his wife.
October	25.	Marie the daughter of Robt yellow & Joann his wife was bapt.
Novemb.	5.	henry the sonne of henry Syir & Beatrix his wife was baptd.
Novemb.	10.	Margret the daughter of John Wright & Marget his wife.
Novemb.	15.	Robt the Son of Edmund Garwood & Jane his wife.
Novemb.	24.	Edmund the Son of George ffitzjefferie & Susan his wife.
Novemb.	26.	Penelope the daughter of Edmond Natts & Elizabeth his wife.
Decemb.	3.	Rose the daughter of James Blyth and Rose his wife Baptizd.
Decemb.	17.	Mary the daughter of Thomas Cowp and Susan his wife.
Decemb.	27.	henry the Son of John Rivers & Catherine his wife Bptz.
ffeb.	18.	John Sorrell the Sonne of Thomas Sorrell and Charity his wife.
ffeb.	18.	Elizabeth the daughter of william Barrow and Anne his wife.
ffeb.	25.	Richard the Sonne of John Bantoffe & Anne his wife.
March	11.	Anne the daughter of Thomas punsett & Marjorie his wife.

1638.   Christnings.

March	26.	Edward the son of Edward Whiting & Margret his wife was baptizd.
Aprill the	8.	Isaac the Son of william Boycok and Avis his wife.
Aprill	22.	Thomas the Son of Thomas Gurny and Lydia his wife.
Aprill	29.	Elizabeth the base borne daughter of Margret Branion.
May	6.	ffrancis Estie the sonne of Jeffery Estie & Elizabeth his wife.

May	6.	William & John the sonnes of Thomas wilshin & Ann his wife.
June	3.	Mary the daughter of Robt ffoxe & Beatrix his wife.
June	29.	Susan the daughter of Thomas Matthew & Elizabeth his wife.
July	15.	Alice the daughter of Peter hardie & Elizabeth his wife.
July	22.	Elizabeth the daughter of John Reyner & Elizabeth his wife.
July	29.	Hannah the daughter of John Denton & Anne his wife.
Septemb.	30.	Anne the daughter of [*blank*] Burnish and Anne his wife.
October	7.	Joseph the sonne of Joseph Arman & Elizabeth his wife.
October	18.	Sarah the daughter of henry truelove & Sarah his wife.
Decemb.	8.	ffrances the daughter of John Pascall & Marget his wife.
Decemb.	9.	Elizabeth the daughter of Henry Pye & Elizabeth his wife.
Decemb.	9.	James the sonne of Symon webber & Anne his wife.
Decemb.	16.	Rebecca the daughter of Richard hust & Rebecca his wife.
Decemb.	21.	ffrances the daughter of John Smithier & Elizabeth his wife.
January	1.	James the son of Thomas Allen & Elizabeth his wife.
January	1.	Elizabeth the daughter of william Brett & Anne his wife.
January	10.	Mary the daughter of Henry Syir & Beatrix his wife.
January	17.	Elizabeth the daughter of William Makrith & Eliz. his wife.
January	27.	Elizabeth & Eliner the daughters of Timothie hervye.
January	28.	william Manship sonn of Stanalles Manship was bt.
March	3.	william Ealsden the son of John Ealsden & Anne his wife.
March	11.	George the son of George Allen & Marie his wife.
March	24.	william the son of william Micklefield and Ann his wife.

1639. Christnings.

Aprill	16.	Robert the son of John Armon & Elizabeth.
Aprill	19.	Alice the daughter of Richard Cutbert & Joan.

Subscribed by { Alex^r Rainold minister of St Nicholas, william shawe Churchwarden.

Page 60. S. Nicholas Ipswich.

Christenings 1639.

Aprill	21.	Marie the daughter of John Warde and Rose his wife.
May	10.	Abigall the daughter of Thomas Molson & Jane his wife.
May	31.	Abigail the daughter of Thomas Molson & Jane his wife.
June	2.	Edmund son of Edmund Brooke & Mary his wife.
June	27.	Dorothy the daughter of John Bragge & Sarah his wife.
Septemb.	1.	Lydia the daughter of Robert Woodhouse & Lydia his wife.
Septemb.	20.	Edward Son of Robert Scales & Sarah his wife.
Octob.	1.	Henry son of Nicholas Bishop & Francis his wife.
Octob.	6.	John the son of Mr Robert Smyth & Catherin his wife.
Octob.	25.	John the son of John Sleter [*blank*] his wife.
Novemb.	17.	Deborah the daughter of Tobith Deadham & Dinah his wife.
Novemb.	27.	Marie the daughter of Thomas Burlingham was bap.
Decemb.	15.	Edward Mali son of Thomas Mali & Elizabeth.
ffeb.	16.	Hannah the daughter of Robert luke & hannah his wife.
ffeb.	18.	Rose the daughter of henry Wright & Rose his wife.
March	8.	Jearg the son of George Allen & Mary his wife.
March	11.	Mary the daughter of Abraham Alberery & Mary his wife.
March	20.	Philip the son of Philip Newton. [*Entry erased*].

1640. Christnings.

Aprill	2.	Marie the daughter of Joseph Denton & Anne his wife bapt.
May	2.	Margret the daughter of Robert yellop christened.
May	31.	Elizabeth Daughter of Clerk [*blank*[.
June	7.	James the son of James Blyth & Rose his wife.
		Bazillai the son of Bazillai huit & Mary his wife.
July the	5.	Ambrose son of Ambrose ffrost & Anne.
July	7.	William son of William ffrost & Elizabeth his wife.
July	14.	Henry Son of John Smythier & Elizabeth.
July the	17.	Robert son of George Smyth & Ann his wife.
August	10.	Christopher the son of Christopher wilkinson and Elizabeth.
August	16.	James the son of Robt Adington & frñs his wife.
August	18.	Elizabeth daughter [*blank*] Matthew.
August	24.	Deborah the daughter of william Boycatt & Avis his wife.
September	8.	henrie the son of henrie Truelove & hannah.

Septemb.	22.	William the son William Micklefield & Anne.
Septemb.	27.	ffrancis son of Adam Mallet & Marable his wife.
October	25.	Elizabeth daughter Richard Nightingale & Mary his wife.
Novemb.	22.	Jeremie the son of Thomas Pamset & Elizabeth his wife.
Decemb.	10.	Mary the daughter of John Burnish & & Mary his wife.
Decemb.	17.	Richard the son of Thomas Wyth & Marie his wife.
ffeb.	7.	Marie the daughter of Thomas Cowper & Mary.
february	17.	John Ward the son of John Ward.

Elizabeth the daughter of John Earman & Elizabeth his wife was baptized march the 8th.

Tho. son of Tho. & Mary Sudgick July 9th.

1641.   Christenings.

May   5. Steuen sone of Steuen & Eliz. Crashfild bapt.

1641.

ffayth the daughter of Robert Boult Musicuner was baptized the 15th of October.

Samuel Nitingale sonn of Marye Nitingale widowe was baptized the eightenth daye of November 1641.

January   4th. Ann dauter of George & Ann Smith was baptised.

Page 61.   1642.

Aprill	11.	{ Thomas the son of John & Brigit Creswell baptized. { Joan the daughter of Edmund & Jane Garwood bapt.
May	i.	Elizabeth the daught. of Charles & Susan Eldred.
	29.	{ Daniel the son of Thomas & Eliz. pouncet bapt. { John the son of John Salmon bpt.
July	31.	Richard son of Richard Cutbert & Jane his wife bapt.
		[*Blank*] the daughter of John Smith.
October	9.	Steuen son of Edmund Brooke & Mary his wife bapt.
	16.	Eliz. daught. of Philip & Ann Newton bapt.
Sept.	7th.	Robte Hollwell sonne of John hollwell baptized.
November	18.	Ann daughter of Ambros ffrost was bapd.
Decem.	3.	Ann daughter of Robert and Jane yellop bapt.
	14.	Tomas the son of Abraham Smye bapt.
		[*Entry erased*].
Januar.	1.	Marie the daughter of Williā Derson & Mary his wife bap.
January	15.	John son of John Sawier of St Peters parrish bapt.
Jan.	22.	Susan Nun baptized ye daughter of Will Nun.

1643.

March	12.	William son of Nathl. Cooke b.
Ap.	16.	Thomas son of Bohl Huit bapt.
Apr.	26.	Susanna Browne bapt.

May	4.	Ann daughter of Thomas Blichingam bapt.
May	21.	George Simpson Baptized.
June	6.	Elizabeth Smart baptized.
	25.	Thomas fford son of John fford bapt.
	29.	Henry Wright bapt son of Henry wright.
July	10.	James Hall son of James & Liddy Hall bapt.
July the	18.	Sarah the daughter of Robard [*blank*] baptized.
August	21.	Thomas Ardom son of Thomas Ardon.
Octob.	4.	Matthias Dedham bapt.
Nouemb.	16.	Lucy daughter of Bart Clarke bapt.

Page 62.   1644.

Nouvmb^r	27.	Marie Tillott dauter of Robt Tillott and Mary his wife baptized.
October	8th.	Thomas Thirtle sonn of Michael Thirkell & Anne his wife was baptized.
October	24.	John the sonn of Richard Wilder was baptised.
ffeb.	7.	James the sonne of Ambros ffrost & Anne his wife was baptized.
March	5th.	Nathanell the sonne of Nathanell Smart & Elizabeth his wife was baptized.
March	6.	George the sonne of william Nune was baptised 1644.
April 12 1645.		Robert sonne of Robert Moulson and Katherine his wife was baptized.
1645.		Mary daughter of Edmond Brooke and Mary his wife was baptized.
December	16.	Thomas son of Thomas & Mary Cowper was baptized.

March ye 10th 1644 Micheal the son of Micheal and Martha Palmer was Baptized the 15th of ye same.

March	16.	John the son of William & Martha Coke was baptized.

Memor. Joseph & Benjamin Jackson the sonns of Isaak Jackson & Elizabeth his wife were baptised June 23 in the yeere 1644.

1645.

March ye 17.	Sary Clopton Dauter of Richard Clopton and was by Sary his Wife.

1646.

April		[*Illegible*] wathwhit was baptized.
May	3.	John Simpson the son of George & Elizabeth Simpson baptized.
		Elizabeth the daughter of Robert Moulson And Kthrin his wife was Baptised y^e [*blank*].
Oct.	20.	Benjamin the son of Williã Nun & Elizabeth his wife Baptised.
		[*blank*] the daughter of Richard Wilder & [*blank*] his wife baptized.
January	17th.	Ann the dauter of Michell & Ann Thurkell baptised.

John the sonne of James Cantinge & Elyzabeth his wife was borne the eyste Day of ffebruary & Baptized the sixteenth Day of the sayd ffebruary at Peters pish in An° Dom. 1646.

1647.

Hannah Smart daughter of Nath. Smart & Eliz. Bapt. Dec. 14 1647.

July	18.	Mary the daughter of Isaak Jackson & Elizabeth his wife was Baptized.
Aug.	8.	Thomas son of John Holder & Susan his wife was baptised.
Aug.	20.	Elizabeth daughter of Richard Clopton & Sara his wife.
Aug.	24.	Anne daughter of Mr John Sicklemore & Anne his wife.
Aug.	31.	Williã son to Williã Burrage & Anne his wife.
Sept.	7.	Joseph son to Joseph Wantwhait & Anne his wife.
Octo.	6.	Edward son to Edward Donlin & Catherine his wife.
Octo.	24.	Margeret daughter to Isaac Alborow & Margeret his wife bapt.
Novem.	7.	Walter the sonne of Tho. Allen & Elizabeth his wife was Bap.
Dec.	16.	Tobias the son of Tobias Dedham & Diana his wif. ws Bap.
Dec.	24.	Elizabeth daughter of Georg Smith & Anne his wife.
Januar.	9.	Thomas son of George Bumsted & Anne his wife.
Febru.	4.	Debora daughter of Edw. Whiting & Marget his wife.
the	27.	beniaemin the son of Robard [*blank*] babtized.

Page 63.

Christenings Anno Domini 1647.

Febr.	6.	Mary the daughter of Will. Smith & Francis his wife.
Febr.	13.	Isaac son of John Burnish & Mary his wife.
Feb.	27.	Thomas the son of Thomas Pounset & Elizab. his wife Baptised.
March	1.	Elizabeth the daughter of Tho. Coop & Marie his wif. Baptis.
March	19.	Rose the daughter of Thomas Hobson & [*blank*] his wife Baptised.

Anno Domi 1648.

March	26.	Elizabeth the daughter of Henry Breame & Parnel his wife Bapt.

April	16.	Robert the sonne of Robert Hardwick & Abigail his wife baptised.
June	11.	Sarah the daughter of John Creswell & Briget his wife Bap.
June	8.	John Lany sonne of Mr John Lany Esquier & Anne his wife was baptised.
June	18.	Timothy the sonne of Robert Wade & Mary his wife was baptised.
Aug.	13.	Susan the daughter of Thomas Daniel & Mary his wife baptised.
Aug.	20.	Debora the daughter of Williā Whitmor & Abigal his wife.
Sept.	3.	Mary the daughter of John Chapman & Anne his wife baptized.
Sept.	13.	Edward the sonne of Edward Hitchbone & Prudence his wife bap.
Sept.	17.	Abigaile the daughter of John Hale & Abigaile his wife baptized.
Sept.	26.	Mary the daughter of Henry Cosens & Anne his wife of Peters parish.
Octo.	22.	Thomas the sonne of Williā Cooke & Martha his wife baptised.
Oct.	26.	Edward the son of Christopher Richardson & Joane his wife.
Nov.	1.	{ Elizabeth the Daughter of Thomas Cooke & Marian his wife Bapt. Hellen Daughter of James Mills & Marget his wife Baptized.
Nov.	17.	{ Daniel the sonne of James Canting & Elizab. his wife was bap. the 7th of the said moneth he was borne. John the sonne of John Canhā & Marget his wife was baptised.
Dec.	28.	Richard the sonne of Richard Annis was baptized.
Jan.	21.	Williā the sonne of John Daniel & Mary his wife was baptised.
Jan.	25.	Williā the son of Williā Longley & Sarah his wife Baptized.
Jan.	29.	Anne the daughter of Isaak Jackson & elizeth. his wife Bapted.
Febr.	18.	Coker the sonne of John Bennit & [blank] his wife was baptised.
Feb.	19.	Elizabeth the daughter of Edward Garrard & [blank] his wife was bapt.
March	4.	John Mixter the sonne of John Mixter & eliz. his wife was baptisd.
March	11.	Debora the daughter of John Somes & [blank] his wife was baptised.
Feb.	11.	George the sonne of Michael Thirkle & Anne his wife was baptised at the Tower parish about the 11 of February 1648.

Anno Domini 1649.

March	25.	{ Richard the sonne of Richard Coe & Alce his wife was baptiz. Elisha the sonne of Elisha Elinot & Elizabeth his wife of the Key parish baptized. Sarah the daughter of Thom. Blasby & Sarah his wife Bap. Mary the daughter of Ambros Elden & Marget his wife.
March	27.	Thomas the sonne of Richard Trowloue & Sarah his wife.
April	10.	Anne the daughter of Richard Clopton & Sarah his wife Bapt.
April	29.	{ Richard the sonne of Edmund Brook & [blank] } his wife Baptised. Anne the daughter of Georg Pascall & [blank]
May	19.	Thomas the sonne of Thomas Matthews & [blank] his wife Baptised.
May	20.	Elizabeth the daughter of Williã Shaw & [blank] his wife Baptised.
May	29.	Anne the daughter of Anthony Phillips & [blank] his wife Baptised.
June	6.	Edward the sonne of Mr Edward Man & Martha his wife Bapt.
July	1.	Susanna the daughter of Gilbert waters & [blank] his wife Bapt.
Aug.	24.	Anne the daughter of Thomas Withe & Mary his wife Bap.
Sept.	17.	{ Elizabeth the daughter of Michael Palmer & Kimburrow his wife. Williã the sonne of [blank].
Novemr	1.	{ elizabeth the daughter of Rich. Wilder & Mary his wif. Bapt. Mary the daughter of Caleb Browne & [blank] his wife Bapt.
Novem.	11.	Elias the sonne of Elias Thirrston & Sarah his wife Bapt.
Novem.	23.	Samuel the sonne of Samuel Fuller & Anne his wife was Baptized.
Decem.	16.	Mary the daughter of John Lord and [blank] his Wife Bap.
Dec.	27.	John the sonne of Zacheus Catlin & Eliz. his wife Bap.
Jan.	27.	Margery the daughter of James Creswell & [blank].
Febr.	1.	Sarah the daughter of Nathanael Smart & Eliza his wife Baptise.
Feb.	17.	Anne the daughter of Williã Risby & Anne his wife Bap.

March	18.	{ Marthey } twins daughters of Isaack Jackson & eliz. { Mary } his wife.

Anno Domini 1650.

March	25.	Edward Veale sonne of Edward Veale & Jane his wife.
March	31.	Elizabeth the daught. of Thomas Paunset & Elizab. his wife bapt.
March	31.	Mary the daughter of Thom Harper & Mary his wife bapt.
April	9.	Williā the sonne of Williā Mutley & Alce his wife bap.

Page 64. ## Christenings Anno Doñii 1650.

Feb^ry	29.	Seanie doughter of robart moulson borne.
April	14.	Margeret the daught. of Ambros frost & Anne his wife Baptised.
April	16.	John the sonne of Thomas Bellamor & Susan his wife.
April	21.	{ Richard Son of Richard Annis & Eliz. his wife Bapt. { Robt Sonne of Robt Seman & Anne his wife Bapt.
May	3.	Nicholas the Son of Anthony Phillips & Anne his wife Baptised.
May	17.	Thomas the sonne of George Smith & Anne his wife Baptiz.
May	19.	{ John the son of John Cope & Elizabeth his wife Baptised. Anthony the sonne of Richard Frost & Martha his wife Baptised. Margeret the daughter of Edward Cosens & Margeret his wife Baptized.
June	11.	Georg the sonn of Georg Cutbert & Mary his wife was Baptized.
June	21.	Katherine the daughter of Mr Francis Bacon & Katherine his wife Bapt.
June	28.	Alce the daughter of Michael Thirkle & Anne his wife Baptised.
Aug.	11.	Thomas the sonne of Thomas Wilchin & Anne his wife Baptised.
Aug.	25.	Mary the daughter of Will. Nun & Anna his wife Baptised.
Sept.	8.	Anne the daughter of Georg Bumsted & Anne his wife Bap.
Sept.	15.	Mary the daughter of M^r [Flank].
Nov.	3.	Josuah the sonne of Robert & Mary wade baptised.
Nov.	6.	Thomas the sonne of Thomas Cooke & Marian his wife Bapt.
Nov.	12.	Elizabeth the daughter of James Canting & Elizab. his wife Baptiz.
Nov,	16.	John the son of Edward Whiting and Margeret his wife was Baptised.

[Nov.]	27.	James the sonne of Mr Edward Mann & Martha his wife Baptised.
Febr.	9.	Matthew the daught. [*sic*] of Thomas Blasby & Sarah his wife Baptiz.
	23.	Anthony the sonne of Anthony Lewis & [*blank*] his wife Baptized.
Apr.	28.	Sarah the daughter of Robt. Monsen & Katheren his wife Baptized.
March	16.	James the sonne of Richard Coe & Alce his wife Baptised.

Anno Dom 1651.

April	16.	Timothy the Son of Timothy Carter & Margery his wife w^s bapt.
May	11.	Martha the daughter of Richard Clopton & Sarah his wife was bap.
May	24.	Robert the sonne of Thomas Harper & Mary his wife Baptised.
June	1.	Elizabeth the daughter of [*blank*] Dasone & [*blank*] Baptiz.
June	15.	George the son of James Gosnell and Mary his wife was Baptized.
Aug.	9.	Margaret the daughter of George warren & Margaret his wife was Baptised.
Sept.	3.	Elizabeth the daughter of Richard Wilder & Mary his wife Baptised.
Sept.	10.	Sarah the daughter of Richard Truelove & Sarah his wife Bap.
August	25.	William sune of francis goodwine & Dorothe his was [*blank*].
Sept.	11.	Robert the illegitimate son of Williā hul & Anne Deay baptized.
Sept.	21.	{ James the sonne of Thomas Daniel & Susan his wife Baptized. Williā sonne of John Bret & Elizabeth his wife Baptized.
Octob.	14.	Susanna the daughter of Isaak Jackson & Elizabeth his wife was Baptizd.
Octob.	6.	Josuah the sonne of Williā Nun & Hanna his wife was Bapt.
Octob.	22.	Jacob the sonne of Isaac Alebery & Marget his wife was Bapt.
Novem.	5.	John the sonne of John Daniel & Mary his wife was Baptized.
Novem.	24.	Sarah the daughter of John Garward & Sarah his wife was Bapt.
Novem.	30.	John the sonne of John Pais and Elizabeth his wife was Bapt.
Janu.	12.	Mary the daughter of James Canting & Elizab. his wife Bap.

| Jan. | 27. | John the sonne of Richard Annis & Elizabeth his wife Bapt. |

Jan.   27. John the sonne of Richard Annis & Elizabeth his wife Bapt.

Jan.   30. Briget the daughter of Anthony Phillips and Anne his wife B.

March 14. { Marget the daughter of Thomas Wilchin & Anne his wife Baptized.
Anne the daughter of Williã Lachy & Mary his wife Baptized & liveing and being of Peters Parish.

March 21. Sivine the daughter of Robert Towne & Mary his wife Baptized.   baptized

Anno Dom̃ 1652.

March 26. Francis the sonn of Mr Edw. Man & Martha his wife Bapt.

April 4. Joseph the sonne of Robert hardwick & Abigail his wife bapt.

William the son of ffrancis Goodwyne & Dorothy his wife w^s Bapt. Aug. 25, 1651.

William the son of John Corball & Mary his wife was Bapt. Nouembr 21, 1651.

John the son of Michaell Palmer & Kimborow his wife w^s bapt. Januar. 11, 1651.

Margaret the Daughter of Thomas Wieth & Mary his wife w^s bapt. Januar. 30, 1651.

Susan the daughter of John Mixter & Elizabeth his wife w^s bapt. ffebr. 6, 1651.

Susan the daughter of John Hammond & Elizabeth his wife w^s bapt. ffebr. 28, 1651.

[*Entry erased*].

May 9. Elizabeth the daughter of Michael Thirkle & Anne his wife was Bapt.

May 12. Basil the sonne of Basil Breame & Hellin his wif. was Baptised.

May 18. Henery the sonne of Henery Sley & Sarah his wife was Bapt.

June 6. Richard the sonne of Edward Hulin & [*blank*] his wife was Baptised.

June 10. Martha the daughter of Mr John Sicklemore & Martha his wife Baptised.

July 8. Williã the sonne of Edmund Garward & Anne his wife Baptis.

July 11. Mary the daughter Jemes Goslin of the Key pish & [*blank*] his wife B.

Aug. 22. Mary the daughter of George Bumsted & Anne his wife Baptised.

Sept. 5. Isaac the sonne of William Longley & Sarah his wife Baptised.

Sept. 13. Elizabeth the daughter of Mr James Gosnell & Mary his wife was baptized.

1652.

June   10th.   henery Moulson son of henery moulson & Sarah his
                 wife baptized.

Decem.   1.   Mary the daughter of Edward Gates & Briget his
                Wife Bap.

Decem.   19.   Francis the sonne of Thomas Bellamore & Susan his
                 wife Bap.

Dec.   28.   Samuel the sonne of Isaak Jackson & Elizab. his
                 wife was Bap.

Jan.   9.   William the sonne of Anthony Lewis & [*Blank*] his
                 wife Bapt.

Jan.   11.   John the sonne of John Garward & Sarah his wife
                 was Bapt.

Jan.   12.   Mary the daughter of James Houlton & Joan his
                 wife was Bapt.

Jan.   30.   { Samuel the son of Michael Palmer & Kimborow his
                   wif. was Bapt.
                   Samuel the son of Edward Garward & [*Blank*] his
                   wif. was baptised.

Febr.   9.   Abigaile the daughter of Samuel Swan & [*Blank*] his
                 was Bap.

Tho. Townes sonne of Rob. Townes and Elizebeth his wife baptised
    22 Sept.

1653.   Anno Dom. 1653.

May   5th.   Richard the sone of James Canting & Elizabeth his
                  wife baptised.

June   17.   Hanna the daughter of Thomas Cap & Hanna his
                  wife Bap.

August   15.   marie the daughter of Samuell Boycatt & Marie his
                  wife was baptised.

July   30.   mary daughter of Michael Osbourne & Elizabeth his
                  wife was Baptised.

Aug^t   25.   richard son of [*Blank*].
Octob. ye 25.   John sonne of John Lucas and Margarett his wife
                  Bapt.

Jully ye 25.   Robert sonn of Robert Cooke & Deborah his wife
                  Baptized.

Janua.   5.   tomas sonne of tomas blasby was baptised.
Janv.   8.   Ealse Thvrston daughter of lias thvrston & Sary his
                  wife baptised.

                         1653.

Septe.   11.   Thomas the sonne of Thomas mvlender & martha
                  his wife.
                  daughter of Jefre Browne of devbeg [? Debbidge]
                  baptiesed.

Janv.   27.   william the sonne of Richard Annis & Elizabeth
                  his wife was babtised.

Mar.	6.	william the sonne of william Lister &davkes his wife Bab.
Mar.	6.	Abegeall the daughter of frances Gooden & of dorothe his wif. b.
feb.	3.	John Gladon the sonne of John gladon & Elizabeth his wif. ba.
mar.	8.	Ann the daughter of John billemer & of Elizabeth his wif. bab.
mar.	9.	Elizabeth Payse the daughter of John Payse & Elizabeth his wife.
mar.	24.	Jeames the sonne of Jeames Gosnall & of Mara his wif. babti.

Elizabeth the daughter of [*blank*] Ruff and Rose his wife was Baptiz. the 22 August 1654.

Baptizings Año 1654.

Aprill the first.		Elizabeth the daughter of James Houton & of Jone his wife was Baptized.
May	1.	John hewling sonne of John hewling & Elizabeth his wife was babtised.
Maye	30.	Jeames the sonne of Jeames Canton & of Elizabeth his wife babti.
June	11.	Thomas sonne of John Daniell & of mara his wife babtised.
Augv.	ii.	Phillip sone of Jn⁰ Sichelmor Esq. & martha his ws. bap.
Octõ	23.	Elizabeth daughter of Edward man & [*blank*] baptized.
Octõ	23.	Stephen sone of Stepēn dyer & Eizebath his Wife bã.
Septeʳ	25.	legddea daughter of Tomas lamebe baptised.
		baptised. }
N.	20.	John Sone of tho. tower wase Borne. }
Jan.	7.	John blasebye Sone of tho Clasbye Baptized.
D.	13.	Samvell Sone of Nathan Smarte & Ruth his Wiffe was Baptized.
Jan.	12.	Thomas son of Tho Billiman was Bap.
Jan.	14.	Mary daughter of will Mondie was Bap.
ffeb.	6.	Elizebeth daughter off Joseph wittum was Bap.
March	11.	Anne daughter Robᵗ Reader was borne.
March	23.	John son of James Gosnell was bap.
March	25.	Sarah daughter of Henery Sley was Bap.

Page 66. December the 19th 1653.

Ambrose ffrost of S. Nicholas pish beinge Chosen Register for the said pish by the Inhitants thereof was sworne before us whose names are subscribed Bayliffes of yᵉ towne of Ipswich to execute the office of Register in the aforesaid pish accordinge to the Act of Parliamᵗ in that case pvided. Jo. Alldus.
Manuell Sorrell.

Septembr the Elizabeth the Daughter of John Margeund and Eliza-
17 1655. beth his wife was Baptized.
Susan the Daughter Robert Wade & Ellin his wife was bapt. Octbr the 5th.

G

Babtizinge 1655.

April	8.	John sonne of John hubberd & [blank] his wife baptized.
		his wife baptized. }
Aprell	9th.	Elizabeth daughter of John brett baptised. }
June	5th.	Ben son of Bassell Brame was Bap.
June	10th.	Elzebeth daugher of Tho. Ha^{r}per was Bap.
Augst	5th.	Hannah daughter of Peter Baker was Bap.
Sept.	14.	ffrancis sonne of ffrancis Lemmon Baptized.
Sept.	14.	Susan Dawghter of Thomas Cooper & Anne his wife.
Sept.	24.	John sonn of henry Molson & Sarah his wife.
Sept.	23.	Mary daughter of William Thorne & Mary his wife.
Octob.	8.	Jacob sonne of Jacob Waitwhatt & Ann his wyfe of Nicholas pish was baptised.
Octob.	3.	George sonn of George Warren & Margarett his wife.
Octob.	23.	Robt lakelyn his dawghter Elizabeth was baptized.
Sep.	25.	[blank].
Novemb.	4.	Thomas & John sonns of Thomas Wilehyn & Anne his wife.
January	4.	Edward sonn of Edward Gates was baptized.
January	6.	Elizabeth Dawghter of John Billamor and Mary his wife.
January	14.	Mary dawghter of Richard Annis & Elizabeth his wife.
January	18.	Mary dawghter of Miell Osbourne baptized.
January	18.	Elizabeth dawghter of Edward hewlyn baptized.
January	28.	Mary dawghter of Edward Mann g^t baptized.
March	2.	Anne dawghter of Robert Cooke baptized.
March	2.	Anne dawghter of John Payse baptized.
Octob^r	25.	Richard son of Richard Warren & Sarah his wife was bapti.

Babtizinge 1656.

September the 17.		Susan Dauter of John Waller was baptised.
March	29.	Mary Dawghter of Christopher Milton baptized.
May the 8.		Robt sonn of Robt Reader borne.
May	11.	Pheby Dawghter of John Tilleson baptized.
June	16.	Anne Dawghter of Robt. frost baptized.
July		Margarett Dawghter of Tho harper baptized.
July	14.	Elizabeth the daughter of Bazaliell Brame borne & baptized the 27th same month.
June	7.	Elizabeth daughter of Willm Curd Baptized.
August	24.	Margarett daughter of Joseph Lindson baptized.
August	23.	Hannah Daughter of Thomas Wythe Baptized.
Sept.	18.	Rose dauter of John & Rose Malster bapt.
	19.	Sarah dauter of William & Sarah Longly bapt.
	14.	William sonne of William & Alice Skeete bapt.
Octo.	28.	Robt Clinch sonn of Mr Robartt Clinch & Marg^{ret} his wife bapt.
Nov.	24.	William sonn of William & Mary Mowdy baptized.
	27.	Thomas sonn of Thomas Lewis & Lidda his wife bapt.

Decem. 2. Mary dauter of Mr John Sicklemore Esq. & Mar^tha his
wife baptized.

10. Sarah Dauter of henery Moulson & Sarah his wife
baptized.

Jan. 11. Nãth. sonne of Nathaniell hill baptized.

Page 67. 1656.

Jan. 18. Ruth Smart daughter of Nath Smart & Ruth his wife
was Bapt.

Jan. 21. Edward leuc son of Edward Luce.

March 15th. Isaac Mixer sonne of John Mixer was Baptised.

March 17th. hannah daughter of Edward Mann gent. & Martha
his wife was Baptised.

1657.

Aprill 17th. Mary daughter of Richard Wilder & Mary his wife
was baptised.

Jan. 14. John Reder son of Robart Reder was borne.

Aprill 26. sonn of Edw. Gates.

Aprill the 8th. Abagale Daughter of george Robertson and Abagal his
wife babtised.

May 30. [*blank*] daughter of Michael osburne.

ffeb. 28. John waller sonn of John waller baptyed. 1658.

June 4. Susan daughter of Roger Younge Clerke.

June 3. Stephen sonn of Stephen Dyer borne.

July 6. Abraham sonne of Jacob Waitwhait & Anne his wyfe
baptized.

Aug. 9. Willm sonne of Robt Cooke baptized.

Aug. 9. Thomas sonne of John Billomor baptized.

Nov. 2. Sarah daughter of Simon Row baptized.

Nov. 2. Mary daught. of Robt Thorpe baptized.

Nov. 28th. Katherine daughter of John brooke & Katherine his
wife.

Decemb. 19. Mary daughter of Thomas Willchin bapt.

Dec. 24. Thomas sonne of Thomas Torner borne & Baptised.

Dec. 26. John wolltum sonne of John wolltum bapt.

March 2. Ann daughter of william Curd bapt.

feb. 28. Petur sonne of Petur Baeker bapt.

March 22. Elizabeth daughter of William Thorne bapt.

1658.

Aprill the 9 ffrancis Clopton sun of Ric. Clopton and Sary his
1658. wiefe.

[Lidia the daughtur of James Carting & of Elyzabeth his wife was
[borne the xith of March An° 1657 and Baptised the 18th day
[of the saide march].

August 22. Tho. sonn of Tho. Lewes baptized.

10th Sept. John sonn of John Skeete baptized.

Sept. 28. John sonn of John Rivers baptized.

Novemb. 14. John sonn of Tho. Elsden baptized.

Decemb 22. Mary daughter of Tho. Cooper baptized.

G ^2

Decemb	26.	henry sonn of Robert Cooke baptized.
March	20th.	Richard and Benjamine sonnes of Mr Jeremy Cole baptized.
Aprill ye	23.	maudlin the daughter of Isaac Gates and Elizabeth his wife.
March	20th.	Thomas sonne of John Tilleson bab.

1659.

Aprill	14.	hannah daughter of Edward Mann Esq. baptizd.
Aprill	17.	Margarett dawghter of Samuell Richardson.
May	forst.	John sonne of Thomas hardy & Abigall his wife baptized.
May	29.	Philip sonn of Thomas harper.
June 16	1659.	Thomas Sonne of Wm Stockton Borne and Christened ye Same day.
June	22th.	Susann Daughter of Thomas Searles Baptized.
Jule	10th.	thms sonne of thoms Smith.
September	24.	Abigall Daughter of John Pink Baptized.
September 2 day.		John son of John pricke baptised.
October	9th.	[*blank*] Daughter of Isaac Albree Baptized.
October	12th.	Lidda Daughter of Thomas Lewes Baptized.
December	18th.	James sonne of John Dyer Baptized.
January	29th.	Sarah Dawghter of William Thorne Baptized.
february the 10th.		Henry so. of Jemes [*blank*].
ffebruary	14.	William Sonne of William Curd Baptized.
March	12th.	Hannah daughter of John brooke and Katherine.

Page 68. ### Baptizings.

| March | 20th. | Ellen daughter of Robt Thorpe baptized. |

1660.   1660 tie.

March	26.	Marey daughter of John Mixter baptized.
March	30.	Charles sonn of Brian & Susun Smith baptized.
Aprel the	23.	John leuc son of Edward.
Aprill	1th.	Otho sonne of Edward Mann Esq. baptized.
January the 24th.		Heaster ye Doughter of Tho. & lidia Torver Baptized.
December the 26 1660.		mary the daughter of John Daniell and Mary his wife was borne.
Aprill	22th.	Thomas sonne of Widdy Poyse baptized.
Aprill	29th.	Phillip sonne of Phillip Wright baptized.
Apr.	29th.	John sonne of Edward Lewes baptized.
May	6th.	Elizabeth daughter of Thomas Brond bap.
May	6th.	Susan daughter of Simon Rowe baptized.
September	16th.	Willm sonne of Elias Thurston baptized.
September	16th.	Mary daughter of Jon Browne baptized.
September	23th.	Mary daughter of Thomas Allard baptized.
September	23th.	James sonne of Robt Townes baptized.
September	26th.	Margrett daughter of Tho. Cooper baptized.
October	6,	Edmunt sune of John yongs babt.

October	7th.	Thomas sonne of Tho. Searls baptized.
November	8th.	Peter sonne of Tho. hardy baptized.
November	11th.	Thomas sonne of Tho. Daniell baptized.
November	25th.	Samewell sonne of Peter Baker baptized.
December	2.	Sarah daughter of Rosmus[*Erasmus*]Gossebaptized.
December	2.	Edmund sonne of Edmund Garrard baptized.
December	16th.	Susan Daughter of Ric^d Pippyn baptized.
December	23th.	Sarah Daughter of John Daniell baptized.
June	27th.	Ann the Daughter of Robte Youngs Baptised.
March	17th.	Mary Daughter of Robte Cooke Baptized.
March	17th.	Elizabeth Daughter of Edmond Garrad baptized.
March	17th.	William sonne of John Brett Baptized.
Octob.	16.	Mary 1° Daughter to Rob. Cooke and Deborah his wife baptised.

Baptizings 1661.

March	31th.	William sonne of John Knights Baptized.
Aprill	21th.	John Gray sonne of [*blank*] Gray Baptised.
		Mary Daughter of John Tilleson Baptized.

Roger the sonne of Roger Young and Susan his wife was baptized April 21th 1661.

Elizabeth the Daughter off William Stockton Baptized ye 14 June 1661.

Novemb	18.	John sonne of John Brooke Esq. & Katherine his wife baptized.
Decemb	12th.	Eleanor daughter of Edward Mann Esq. & Martha his wife baptized.

Willm Roleson son of Will. Roleson & Jone his wif. was born the 3 day of July 1661.

Page 69.

March the 22 1661. Thomas Margerum sonne of John margerum and Elizabeth his wife was Baptized.

Baptizings 1661.

October the	23.	thomas leuc son of Edward Luce.
July	7th.	Elizabeth daughter of John Boston Baptized.
July	14th.	[*blank*] daughter of Thomas Steddie Baptized.
Aug.	11th.	Ann daughter of Phillip Wright Baptized.
Nov.	10.	Samuell sonne of John Simpson Baptized.
ffeb.	23.	Mary daughter of Thomas Daniell baptized.
ffeb.	23.	Mary daughter of John Garwood baptized.
Aprill the	27.	Elizabeth daughter of John King and Elsabeth his wife babtis 1662.

Baptizings 1662.

Aprill	10th.	Samuell Son of Thomas hardy & Abygall his wife Baptized.
May	25°.	Susan Daughter of William Labis baptized.
June	8".	Margarett daughter of William Thorne baptized.

July	27°.	John sonne of Robte Johnson baptized.
July	27ⁿ.	Christian daughter of John Browne baptized.
Sept.	3th.	Ann Daughter of Robert Reader borne.
Sept.	9th.	Stephen sonne of Thomas holliwood baptized.
Sept.	26th.	Robte sonne of James Canting and Elizabeth his wife baptized.
Novemb	2ᵈ.	Mary daughter of Willm Sudbury baptized.
Novemb	17th.	Elizabeth daughter of John Boston baptized.
Novemb	30.	John sonne of John Hudgwell baptized.
Decemb	6th.	John sonne of Edward Mann Esq. baptized.
March	9th.	Thomas sonne of John Brooke Esq. and Katherine his wife baptized.
January yth	10.	Marthe daughter of thomas Smith bap.

Anno 1663.

March	27°.	henry Peake sonne of John Peake Baptized.
July	17°.	Edward sonne of Edward Pilkington and Eliz. his wife baptized.
Sept.	20°.	Hannah daughter of Lias Thurston baptized.
Novemb	8°.	Susanna daughter of Robert Death Baptized.
Novemb	23°.	Thomas sonne of Thomas Billamore baptized.
Septemb	2°.	Elizabeth daughter of Thomas Searles Baptized.

Novemb. first of the year abovesaid Thomas sonne of Thomas hardy & Abigall his wife Baptized.

Thomas Son of tho Creswell & Sarah his wife was Babtized September yᵉ 18th 1664.

Susen Roloson dafter of will Roloson and Jone his wif. was born Aprill the 16th 1664.

Anno 1664.

1664. Elizabeth Whiting davghter of Edward & dority his wife was Baptized 23th of Aprill.

March	27°.	Bridget daughter of Edmond Garwood baptized.
Nouvmᵇ	17th.	Tho. Gattes Son of Isack Gattes & Elizabeth his wife was baptised n. Affore said.
Aprill	5°.	Phillip sonne of Phillip Wright Baptized.
Apr.	10°.	Anne daughter of William Thorne Baptized.
Apr.	25.	Thomas sonn of Edward Mann Esq. & Martha his wife Baptized.
June	5.	Robt sonn of Rob. Wale & [*blank*] his wife Baptized.
June	11th.	Thomas sonn of John Broke Esq. & Katherine his wife Baptized.
June	19.	Elizabeth dauter of [*blank*] Eades & [*blank*] his wife Baptized.
July	3.	John sonne of John Barber & [*blank*] his wife Baptized.
July	10.	Mary dauther of Christopher Wilcock Baptized.
July	13.	Mary daughter of George Warren & [*blank*] his wife Baptized.

Septem.	8.	John sonn of Peter Baker & hannah his wife baptized.
Novem.	17.	Georg sonn of Edward Pilkitton gent. & Eliz. his wife baptized.
Novem.	27.	John sonn of Thomas Smyth & Martha his wife baptized.
Decem.	16.	Penellope dauther of Thomas Blose & Penellope his wife bapt.
Decem.	25.	ffrancis sonn of ffrancis Turner & Mary his wife Baptized.

Anno 1665.

April	9th.	Richard sonn of John Hudgwell & [*blank*] his wife Baptized.
Aprill	23.	Ann daughter of Symont Smyth [*blank*] baptized.
April	30.	John sonn of John King & Eliz. his wife baptized.
May	14.	Joseph sonn of Thomas Hardy & Abigal his wife baptized.
July	5.	Mary daughter of Edward Man Esq. & Martha his wife baptiz.
July	16.	Ann dauther of William Cowper & [*blank*] his wife baptized.
July	21.	Mary dauther of Nathaniell Branson [*blank*] Baptized.
Jvne the 29th.		Sary dooghter of henry bvckrum baptised.

Page 70.

Aug.	4th.	John sonn of John Broke Esqʳ & Katheren his wife Baptized.
	20th.	Thomas Sonn of John Brett [*blank*] baptized.
	27.	Georg sonn of Georg Allin & Brigitt his wife baptized.
Octo	22.	ffrancis sonn of Andrew Cremer & [*blank*] his wife after her death.
	29.	Digby Sonn of Thomas hardwick & [*blank*] his wife baptized.
	29.	Danill Sonn of John Waller the same day baptized.
Martha daughter of Edmond genens. Baptised Dec. 2th.
ffeb.	14.	John sonn of ffrancis Canny baptized.
March	13.	John sonn of Phillip Wright & Ann his wife baptized.

Anno 1666.

Augustyᵉ 17th.		Alice the Dafter of Will and Alice Sare was Babtised.
May	20th.	Jesuway Son of george Warren & Margate his wiff. baptized.
Septe the 4th.		Charele King son of John King babtiz.
Octo. yᵉ 7th.		mychal Sonn of Thomas Danill & Mary his wife baptiz. the 7 October.
Noue.	13th.	Babtized was John Sonn of John Laurance.
Novem.	2.	Robt Sonn of William Rawlison & Joone his wife bapt.

January   18.   Rachell daughter of William Chinnery baptized.

March   11th.   James the sonne of Thomas Hardy & Abigal his wife bapt.

Aprill y⁶ 7.   william Son of william Branson and mari wife was baptized.   march the 12.   daughter of Roberd Cook Borne October 3 1667.

June 16th day.   Robrt Sone of William Cooper & Sewsanah his wife baptised.

Thomas Huitt [*blank*] Thomas the son [*blank*] baptised. and Mary [*blank*].

Mary wright daughter of Phillip and Ann Wright was Baptised the 26th day of September 1667.

October the 6.   John stone sonn of John Stone baptised.

Martha the Davghter of John warne and Martha his Wife was Borne the fourth Day of Jully 1667. |: John the sonn of John harper & Eliz. his wife was baptized Jvary 1° 166—.

Octo. the 5ᵗʰ.   John Son of John Monson was baptized.

Elizabeth daughter of Philip Candler and of Deborah his wife was borne March yᵉ 2 and Baptized March the 10th 1667.

March yᵉ 4th. ⎧ Robert yᵉ Son of Robert bond was baptized—1667.
          1 ⎨ Mary daughter of George Alberie And Bridget his
            ⎩ wife Bapt. August yᵉ 10.

March   15th.   Hana daughter of Robᵗ Keeble & margaret his wife baptized.

fr.   , 8th.   simon sonn of simon smyth baptised.

michel Palmer and elizabeth his wif. Elizabeth his dauter was born o.

1668.

October the 2.   basel the Son of Basell huet and Susan his wife Born [*or Baptized, uncertain*].

Elizabeth the dafter of mickaell Palmer and Elizabeth his wife was baptized June 8th 1668.

October the 18th.   Thomas son of Thomas bond & mary his wife.

November yᵉ 19 1668.   Elizabeth the daughter of William Boycatt and Elizabeth his wife was born and baptised yᵉ sᵈ nineteenth day of Novᵇ anno Dñi 1668.

William sone of william crinnery and margret his wife 25th october was born.

ffrances sonn of ffrances Leg was baptized August the 11th.

Jan.   29.   Christian Norton dauter of John Norton & Susan his wife.

1669.

Aprill the 10th.   Edmond son of Edmond Lvffe baptised.

June yᵉ 15th.   Elizabeth daughter of Willm̄ Green was born & baptised.

¹ These two entries are interpolated or mixed up with the preceding and succeeding ones.

Sep^t the 8°. Thomas Allen the son of George Allen And Bridget.
Nove. the 19. George the son of ffrances Turner was born and
    baptised the same day.
 the 25. Mary davter of John Movson & mary his wife was
    bap.
Decem. the 14. Susan Cliford dafter of Joseph Clifa.
  Margret daughter of Peter Bigsiby and [*blank*] his wife
   Baptized the 11th day of march 1669.
  [*blank*] sonn of Richard whiteng & Joan his wife.
Ann the Daughter of Robt Wales.

 Page 71.

  Mary davghter of Edmond Jenings baptid march ii.
  Richard son of Thomas heere Cocke and Prudence his wife
   was babtid 10th March 1669.
June 5 1669. Bazillay [*blank*] of Thomas Huitt & Mary his wife
   Bapt.
  Tho. Cooke Sone of Robt Cooke and Sarah his wife was
   baptised the 20 of August 1669.
  Mary Skeet Daughter of Wm Skeet & Mary his wife w^s babtz.
January ye 20th 1669. Peter sonn of Peter strong was baptized
   January 30th.

Baptizeing An° 1670,

Thomas Shuckforth son of Tho. Shuckforth and Sarah his
  wife was Borne The 8 day of february 1670.
Rich. Newton son of Rich. Newton Gent. & Lettice his wife
  was borne the 12th of march An° 1669 And was
  Baptized the 31th of march An° 1670.
1668 John Harper the sun to John Harper was born the 10 day
  of Jewary 1668.
  Mary the dafter of michaell Palmer and Elizabeth was
   baptized the 22 of march 1669.
  Mary Larance the dafter of John Larance was baptised
   febrwary the 28.
1669 Robart Pulbroo the sun of Robart Pulbree & Thomazin his
  wife was baptized the 12th of Aprell.
  Abraham sone of william chinnery was born Anno 1670
   and baptised Apriel the 19th.
  Phillip Sonne of Phillip Wright & Ann his wif. was borne
   April 17th 1670 was Baptized April 19th 1670.
June 24th. Robt sonn of Robt Lakeland & Eliz. his wyfe was
   Baptized.
July 17th. Elizabeth daughter of John & Elizabeth Harper was
   baptised.
  Thomas son of Bazell huitt & Susan his wife was bapt.
  Sept. 19th 1670.
August the 6 1670. Peter hovgrav and alic. his wif.* had their
   their dafter was babtised the 6 of augst.

Daniell Richer and Elezebeth his wife and Elezebeth ther daughter borne 25 September 1670.

Novem. 6th. a base child of Ann Cowper wid. was born & bapt. 9th nouem. following.

Nouem. 27. Alixsander son of ffrancis Lee & of Eliz. his wife was baptized.

March 10th. Elizabeth daughter of John Rye & Eliz. his wife was baptised.

John Stroggin Sonne of Thomas Stroggin and Elizebeth his wife was baptised the 1th october 1670.

Danell son of Thomas Crissell and Sarah his wife was baptised the 11th day of nouember 1670.

ffebruary the second. John Smyth the sone of Symond and Ann his wife baptized 1670.

Aug. 23 1670. Mary dauther of Edmund Luffe & Mary his wife was baptized.

1670.

January the 28. Lydia the Daughter of John margerum and Elizabeth his wife was Baptized.

Page 72.

Año Doṁi. 1671.   Christenings.

1671. April 16. Ann Daughter of William Rogers & Jane his wife baptized.

Beniaman sonn of William Skeet & Mary his wife was baptized April 23th 1671.

May 17. henrey orger sonn of Georg orger and Marey his Wife was Borne and Baptied.

June 9. Samuell Son of Henry Goodin And Martha his wife was baptized 1671.

July 12. Dorkas Daughter of Robt Houell Als Smyth And Dorkas his wiffe was baptised 1671.

September the 3ᵈ 1671. } was baptised Elezebeth the Daughter of Francis and Sarah Garway his wife.

August the 9° 1671. } John the Sonn of John Margerum and Elizabeth his wife was Baptized.

August the 13 1671. } Elizabeth the Daughter of David Richardson and Susan his wife was Baptized.

September the 11 1671. } elezabeth the daughter of Robert Lackland and elezabeth his wife was baptised.

September the 7 1671. } Robert the sonn of John Harper and Elizabeth his wife was baptized.

October the first 1671. } John Baker the Sonn of John Baker and Ann his wife was baptized.

Octo. 15th. Henery sonn of William & Joone Rawlinson bapt.

1671. Robart Harper the sun of John Harper was born the 7 Day of September 1671.

Nouember 12th. Dorety the daughter of Edweard Whitin and Dorety his wiffe bapt.

December the 8th 1671°.	Isaac the sonn of Isaac Boyket and Mary his wife was baptized.
March the 3 1671.	Then was Babtized John Turner Sunn of ffrancis Turner and Susan his wife.

1671.

february the 18.	then was babtized Josepth movson sonn of John movson and mary his wif.
ffeb' the 18.	Thomas the Sonn william Boranson [*Branson*] and Margaritt his wife was Baptized.
March the 1.	Catherine the daughter of Robert Jewrey and Elezabeth his wife.

Elizabeth y' daughter of Marten Wheler and Lidy his wife was borne July the 2. 1671.

March y° 31 1672.	Mary the Daughter of ffrances Sames and Mary his wife was Baptized.
Aprill the 9 1672.	Then was Baptized nicklolas Wright son of Phillip wright and Ann his wife.

Page 73.

Anno Dn° 1672. Christenings.

James Newton the sonn of Richard Newton & Lettis his wife was borne the 30th of May and christened the fourth of June 1672.

1672. Suann daughter of thomas Strogin and Elesebeth his wife baptised ffeb. the 2 daye.

June	23.	Thomas the Son of Daniell Richer and Elizabeth his was Baptized.
June	23.	Steven the Son of John Stone and Sarah his wife was Baptized.

John Brame was Baptised Nov. y° 19 1671.

August 2th 1672.	was Borne Robt Houele Als Smyth Sun of Robt houele Als Smyth And Dorkas his wife And Babtised August the 4th 1672.

Tamissin daughter of william Chinnery was born & bapized 20th aygust.

July 26 was bptised mary the daughtare Basseill hewate and sheusana his wife 1672.

August y° 20th was baptised Ann Elsden y° Dufter of Rob. Elsden and Ann his wife.

October the 5 was Richerd Lackland baptised the sonn of Robert Lackland and elzebeth his wife 1672.

Mihell palmer Son of mihell plamer [*sic*] and of elisebeth his wife was born the 9th of october 1672.

Jeremiah focha the son of Jeremiah focah and of Serah his wife was born the 3 of december 1672.

Mary huet daftere dafter of thomas huet & mary his wife was babtised on Januery the 10 1672.

Bredget the dafter of gorg Alen and Bredget his wife was born Janawary 21th 1672.

feb. the 5th   Witt Skeet son of witt skeet & mary his wife was 1672.   baptised.   william Crisell son of Thomas Crisell

{ 1671.   and Sarey his wife wase born Jannav^ry_{av}
{ 1672.

Micell Pamer this yere 1673 was chosen Sexton.

Mary Coke daughter of Edward Coke & mary his wiffe was baptised April 13th.

Elizabeth Sames the daughter of ffrances Sames and Mary his wife was baptised May ye 11.

Ales the daughter of Peeter Hoggrafe and Alse his wife was baptized June ye 10.

Auis the daughter of William Boicett and Elizebeth his wife was baptized July ye 6.

Samuel ye sonne of John Herper and Elizebeth his wif. was baptized July ye 8.

James the sonne of thomas Coocke and Elizebeth his wif. was baptized August ye 17.

Page 74.

1673.   Chriseninges.

Thomas ye sonne of ffrances Turner and Susan his wife was babtized August the 29.

John ye sonne of William Rorgers and Jane his wife was babtized September ye 9.

John the sonne of Robert Wales and Ann his wife was babtized September y^o 10.

Mary the daughter of Robert Elseden and Mary his wife was babtized September y^c 14.

Elizebeth the daughter of John Crouder and Elizebeth his wife was babtized September y^o 22.

Edward the sonne of Thomas Heere Cocke and Prudence his wife was babtized September y^c 23.

David the sone of David Richerson and Susan his wife was baptiz february 8th.

Mary the daughter of John Duse and Mary his wife was babtized September ye 24.

Robert the sonne of Robert Jurie and Elizebeth his wife was babtized September the 15.

Thomas the sone of Marten wheler and Liddy his wife was babtized October the 10.

Edmund ye sonne of ffrances Lee and Elizebeth his wife was babtized Desember the 7.

Jacob the sonne of Thomas Daniell and Mary his wife was babtized May the 9.

Nathenell the sone of William Branson and Margrett his wife was babtized January y^o 27.

ffeberywary the 19th was borne Ann houele Als Smyth Ann Elizabeth houele Als Smyth both daughters of Robt houele Als Smyth And dorkas his wife ware Babtised the Nine and Twenth of ffeb 1673.

1674. ## Chrisenings. 1674.

Mary the daughter of Henery Birde and Marcy his wife was babtized Aprill the 14.

Robert Newton sonn of Rithund Newton and Lettis his wife was borne the 3th of Aprell & Baptized the 29th of Aprill 74.

ffrantces the Dauter of Staphen kebell and mathew is wif. was baptised march 20.

Jane yᵉ Daughter of Thomas browne and Rose his wife was babtized Aprill the 23.

Page 75.

1674. ## Chriseninings.

ffrances the sonne of William Roldeson and Jone his wife was babtized May the 11.

Mary the daughter of James Birde and Mary his wife was babtized June yᵉ 9.

Vallintine the sonne Vallintine More and Margret his wife was babtized June yᵉ 11.

anna the dafter of Edmund Luffe and Mary his wife was babtized June the 24.

Mary the dafter of arnold tilison and susan his wif. was babtised september the 11th.

ann the dafter of nathinel brown and mary his wif. babtised october the 11th.

Mary the dafter of thomas Iven and Ivcy his wif. was baptised october 23.

Ann the dafter of William genry and margret his wif. was babtised november the 7th.

An the daughter of Peter Stronge and Mary his wife was baptized the 25th of Nouember 1674.

Edward son of Edward Coke and mary his wiffe was baptised nouerber 26th.

Elizabeth daughter of Jonas tvnmer and Elizabeth his wiffe was baptised no. 27.

John sone of John balderson and Elizabeth his wiffe was baptised dec. 6th.

Edm. sune of Edm Cochpoll and Ame his wife bapt. dec. 14.

Deborah Dafter of henry hocker and Deborah his wife was Baptised Janua yᵉ 12 1674.

Elizabeth daughter of Edmond fewnes and martha his wiffe was baptised feb. 15th 74.

William son of ffrancis Turner and Susan his wiffe was baptized feb. the 31th [*sic*].

Elizabeth daughter of John browne & Elizabeth his wiffe was baptised ffeb. 14th.

Ann the Dauter of william Copper and Ann his wife was Baptised ffeb. 28.

JohnHouton was baptised march 3 son of JohnHoutonAndSusan his wife.

Mathew the Dauter of William Sket & marey his wife was baptise march the 14.

Tho. The Sunn of Will may and Susan his wiffe was babtised march the 14th 1674.

Ann morden Daughter of Will morden Ann his wife was borne and baptised march the 16 1674.

Martha the daughter of Phillipe Wrighte and Anne his wife was baptized March the 4th 1674.

Page 76.

1675.   Christnings.[1]

Elezebeth the dauter of henrey Lockwod and Elezebeth his wife was baptized Aprell the 4 daye.

Charles the sonne of Charles stubs & francies his wife was baptised Junn the 14 daye.

Elezebeth the dauter of John harper and Elezebeth his wife was baptised August 21.

William the sonn of ffrancis luck & marey his wife was baptised August the 20 day.

Edward the sone of Samuel ffeveyore and Ann his wife was baptiz. Septemb. 3th.

Robeart sonn of thomas Cresell & Sarey his wife was baptised septemb. 12 daye.

An the Daughter of James ffrost & Sarah his wife was baptized the 24th of September 1675.

John the sonn of John smith & marrey his wife was baptised octob. the 31 day 1675.

Sarah the daughter of Richard hayward and Sarah his wiffe was babtised n°. 10. 75.

william the sonn of william boycatt and margritt his wife was baptised nouemb. the 9 day 1675.

John the sonn of John Duce & marey his wif. was baptised nouemb. the 16 day 1675.

Ann houell Als. Smyth Daughter of Robt houell Als. Smyth And Dorkas his wiffe borne this Janewary the 25 Baptised Janewary the 30th 1675.

Henery the sonn of John wayth And mary his wiffe was Borne Janewary the 11th babtised Janewary the 30th 1675.

Sary The Daughter of Edward Cooke And mary his wiffe was Borne Janewary the 28th Baptised the thirty 1675.

Robartt sonn of Robeartt Elsden & marey his wife was baptised ffeb. the 13 daye 1675.

John the sonn of thomas harecoke & prudence his wife was baptised march the 4 day 1675.

John the sonn of ffrances Lee & Elezebeth his wife was baptised march the fiiue day.

william the sonn of william branson & margrett his wife was baptised march the 12 day.

[1] See an entry on page 96 that belongs to the year 1675.

Edw. sonn of John Cruder & Elzebeth his wife was baptised ffeb. 15 day 1675.

1676. Christnings 1676.

ffrancies sonn of Edw. Catchpole and Ame his wife was Baptised Aprell 2 daye.

Edw. sonn of thomas Strogin and Elezeb his wife was baptised Aprell the 2 day.

Page 77.

Thomas the sone of ffrancis Turner And Susan his wife was baptiz. May 7th.

Robert the sone of John Wade and Elizabeth his wife was baptiz. May 7th.

Mary the Daughter of Thomas Clarke And Bridgit his wife was baptiz. May 7th.

Lettis the Daughter of Richard Newton and Lettis his wife was borne June 12th and baptized June 18th.

John the sone of John Browne and Elizabeth his wife was baptiz. June 18th.

Mary the Daughter of William Daniel and Mary his wife was baptiz. June 22th.

John the sone of George Allen and Bridgit his wife was baptiz. July 16th.

Jonathan the sone of Martin Wheeler and Lydia his wife was baptiz. July 18th.

Susan the daughter of David Richerson and Susan his wife was baptiz. August 13th.

Anthony the sone of Thomas Cushion and Margaret his wife was baptiz. August 28th.

Elizabeth the Daughter of Henry Bird and Elizabeth his wife was baptiz. Septemb. 24th.

Henry the sone of Samuel ffeveyeare and Ann his wife was baptiz. octob. 8th.

Ann the Daughter of William Rolison and Jone his wife was baptiz. octob. 8th.

Elizabeth the Daughter of Phillip wright and Mary his wife was baptiz. October 22th.

Mary the Daughter of Peter Strong and Mary his wife was baptiz. November 19th.

Robert the sone of Robert Ellsdin and Mary his wife was baptiz. november 19th.

Margaret the Daughter and Base child of Margaret Germee was baptized December 31th.

Ann the daughter of Jonas Tunmer and Elizabeth his wife was baptiz. January 4th.

Mary the Daughter of John Woods and Margaret his wife was baptiz. December 10th.

Elizabeth the Daughter of John Norton and Susan his wife was baptiz. January 25th.

Robert the Sone of Simon Willkenson and Margaret his wife was
baptiz. January 28th.

December 17th.   Abigal daughter & Base Child of Abigal ffl . . r
was baptized.

March   14.   Susan daughter of Henry Morris & Susan his wife
was baptized.

Page 78.   Christenings   1677.

Ann the Daughter of ffrancis Turner and Susan his wife was
Baptized May 20th.

Elizabeth the daughter of John Wade and Elizabeth his wife was
Baptized June the 5th.

Jane the daughter of William Rogers and Jane his wife was Baptized
June the 6th.

Thomas the son of Valentine Moore and Margret his wife was
Baptized June 17th.

Elizabeth Houell Als. Smyth daughter of Robt Houell Als. Smyth
and Dorkas his wiffe was Borne June the 21 Baptised July the
first.

Mary Wakefield the Daughter of Jeffery wakfield and Martha his
wife was Baptized August 12 1677.

Sarah Cressell the daughter of Thomas Cressell and Sarah his wife
was Baptised August 26 1677.

Mary ye daughter of Jeremiah Cole and Jane his wife was christened
the 3d day of August 1677.

Mary Danill Daughter of William Dainell and Mary his Wiffe was
baptized 26 June 1675.—*thur was not Rome in 75.*

Willm ye sonne of Robt Ellsden and Mary his wife was babtised
Sept. 23d.

Thomas sonne of Thomas Lewin and Lusee his wife was baptised
October the 7th.

ffrancis sonne of ffrancis Huck and Mary his wife was baptised
october 21th.

John the Sun of Wm Copper was Baptized and An. his oct. 12 1677.

Edmond sonne of Edmond Janneas and Martha his wife was
baptised october the 24.

Elizabeth Newton Daughter of Richard Newton & Lettis his wife
was borne the 28th of Nouember and babtized the fflrst of
December.

Elizabeth the Daughter of Bazahell hewett & Elizabeth his wife was
Bapt. December the 16th Annvys Dn^o vt super.

Mary the Dafter of Edward Coock & mary his wife was babtised
Janvery the 27th.

William son of william branson ad Margrat his wiffe was baptised
ffeb. 24.

Ann the dafter willam Jannry and margret his wife was baptized
december the 25th.

Willam the sonn of francis Lee and Elizabath his wife was baptized
March the 10th.

John the sonn of John billemer and Elizabeth his wife was baptized March the 10th.

John the sonn of Susan daniell was baptized March 10th.

Elizebeth the Davghter of Wm Daniell Mary his wiffe was Baptized 27 March 1677.

Page 79. Christenings 1678.

Nathaniel son of John brown and Elizabeth his wife was baptized April 7th.

Elizabeth the dafter of Samuel feveyeare and Ann his wife was baptised May 5th.

Ephraim the sonn of Thomas Baker and Mary his wife was born the 9th and baptized the 21th of April.

Samuel sonn of Phillip wright and Mary his wife was baptized Jun the 30th.

Susan the dafter of daniel Smith and Elizabeth his wife was baptized July 28.

John the sonn of Thomas Cushion and Margret his wife was baptized August 11th.

John the sonn of William Skeet and Mary his wife was baptized August 11th.

William the sonn of ffracis Turnner and Susan his wife was baptized August 12th.

Samuell the sonn of Samuell foster and Sary his wife was baptized August 12th.

William the sonn of Francis Blois and Mary his wife was baptized August the 16th.

Elizabeth the dafter of Nathaniel brown and Mary his wife was baptized August 25th.

Jaffry the sonn of Jaffry wakfield and Martha his wife was baptized Septem 8th.

James the sonn of James ffrost and Sary his wife was baptized October 6th.

Sary the dafter of William Comman and Sary his wife was baptized october 6th.

Thomas the sonn of thomas Goldbrough and Mary his wife was baptized november the 3.

Jonas the son of Jonas tumner and Elizabeth his wife was baptized febavary 6.

Margret the dafter of Valentin More and Margret his wife was baptized febrvray 23.

Sammuell son of william branson & margot his wife baptised march the 23th.

1679.

Elizabeth dafter of Robart Elsden and Mary his wife was baptized April 6.

Elizabeth the dafter of william daniell and Mary his wife was baptized April 17.

Dabory the dafter of Edward Goslen and Ann his wife was baptized Aprel the 18th.

H

dabory the dafter of Jaffry bloumfeld and dabory his wife was baptized
    May the 19.
Rose the dafter of John Mooson and Rose his wife was baptized
    July the 6.

Page 80.

Sary the dafter of william Dyer and Hannah his wife was baptized
    July 13.
Joseph the sonn of John Brown and Elizabeth his wife was baptized
    July the 27.
Susanna the dafter of ffrancis Turner and Susan his wife was baptized
    october the 5th. .
Ann the dafter of william Rolason and Joan his wife was baptized
    October the 21.
Thomas the sonn of thomas Breatt and Ann his wife was baptized
    November the 2th.
ffrancis the sonn of thomas Cushing and Margreet his wife was
    baptized desember the 14.
Samuell the son of Phillip wright and Mary his wife was baptized
    desember the 28.
Edward the son of Edward Mann Esquir and Ann his wife was
    baptized Janwary 22th.
James the son of George Allen and bregget his wife was baptized
    Janvary 25th.
Thomas the sonn of Thomas Barker and Sary his wife was baptized
    febauary the 25th.
Mary the dafter of thomas Baker and Mary his wife was baptized
    febauray the 25th.
Elizabeth the dafter of Androw finly & Elizabeth his wif. was baptized
    March 7th.

Christening Ano domo 1680.

Ester the dafter of Samuell ffoster and Sary his wife was baptized
    Aprill 18th.
Elizabeth the dafter John Belemer and Elizabeth his wife was baptized
    Aprill 18th.
Simond the Sonn of Simond Willkingson and Margreet his wife was
    baptized May 16th.
Lettis Daughter of Richard Newton & Lettis his wife was baptized
    the 26th of May 1680.
Mary the Daughter of Robt Houell als Smyth And Dorcas his wiffe
    was Baptised June the 2 1680.
Christopher Chamberling the sonn of Christopher Chamberling and
    Hannah his wife was baptized June 27.
Rebake the dafter of Abraham Blichingden and Mary his wife was
    baptized June 27.
Some few entries following quite obliterated but the figures remaining—
    20 1680.
Elizabeth Daughter of William Coleman was baptized the twenty-
    eight of Nouember 1680.

Margret ye Dafter Of Thomas Cvshing And margret his wife was
Born march ye 11th and was Babtized march ye 13th Ano Dm̃m
1680.

Osborne Rolfe the sune off John Rolfe and Ester His wiffe was
Borne the 14th Day off October and Babtised the 20 day off
October 1680.

Page 81. Christinings An° Dom̃ 1681.

Mary the daughter of Robert Symons & Mary his wife was borne
Aprill the first & was baptised Aprill the third.

1681 { Thomas the sun of Wm Coper ann his Wiffe was Babtizied
         { the 12th of ffeb 1680.

Samuell the sone of Jeffrey blomfield & Deborha his wif. was baptised
Aprill the 16 1681.

Susan the daughter of thomas luwin & lucy his wif. was baptised
April the 16 1681.

Henry ye Son of Henry Bird And Elizabeth his wife was Born Aprill
ye 29th & was Babtized may ye ffirst Anno Dom̃ 1681.

Mary Daughter of Francis Turner & of Susan his wife was 1681 born
the twentyninth of May & was baptized the same day.

Mary Daughter of Andrew Tendlye & of Elizabeth his wife was born
the twenty eight of May & was baptized the first of Jun. 1681.

Sarah the Daughter of Philip wright & of Mary his wife was borne the
third of July & was baptized the tenth day of the same month 1681.

July the 24th 1681.

Dorcass the Davghter of thomas Heareby And willinkin his wife was
Babtized Anno 1681.

Judeth Baddeson Davghter of philep Baddeson And Judeth his wife
was Babtized August ye 7th Anno Domiñ 1681.

William Daniell Son of william Daniell And mary His Wiffe was
Babtized September ye 4th 1681.

Henery Ventris son of Peyton Ventris and Margaret his wife was born
September 16th and was Babtized September the 18th Anno
Dom. 1681.

Sarah the Daughter of Samewell ffoster And Sarah his wife was
Babtized October the 2^d 1681.

John Rolfe the sune off John Rolfe and Ester His wife was Borne
the 14 off October and Babtised the 20 day off October 1681.

Mary the Daughter of John Moulson And Rose his wif. was Babtized
Nouember ye 25th 1681.

Page 82. Babtizings in ✠ 1681 ✠

Elizebeth Daughter Of Robt Reder and Elizebeth His wife was Born
Janewery ye ffirst And was Babtised Jan. ye 12th 1681.

Sarah the daughter Of marke Barit And Sarah his wife was Babtized
Jan. ye 12th 1681.

Mary the Davghter Of John Smith And Mary his wife was Babtized
ffeb. ye 19th 1681.

March 5th. William Chamberlin Son of Christopher And Hanah
His wife was Babtized.

H^2

March 5th 1681. Sarah y⁰ Daughter of Thomas Clarke and Bridget his wife was Babtized.

Elizabeth the daughter of John Girling and Elizabeth his wife was baptized march 16 1681.

Anno yᵉ 1682.

Sarah the Daughter of James ffrost And Sarah his wife was Babtized may yᵉ 28th.

John the Son of John Cushing And Elizebeth his Wife was Babtized may yᵉ 28th.

Elizebeth the Daught. of Abraham & mary Blisingham was Babtized June yᵉ 15th.

[*In margin*]. Wᵐ the sunne of william Coper and ann his wiffe was Baptized July 12th 1682.

Mary yᵉ Daughter of Sam ffeveryear And An his wife was Babtized July yᵉ 23th 82.

Whibro Davghter of Tho. Brett And Ann his Wife was Babtized June yᵉ 2ᵈ 1682.

[*In margin*]. Michaell yᵉ sonn of Michaell Lech and Ailce his wife was Babtized August 10th 1682.

Nickolas Smaledg son of Nickolas Smaledg And grace his Wife was Babtized Avgust yᵉ 20th 1682.

Margret the Daughter of peyton Ventriss Esqʳ And Margret his wife was Babtized October yᵉ first 1682.

An the Davghter of Robert Elsden And Mary his wife was Babtized November the 5th 1681.

Page 83.

Edward the Son of Edward may & of Mary his wife was Babtized the first 1682.

Thomas the son of peter Strong And of mary his wife was Babtized October the 3ᵈ 1682.

John the Son of Phillip Baddesun And Judeth his Wife was Babtized October the 26 1682.

Sarh the daughter of Stephen Dansie & of Elizabeth his Wief was Babtized Nouember the 12th 1682.

Edward Son of Lenoard Tillott And of Martha his Wife was Born Nouember the 19th And was Babtized Nouember the 25th 1682.

Thomas Cushing Son of thomas And Margret Cushing was Babtized Janvery yᵉ 6th 1682.

John Tolsbury Son of thomas Tolsbury & of Mary his Wife was Babtized Janvery yᵉ 7th.

Presillia Allin Davghter of Robt Allin And Mary his Wife was babtized ffeb the 4th 1682.

Sarah the Davghter of Wiłłᵐ Daniell And Mary his Wife was Babtized March the 3ᵈ 168⅔.

Susan the Davghter of ffrancis turner And Susan his Wife was Babtized march the 20th 168⅔.

[1683.]

John Willkison the son of Simmond Willkison and Margret his wiff, Babtized Aprill the 18 1683.

Thomas the son of Robert semons and Mary his wiffe was babtized
Apriell the 29 1683.
William the sun of William Trusun and Judeth his Wife was Bab-
tized may ye 1 1683.

Page 84.

John Girling the Sone of John Girling and Elizabeth his wife was
baptized may the 13 1683.
Elizabeth and dorithea daughters of John Chushing and Elizebeath
his wife was babtized July ye 9. 1683.
Entry obliterated.
Mary the Davghter of John Marshall and Mary his Wife Baptized the
16th Sep^t 1683.
William ye son of John Simpson & Margret his wife was baptiz^d
Septemb ye 18 1683.
Jane The Daughter of Leonard Tillott And of Martha his wife was
born October The 10 And was Babtized October The 13 1683.
Four lines entirely erased.
Abegell the Daughter of Elazar Elener an Abgell his wiffe was Bab-
tized oct. the 14th 1683.
Samuell the Son of Samuell garrod and of Sarh his wife was Babtized
october 28th 1683.

1683.

Ales the daughter of Michall Cole and Ales his Wife was Babtized
Nouember the 8 1683.
Nicholas the Son of Stephen Dansie and Elizabeth his wife was
Baptized december 23th 1683.
William the Sun of Robert Coke and Jane his wife Was Babtized
december the 23 1683.
Mary the daughter of Edmund Cooke and mary his wife was Bab-
tized december the 01 [*sic*].
Abigail the daughter of Christopher Chamberlin and Hanah his
Wife was Babtized January the 8 1683.
John the Sun of Thomas Brett and Ann his Wife Was Babtized
January the 20 1683.
Sarah the daughter of John moulson and Rose his wife was babtized
feb. the 3 1683.
Anne the daughter of William Ashfild and Elizabeth his Wife Was
Babtized march the 16 1683.

Page 85.   1684.

Sarah the daughter of John Slad and Elizabeth his wife was Babtized
Aprill the 13. John the Son of Richard Sarles and martha his
wife was Babtized Aprill the 27 1684.

1684.

John the Sone of Peyton Ventris Esq. and Margret his wife was
Babtized may the 28.
Vri was borne ⎫ Vri the sone of Tho. Toply and Ailce his Wife
May 30 [*margin*] ⎬ was Babt. June ye 8th 1684.

Sarah ye daughter of John Daniell and mary his wife was Baptized
July ye 8th 1684.

John Baddesun the sune of Phillip Baddesun and Judeth his Wife
was Babtized June the 22 1684.

Elizabeth the daughter of Elazar Elener and Abigall his Wife was
Babtized Nouember the 23 1684.

Ann the Daughter of Thomas Holwell and Katherin his wife was
Baptized August th3 Anno dom. 1684.

ffreneis the daught of will^m Trusum and Judith his wife was Baptized
August ye 17th 1684.

John the sonn of John Hassell and Ann his wife was Baptized
August the 3th 1684 and was born Augt ye first.

1684.

Charles the Sone of James frost and Sarah his Wife was Babtized
July 20.

Mary Steel the daughter of James Steel an Mary his wife was Baptized September the 7 1684.

1684.

John the sune of Thomas Cushing and Margret his wife was Babtized
ber

nouem.

the 9   Babtisings 1684.

John the Son of Robert Reder & Elizebeth his wife was borne December the 3^d & was babtized December ye 7th in ye year 1684.

An the Daughter of philep Wright and mary his wife was Babtized
Janverey the 4th 1684.

                                        Geo. Raymod.

Page 86.   ·

　　　Grace Browne The Daughter of Thomas Browne And of
　　　Grace his Wife was baptised the 7th day of March
　　　1683. The abou^e named Grace was Borne in S^t
　　　Magert parish.

　　　Edward Alderid the Son of Edward Alderid And of Masse
　　　his Wife was baptised The 18th day of Jannweary 1684.

1684.

Jannweary the 25. then was Babtized Hanah the Daughter of
Thomas Goldsbrow and Hanah his wife.

John the Sun of John franses and mary his Wife was babtized
Jannwearry the 22 1684.

1685.

Ann the Dauter of John hall and Ann his wife was Babtized marth
the 29 1685.

Mary the daughter of Peyton Ventris Es^q and of margreat his Wife
was Babtized may the 18 and was Borne may the 6 1685.

Samuel the Sune of Samuel Waladge and of Sarah his wife was
baptized July the 19 1685.

Isack ye Son of Samvell Waythwit & An his wife was babtized Aprill
ye 16th 1685.

Margerett Roffe the dafter of John Roffe and Margerett his wife was Borne the 11 day of July and Babtized the 26 1685 of July.

William harper the Sune of William harper and Elizabeth his wife babtized August the 23 1685.

John the Sune of William Danill and Mary his Wife was Babtiezed August the 30 1685.

Lidia the Daughter of John Carsey and Ledia his wife was Babtized August the 30 1685.

Phillip and mary Sune and Daughter of Samewell foster and Sarah his wife was Babtized September the 10 1685.

John the Sune of John Cushing and Elizabeth his wife was Babtized September the 13 1685.

Geo. Raymond.

Page 87.

Bridget the Daughter of Stephen Bond and of margret his wife was babtized October the 4 1685.

Tho. the Son of Tho. Toply and Alice his wife was babtized october ye 8th 1685. [*In margin*] was borne oct. 27 1685.

Ester the daughter Simond wilkinSon and margret his wife was babtized october the 27 1685.

Robert the Sun of Robert Cooke and Jane his wif. was babtized october the 18.

ffrancis the daughter of William Trusson and Judeth his wife was Babtized nouember the 21 1685.

Ann the daughter of John haset and Ann his wife was Babtized December the 13 1685.

William the Son of thomas breet and Ann his wife was Babtized Jan. the 3 1685.

Sarah the daughter of Christopher Chamberlin and hanah his wife was babtized Jan. the 24 1685.

Sarah the daughter of thomas Garrod and of Sarah his wife was Babtized feb. the 14 1685.

Susan the daughter of thomas Trapnill and Sarah his wife was Babtized march the 7 1685.

mary the daughter of Thomas Goldsbrow and hanah his wife was Babtized march the 14 1685.

John the sune of John Slad and Elizabeth his wife was Babtized Aprill the 4 1686.

Elizabeth the Daughter of Edward Alderid and of Margre his wife was Babtized Aprill the 11 1686.

Robert the sune of Robert Semons and of mary his wife was Babtized Aprill the 18 1686.

Ann the daughter of Richard Newton and Lettis his wife was Babtized Aprill the 19 1686.

Edward the Sune of thomas Lues and Elizabeth his wife was Babtized may the 23 1686.

Page 88. Babtisings 1686.

ffrancis the son of ffrancis gildersleeve and Elizebeth his wife was borne August ye 20th and was babtized August ye 29th 1686.

Mary the Daughter of Samvell Waythwith and ann his wife was
borne August yᵉ 6th and was babtized August yᶜ 22th at yᶜ
pish curch of Sᵗ Lawrence in Ipswich by Mʳ George Raymond
minester 1686.

Willᵐ Son of Willᵐ Moriss and Elezebeth his was borne May yᵉ 3ᵈ
and was babtized May the 8th 1686.

Robert Sone of Robert King and Ann his Wife was borne September
the 4th and was babtized September yᵉ 19th 1686.

John yᵉ Sone of Edward Pattiston and Ann his wife borne September
the 2ᵈ and was babtized September yᶜ 12th 1686.

John yᵉ Sone of John Madcalfe And Ann his wife And Thomas yᵉ
son of John Madcalf And An his wife was Babtized September
yᵉ 12th 1686.

Phillep and Mary the Sone And Davghter of Samvell And Sarah ffoster
wear born September the 11th And wear babtized September the
16th 1685 [*sic*].

Paid Susan the Davghter of John Espin and Mary his wife was Borne
August yᵉ 29th and was Babtized Sepʳ yᶜ 12th 1686.

Sarah the Davghter of Samvell Woledg and Sarah his wife was borne
September yᵉ 21th and was babtized October yᵉ 3ᵈ 1686.

Elisha the Sone of Eleasvr Elonit and Abigall his wife was borne
October the Second and was babtized October yᵉ 3ᵈ 1686.

Mary the Davghter of John Cushing and Elizebeth his wife was borne
October yᵉ 8th and was Babtized October yᶜ 24th 1686.

Robert the Son of Robert Elsden and mary his wife was Borne
November the ffirst and was Babtized November the 5th 1686.

Samvell the Son of Samvell culvin & Jane his Wife was borne october
the 30th and babtized November yᵉ 5th 1686.

Geo. Raymond.

Page 89.   # Babtisings 1686.

Timothy the son of thomas toply and Alice his wife was borne the
11th of november & was Babtized the 15th of December Ano
Dm 1686.

John the Son of Thomas Walsingham and An his wife was borne Janvary the 4th and was Babtized Janvary the 16th Ano p Dm. 1686.

ffrancis the Son of Peyton Ventris Esqʳ and Margaret his wife was
Born the 3ᵈ Day of Janvary and Baptized the 19th Day of the
same month Ano Dm 1686.

Jane the Davghter of Robert Cooke and Jane his wife was born
Janvary the 7th and was Baptized the 20th of the said month
Anno p Dm 1686.

John the Son of John kersey and Lidia his Wife was Borne Janvary
the 27th 1686 and Baptized the same Day.

Mary the Davghter of Roger Sands and Amy his wife was borne
ffebruary the 11th and was Babtized february The 13th 1686.

Ann the Davghter of Robert Reader & Elizebeth his wife was Borne
february the 16th and was Baptized the 27th of the Same month
1686.

William the Son of William Pege & Mary his wife was baptized february ye 27th 1686.

William the Sone of James ffrost and Sarah his wife was borne March the 10th And was baptized ye 20th of the Same 1686.

Baptizings 1687.

Thomas the Son of thomas chamberlin and Mary his wife was Baptized Aprill the 10th 1687.

Susana the Davghter of Thomas golsburovgh and hanah his wife was Babtized Aprill ye 24th 1687.

William the Sone of John Hazell and Ann his Wife was Babtized May ye 8th 1687 And Borne Aprill ye 28th.

Robert the Sone of Edward Cooke And Elizabeth his wife was Baptized Jully ye 17th 1687.

Thomas the Son of Thomas Nulton gente and Sarah his wife was Baptized Jully ye 13th 1687.

Page 90.

Elizebeth the Davghter of WiH^m Harper And Elizebeth his Wife was Baptized Sep^t ye 21th 1687.

Deborah the Davghter of Mr George Raymond Minister and Elizebeth his Wife was Borne October the fifth & was Baptized the Seaventh Of the same Month 1687.

Edmond the Son of Thomas Garwod & of Sary his wife was born the 11th of Decemb. & baptsed the 13th of the same.

John the first S^o of John Leus & of Bridget his wife was born the 31th of Decemb. & was baptd the 5th of January 1687.

Mary the first Daughter of Joseph Gullifor Gent. & of Mary his Wife was born the twelfe of January & was Baptized the nineeth Day of February 1687.

George the Son of George Hill & of Mary his wife was born the fourth of ffebruary & was Baptized the nineteenth Day of the same month.

John the Son of Thomas Brett & of Ann his wife was borne the of [*blank*] february & was Baptized the fourth of march 1687.

Mary the Daughter of Mr. John Walis & of Margret his wife & Docter of Phisick was born the Eleauenth of march & was Baptd the 22 of the same month 1687.

1688.

Sary & Mary Daughters of Philip Baddeson & of Judeth his wife were borne the Eighteenth of march 1687 & were Baptized the thirtieth of the same month 1687 [*sic*].

Elizabeth the first Daughter of Henry Riches & of Mary his Wife was borne the twentieth of march 1687 & was Baptized the first of Aprill 1688.

James Son of George Allin & of Bridget his wife was born the 19th of March in 1687 & was Baptized the Eight Day of Aprile 1688.

Also Abigall the Daughter of John Moulson & of Rose his wife was born the twenty seaven of march & was Baptized the same Day ye 8 Aprile [*sic*].

Henry the Son of William Trusson was born the Eight Day of Aprile & was Baptized the two & twentyth of the same month.

Mary the Daughter of Robert Cooke & of Jane his wife was born the sixt Day of Aprile & was Baptized the 29 of the same.

Martha the second Daugh. of Samuell Waythwith & of Ann his wife was born the third of May & was Bapt. at St Lawrance the sixt of May.

John the Son of Christopher Chamberlain & of Hannah his Wife was born the ninteenth of Aprile & was Baptized the thirteenth of May 1688.

John the Son of John Daniel & of mary his wife was born the twenty six of Aprile was Baptized Also the same day the twenty six of May 1688.

Mary the Daughter of Robert Seamon & of Mary his wife was born the Eleauenth of May & was Baptized the twentieth Day of May 1688.

Thomas Son of John Whithand & of Ann his wife Was born the twentieth of May & was Baptd the 22 of May at home by Reason of Sickenes 1688.

Esther Daughter of Thomas Toply & of Alice his wife was borne the 17 of March 168$\frac{7}{8}$ & was Baptized the 27 of May 1688 at St Lawrance.

Thomas Son of John Hazell & of Ann his wife was born the ninth of July & was Baptized the twelfe of August 1688.

Stephen Son of Stephen Bond & of Margret his wife was born the nineteenth of July & was Baptized the second Day of September : : 88 : :

Page 91.

Alce the Daughter of Mr George Raymond minister & of Elizabeth his wife was borne the twenty seauen of Sept. & bapt : d ye tenth of October.

Ann the Daughter of Robert King & of Ann his wife was born the tenth of September & was Baptized the fourteenth of Octob : 88.

Elizabeth the first Daughter of Francis Gildersleeue & of Elizabeth his wife was borne the Eleauenth of Octob. & Baptized y^e 21 Octob.

Mercy the Daughte of Edward Aldret & of Mercy his vvife vvas borne the fourteenth of Octob. & was Baptized the 28th of the same 16$\frac{8}{8}$.

Lancalot Son of John Simpson & of Margret his vvife was borne the twentieth of October & was Baptized the Eighteenth of Nouember : 88.

William Son of Thomas Newton Gent. & of Sarah his wife, was borne the tenth of Nouember & was Baptized the eighteenth of Nouemb : 88.

Samuell the first Son of Samuell Hambling & of Elizabeth his wife was borne the twentieight of nouemb. & was Baptized the second of Decemb. 1688.

Rebaca the Second Daughter of John Carsey & Lidia his wife was borne the twentifiue of Nouemb. & Baptized ye 2^d of December.

Roger the first son of Roger Sands & of Amy his wife was borne the fift Day of December & was Baptized the sixteenth Day of the Same month 1688.

Thomas Son of John Cushing & of Elizabeth his wife was borne the fifteenth of December : & was Baptized the twenty sixt of the Same.

Mary the Daughter of John Slade & of Elizabeth his wife was Baptized the thirtyeth of December : 1688.

Robert Son of Robert Reader & of Elizabeth his wife was borne the twelfe of January & was Baptized the twenty Day of the same month.

William Son of John Jolly & of Martha his wife was borne the seauenteen of January & was Baptized the third of february : 88.

Robert Son of Thomas Gouldsbury & of Hannah his wife was borne the twentieth of february & was Baptized the third of March 1688.

Tho. Toply

Baptizings 1689.   ｆｆ   Tho. Toply.

Mary ye daug^r of Tho. Hewett Jou^r and Ann his wife borne ye 30th day of March 1689 & was babtz^d ye 14th of Aprill 1689.

Jeane ye daug^t of Will Rogers Ju^r & Sarah his wife was borne Aprill ye 12th and was babz 28th instant 1689 at St Laurance.

Johnathen the Son of Tho. Brett and Ann his Wife was born May the 2^d and was Babtiz. 19th Instant 1689.

George The Son of Willm Pege & Mary his Wife was borne May 22th 1689 and was bab 25th Instant.

Jeane daug^t of John Moulson baptiz. May 28 day.

John the Son of George Hill & Mary his Wife was borne May ye 29th and was babtz. June ye 2th.

1689.

Sarah the dayghter of Tho. Toply and Alice his Wife was borne May the seuenth 1689 and was babtiz. June ye 30 1689.

Judith ye daugh. of Will Trusson was borne June ye 6th & was Babti. 20th of ye same month 1689.

Geo. Raymond.

Page 92.

Samuell ye son of Tho. Chamberlin and Mary his Wife was borne June 16th and was babtiz^d June ye 23th 1689.

Henry ye sone of Richard Sarles & Matha his wife was borne June 12 and was babtz by Mr Will Knights Rector of St Mathews p^{r}sse.

Susanna a Child of base borne of ye body of Eliz. Hareson was baptiz. June ye 30 1689.

Susan ye daugh. of Abraham Blishingham & Suhan his wife was borne July 30th & was babtz. August ye 30th 1689.

William ye son of Peyton Venteriss Esqr & Margret his wife was borne August 11th Day and was bab. the 30th of ye same month 1689.

Thomas sone of Henry Richers & Mary his Wife was Baptiz. October ye 13th & was borne ye first day of ye same.

Thomas ye son of John Lee & Brigett his wife was baptizt nouemb. ye 3th 1689.

Ledia y^u daug^t of Samuell Hardy & Mary his wife was baptiz. nouemb. 10th & borne octob. y^u 27th day 1689.

Mary ye Daught. of Mr George Raymond Minester and Elizebeth his Wife was borne nouemb. y^e 19th & baptiz. october the first 1689.

Mary y^o daught. of Alexsander Willer & Mary his wife was Baptiz. January y^u 12th 1689.

Sarah y^c daugh. of Tho. Haney & Marg^t his wife in St Peters parrish & was Baptz. January y^c 12th 16$\frac{8}{9}\frac{9}{0}$.

Robert y^u son of Robert Cooke & Jeane his wife was borne Jan^o y^c 16th & was Baptiz. ffeb. y^u 16$\frac{8}{9}\frac{9}{0}$.

Henry y^e sone of Edward Aldret & Mercy his wif. was babtizd March y^u 2th 1689.

1690.

John y^c sone of Phillip Wright & Mary his wife was babtiz. Aprill 11th borne y^e 6th day of March.

Aprill y^c 26. Anes y^c daughter of Jooseph Catlen and Anes his wife.

y^c first Son of Bazzell Hewet & of Judah his wife was borne of & was Baptized the 11th of may 1690.

1690.

Mary the Daughter of Samuell Woledg & of Sarah his Wife was born the fift of may & was Baptized the 18th of the same month.

[*In margin.*] Elizabe^r dag^t of Philipe Baddeson and Judith his wife was born June 20th & baptiz. July 11.

Margret y^c Dafter of Willm Wood And Deborah his wife was borne ye 7th of July and baptized the 27th of y^c Said month 1690.

Elizabeth Dafter of Sam^tt hambling and Elizabeth his wife was borne y^c 15th of June & baptized the 29th of ye Said month 1690.

Jean the Daughter of John Mowson & of Rose his wife Bapt. y^c 27th of July : 90.

[*In margin.*] Jeames son of Isa^{ck} Bennet and marg^t his wife was Babtiz^d July 27 1690.

Elizabeth Daughter of Thomas Chamberlin & of Mary his wife was borne the 31th of August & was Baptized the 14th of September 1690.

October y^o 15th 1690. Mary ye Davghter of Robert Reader and Elizabeth his wife was borne & baptized ye Same Daye.

Geo. Raymond.

Page 93. Baptizings in 1690—1691 [& 1692].

Nouemb.   Mary The Daughter of George Hill & of Mary his wife
ye 23.   was Borne the 15 of Nouemb. & was Baptized the
                23 of the same month.

30.   John the Son of Thomas Garwood and of Sary his
        wife was Borne the [*blank*] of Nouember and was
        Bapt^d y^o thirtieth of Nouc.

Feb.　　4.　William Son of Abraham Blisingham & Susan his Wife.

March yᵉ 8　Mary the Daughter of John Simpson & of Margret his
　　1691.　　Wife was Borne the 25th of feb. and was Baptid
　　　　　　the 8 of March.

May　　4th.　Caleb Brown yᶜ Son of Caleb Browne & Ann his was
　　　　　　borne & Baptiz.

　　　　　　Mary daugᵗ of Stephen Bond & Margᵗ his wife May 3th.

Charles yᶜ Son of Tho. Toply and Ailce his wife was born July j &
　　bapt yᶜ 5th of yᵉ same July 1691.

[*In margin*].　Joseph yᶜ Son of Samuell Wantworth bapt July 5th
belong to Sᵗ Mary Elms 1691.

Ann yᵉ daughtʳ of Mʳ George Raymond & Elizb his wife was borne
　　July yᶜ 27th & was Babt August yᶜ 6th 1691.

Augᵗ　　16.　Rebaca yᶜ daughter Alexsander Willeʳ & Mary his wife
　　　　　　Baᵗ.

Sepᵗ　　6.　Judith yᵉ daugh of Witti Trusson & Judith his Wife.

Sepᵗ　　7.　Elizab yᵉ daugᵗ of Steuen Bedall & Elizb his wife was
　　　　　　born.

Sᵗ　　18.　Samuell yᵉ Son of Samuell Hardy & Mary his Wife.

　　　　　　ffrancis yᵉ sonn of ffrancis Gildersleue & Elizbath his wife
　　　　　　was born Sepᵗ 29th & was Babᵗ octob. 18th 1691.

No.　　13.　John yᶜ son of Tho. Garwood & Sarah his Wife.

Octo. ye 12.　Elizab yᶜ daughter of Samuell FeberYeare & Grisell his
　　169½.　　wife was born Octob. 2th bapti.

Elizabeth daughter of michael Daniel bapt. Octob. 25th.

Janᵒ.　　3.　Ann yᵉ daugᵗ of Edw. Alderid & Mercy his wife.

　　29th.　Isabell yᶜ daughᵗ of Mʳ John Wallace Doct. of Phis.
　　　　　& Margret his Wife was Bapᵗ.

　　　　　William yᵉ Son of Samuell Hambling & Eliz. his wife was
　　　　　borne Janᵒ 15 & Baptized feb. yᶜ i 1691.

Mar.　　24.　William yᵉ sonn of Christopher Chamberlin & Hanah
　　1692.　　his wife was baptized.

Sañ son of Robte Reader bapt. march 20 1692.

Aprill　　10.　Elizabeth daughᵗ of Geoge Hill & Mary his Wife.

John yᶜ son of John Cusing & Mary his wife was born Aprill 21
　　and baptizᵈ May yᶜ 8th 1692.

May 8.　John and Thomas sonns of Robert Cook & Jeane wife
　　where born may yᶜ 4th & baptized yᶜ 8th of yᶜ same.

Au3ᵗ.　　Tho. yᶜ son of Tho. Bretting and Elizb. his wife was born
　　　　August yᶜ 23 day & babt. 28th of yᶜ same.

Isable daugᵗ of Mʳ Geo. Raymond & Eliz. his wife was babti Octob.
　　yᶜ 13th 1692.

Ann daugʰ of Sañ Wantworth & Ann his wife was baptized Sepᵗ
　　yᶜ 3th 1692.

Rachell daugᵗ of William Coeman & Rachell his wife Oct. 25 1692
belonging to Sᵗ Mary Elms.

Elizb daught. of Rob King & Ann his wife Was born octo. 10th &
　　bapt. 13th of yᶜ sam. 1692.

[*In margin.*]　Sarah daugh. of Phillipe Church & Deb. his wife was
October 29th 1692 Bap.

1692.   Thomas ye sonn of Thos. Shuckforth Ju^r & Sarah his wife
        was borne one Thursday July y^e twenty one at two one
        y^e after noone.

                                              Geo. Raymond.

Page 94

Baptizings 1692 : 1693 : 1694.

Decem̃ y^e 25.   Elizabeth daughter of John Buckingham & Jeane
                his wife.
febru 8th 169$\frac{2}{3}$.   Joeseph y^e son of Mr Samuell ffuller & Judeth his
                wife was Baptized feb^y 8th 169$\frac{2}{3}$.
Mar.   5.   hannah daug^t of Joes. Catlin & Anes his wife.
Mar. 20 1693.   Mary daug^t of Steuen Bedwell & Elizb̃ his wife.

1693.   1693.
Mar.   31.   Mary daug^t of John Hayles & Ailces his wife.

                            1693.
May   2.   Joeseph y^e son of Tho. Hewett seo^r & Matha his wife.
            21.   Tho. son of Tho. Billemore & Eliz. his wife.
            28.   Tho. son of Allexsander Weller & Mary his wife.
            28.   ffrancis son of ffran. Welltum & Ann his wife.
June   28.   Robert ye sonn of Samuell Hambling & Eliz. his wife
                was borne June 28th & Bapt July ye second 1693.
Augt 20 1693.   ffoster ye son of Stephen Bond & Margrett his wife was
                borne Augt ye 10th & Bapt ye 20th of ye same.
Oct. ye 2th.   Ailce ye daughter of Tho. Toply & Ailce his Wife was
                borne and Baptized October ye second 1693.
                Ann daug^t of Edward Alderidge & Mercy his wife was
                baptized octob. ye 29th 1693.
                Dorkas ye first daug^t of John May and Dorkas his wife was
                Baptized Decemb̃ 15th 1693.
feb.   9.   Sarah a child base born of ye body of Ann Lines was
                Bap^t feb. 9th.
feb.   25.   Margret daug^t of Jean̄ Latour a french-man & Ann his
                wife was bapt. ye 25th.
                Roger son of Rob̃ Cook and Jeane his wife was born feb̃ y^e
                19th & baptized march ye 4th 1693.
                Richard son of Jno Simpson Bapt. March 9: 1693.
1694.
Aprill 29.   Phillipe son of John Cushine & Mary his wife was borne
                Aprill ye 22th and Baptiz' ye 29th of ye same.
May 23.   Susan daughter of Mr Geo. Raymond and Elizab̃ his wife
                was Baptized May 23th 1694.
May 20.   Elizabeth daugh^t of Sam̃ Walledge & Sarah his wife was
                Baptized May ye 20th 1694.
                William ye son of Witti Coeman & Rachell his wife was
                borne May ye 21th & Bapt June ye first 1692 [*sic*].
1694.   Eliz. daugh^t of Rob. King & Ann his wife was borne Sept.
                ye first and Baptized the second of ye same.

1694. William son of Samuell ffeberyeare and of Grisell his wife
   was borne July y⁰ 1 and bapt y⁰ 8th of y⁰ same.
Augt 24. Sarah daughter of Tho. Shuckforth and Sarah his wife
   was borne Augt 24th 1694.
          Geo. Raymond.

Page 95. Baptizings 1694 : 1695.

Theophilus y⁰ sonn of Mr Theophilus Parson Doct. of
Phi. and of Catherine his wife was borne Augt y⁰
11th and Baptiz. y⁰ 30th day of y⁰ same.
Elizabeth y⁰ second daugh^t of John May and Dorcas his
wife was bap^t Nouemb. 2th.
Richard son of Jn⁰ Simpson & marg^t Bapt. No. 5.
Briget daug^t of Samuell Hambling & Elizab. his wife was
born feb y⁰ 8th and Bap^t 17th of the same feb 1694.
Mary a Child of Base borne of y⁰ body of Mary Scutlell
octob y⁰ 22th & Bap^t feb 24th 1694.
1695. Dorcas daugh^t of Steuen Bedwell & Eliz. his wife Baptized
Aprill y⁰ forth day 1695.
1695. Ann daug^t of ffrancis Welltum & Ann his wife was baptized
Aprill y⁰ 28th 1695.
Anthony son of Robt Cook & Jane his wife born may 10th
was baptized may 19th 1695.
John son of John Lea & Bridget his wife born June 2^d
baptized June 9th 1695.
Samuel son of Samuel Wantworth (of St Mary Elms) born
July 15 baptized July 21 1695.
Robert son of Robt Lakeland & Eliz. his wife born Aug. 21
baptized Aug. 25 1695.
Mary d^r of Tho. Hewit & Martha his wife born sept^r 19th
baptized sept. 29th 1695.
Sarah d^r of Alexander Weller & Mary his wife born
octob. 7th baptized octob. 13 1695.
Joseph son of Michael Daniell & Elizabeth his wife born
nouemb. 6th baptized Novemb 11th 95.
John son of John May & Dorcas his wife born octob. 13 : 95.
George son of Edmund Luff & mary his wife born
octob. 11th 95.
Francis son of francis Fordham & Sara his wife baptized
Novemb. 17th 95⁰.
Abraham son of Will. Cooman born Jan. 4th.
John son of Thomas Brett & Mary his wife born Jan. 24
baptizd Jan. 27 from St Lawrence parish.
          Geo. Raymond.

Page 96.
Thomas son of Thomas Creswell born & baptizd 24th day
of February 169⅚.

1696.
Elizabeth daughter of John Cushing & mary his wife born
April 4th baptized April 12th 1696.

William son of William Osborn & Alice his wif. born &
baptized may 25.

John son of Abraham Blichendeen & Mary his wife baptized
May 31.

William son of William Rogers & Sarah his wife born July
1st baptized July 26th.

Mary daughter of Richard Withe & Margaret his wife born
octob. 1st baptized octob. 18th.

Sara daughter of Thomas Stolery & Elizabeth his wife born
19th of octob. bapt 25th   96.

Benjamin son of Benjamin Skeet & sara his wife born
octob. 19 bapt nov. 18^t 96.

Henry son of Henry Rawleson & sara his wife born octob. 26
bapt Nov. 1st   96.

Deborah daughter of sam Hamblin & of Eliz. his wife born
novemb 2^d bapt 8th.

Sarah daughter of Robert King & of Ann his wife born
novemb. 2^d bapt 8th.

Thomas son of George Hill & of Mary his wife born Nov.
21st bapt 29th.

Elizabeth daughter of Tymothy Wode born febr. 2^d baptized
febr. 7th.

William son of William Green about 2 years old baptized feb. 10th.

Sarah daughter of ye s^d Willm Green born febr. 4th baptized febr.
10th.

1697.	1697.

Mary daughter of Michael Daniel & Eliz. his wife born
March 30th baptized April 4th.

Daniel son of Thomas Creswell baptizd. May 10th.

David son of David Morgan & Mary his wife born May 15th
baptized May 18th.

Ann daughter of Abraham Chenery & Ann his wife born
July 4th baptizd. July 6th.

Page 97.

Thomas son of Thomas Billamer & Elizabeth his wife borne
July 10th baptized July 11th.

Ann daughter of James Newton & Ann his wife born July
22^d baptizd August 8th 97.

Alexander son of Alexander Weller & Mary his wife born Aug. 23
baptizd Augt 29 97.

Isaac son of Stephen Bond & Mary his wife born Septemb
22^d baptiz'd Septr 29.

Nathan son of Nathan Harvey & Mary his wife born Sept^r
26 baptizd octob. 3^d 97.

John son of Robert Lakeland & Eliz. his wife born octob.
28 baptized octob 31 97.

Boycat son of Peter Proster & Eliz. his wife about 18 months
old baptized octob. 31 97.

samuel son of Francis Welton & Ann his wife born octob. 24 baptized Novemb 7th 97.

George son of George Raymond clerk & of Eliz. his wife born novemb. 29 baptized decemb 16.

Nathaniel son of Basil Hewit & Margaret his wife born January 19th baptized Jan. 23.

Sarah daughter of James Pinborough & Martha his wife born febr. 5th baptized febr. 20th.

1698.

Alice Daughter o Willm Osborn & Alice his wife born febr. 26 baptized April 1st 1698.

Thomas son of Thomas Stolery & Elizabeth his wife born April 15th baptizd may 12th.

John son of Michael Daniel & Elizabeth his wife born may 12th baptizd June 19th.

Jonathan son of Willm Green & Ann his wife born may 12th baptizd may 20th.

Roger son of Thomas Brett & Mary his wife born may 17 baptizd may 22.

John son of John Smith & Elizabeth his wife born June 19 baptized July 3^{d}.

Elenor daughter of John Sympson & Margaret his wife born june 22 baptizd Jue 30.

Mary daughter of Abraham Blichenden Ju^{r} & Mary his wife born jly 4th baptizd July 10th.

Jeremiah son of Jeremiah Sicklemore & Mary his wife born July 22 baptized July 31.

Elizabeth daughter of Peter Procter & Eliz. his wife born Augt 29 bapt. sept. 4th.

Elizabeth Daughter of Barzillai Hare born Septr 25 bapt. octob. 9th.

Geo. Raymond.

Page 98.

1698.

James son of James Newton born Septr 30 bapt. octob. 9th.

Charles son of Nathan Harny & Mary his wife born Novemb. 3^{d} bapt. 6th.

Sarah daughter of Benjamin Skeet & Sarah his wife born Novemb. 5 bapt. Novr 6th.

John son of Samuel Hamblin & Eliz. his wife born novemb. 23 bapt. dec^{r} 9th.

Edward son of Jonathan Cook & Ann his wife born January 16 bapt. Jan. 22.

Dorothy daughter of Joseph Hudson & Dorothy his wife born march 2^{d} baptized mar. 5th.

1699.

Martha daughter of James Pinboro & Martha his wife born mar : 29 bapt. April 9.

Finie daughter of Thomas Creswel born Apr. 10th bapt. June 2^{d}.

I

Margaret daughter of Stephen Bond & Margaret his wife born Apr. 12 bapt. Ap. 23.

Elizabeth daughter of Thomas May & bridget his wife born Apr. 18 bapt. Apr. 23.

William son of George Hill & Mary his wife born June 23 bapt. June 25.

Mary Daugh. of Edw. Syer & lydia his Wiffe born July 26.

Henry son of John Booth & Hannah his wife born July 16 baptized Septr 15.

Mary daughter of James Latour & Ann his wife born Septemb. 4th bapt. 7th.

Margaret daughter of Richard Wyth & Margaret his wife born Septemb. 28 baptizd octob. 16.

Abigail daughter of Francis Goldersleev & Eliz. his wife born octob. 15 bapt. 29.

Barthol son of Basil Hewet & Margaret his wife born decemb. 15 bapt. 24.

Edward son of Michael Daniel & Eliz. his wife born decemb. 17 bapt. 31.

James son of James Kerridg & Ann his wife born febr. 14 bapt. 25.

1700.   1700.

James son of James Pinborow & Martha his wife born march 29 bapt. Apr. 7th.

John son of John Boycat & Mary his wife born 8 bapt. April 14.

                                        Geo. Raymond.

Page 99.

Sarah daughter of Abraham Blitchenden & Mary his wife born Apr^l 23 bapt. Apr. 28.

John son of Alexander Weller & Mary his wife born may 5 bapt. may 12.

Elizabeth daught^r of James Newton & Ann his wife born may 10 bapt. may 26.

Ann daught^r of Peter Proctor & Elizabeth his wife born June 3^d bapt. June 9th.

James son of Thomas Creswel & [*blank*] his wife born June 7th bapt. June 16.

William son of William Howard & [*blank*] his wife born July 5 bapt. July 28.

George son of Sam Hamblin & Elizabeth his wife born Aug. 6th bapt. Aug. 11th.

Henry son of Henry Snell & Elizabeth his wife born Aug. 22^d bapt. Septr 1.

A base child born of ye body of Susan Richards Aug. 27.

Mary daughter of William Boycat & Mary his wife born sept^r 1st bapt. sept. 5th.

John son of John Batter & Mary his wife born novemb. 6 bapt. Novemb. 10th.

William son of John Whayman & Elizabeth his wife born Novr 21 bapt. decem^r 25.

William son of Thomas May & Bridget his wife born decemb[r] 18 bapt. dec[r] 22.

Henry son of Thomas Stolery & Elizabeth his wife born dec[r] 18 bapt. dec[r] 22.

Mary daughter of Joseph Hudson & Dorothy his wife born febr. 3[d] bapt. febr. 9th.

William son of William Osborn & Alice his wife born febr. 22 bapt. Mar. 2[d].

Samuel son of Jeremiah Sicklemore & Mary his wife born feb. 22 bapt. Mar. 2[d].

Elizabeth daughter of George Mayer & Eliz. his wife born March 3[d] bapt. Mar. 9th.

1701.   1701.

Elizabeth daughter of Robert Cooke & Ann his wife born & bapt. April 1st.

Sarah daughter of William Green & Ann his wife born April 9th bapt. 27.

Samuel son of Francis Welton & Ann his wife born April 24 bapt. Apr. 27.

'   Geo. Raymond.

Page 100.   1701.   Christenings.

Thomas son of Thomas Frogget & Rose his wife born & bapt. July 7th.

John son of John Reynols & Martha his wife born July 11th bapt. 20th.

Thomas son of Michael Daniel & Elizabeth his wife born July 27 bapt. Aug. 3[d].

Isaack son of Stephen Bond & Margaret his wife born Sept[r] 22 bapt. Sept[r] 28.

Thomas son of Thomas Cole & Ann his wife born & bapt. octob[r] 17th.

Mary daughter of James Newton & Ann his wife born octob[r] 20 bapt. 26.

William son of William Rogers & Jane his wife born december 20th bapt[d] febr. 15.

Elizabeth daughter of Mary Boycat relicta of William Boycat born March 15th bapt. 22th.

1702.   1702.

Anne daughter of Samuel Hambling & Elizabeth his wife born June 16 bapt[d] y[e] 21.

Bridget daughter of Tho. May & Bridget his wife born June 20 bapt[d] 29.

[*An entry erased here*].

George son of George Mayer & Elizabeth his wife born Aug. 19 bapt. 23[d].

Jacob son of Michael Daniel & Elizabeth his wife born Septemb 4th bapt. 13.

Priscilla daughter of George Prat & of Priscilla his wife born Sept[r] 22 in S[t] Clements parish bapt. in this octob. 21.

I[2]

Margaret & Dorothy Twin daughters of Edward Syer & Lydia his wife born 8 bapt. octob. 22.

Thomas son of Roger Read & Elizabeth his wife born Novemb 2^d bapt. 8th.

Mary daughter of John Boycat & Mary his wife born decemb^r 5th bapt. 13th.

Anne daughter of Willm Wright a soldier born febr. 10th bapt. 17th.

Thomas son of Thomas Criswel & [*blank*] his wife born febr. 25 bapt. mar. 3^d.

1703.

John son of James Pinborow & Martha his wife born Mar. 26 bapt. 28.

Nathaniel son of John May born May 30.

A base child of Susan Richerson born April 15.

Geo. Raymond.

Page 101.

1703.

John son of Henry Snell & Elizabeth his wife born April 16th bapt. May 23.

Zechariah son of Francis Welton & Anne his wife born Apr. 29 bapt. May 2^d.

George son of John Reynolds & Martha his wife born June 12 bapt. 20th.

Rose daughter of Thomas Bemish & Rose his wife born June 16 bapt. 20th.

Joseph son of Joseph Hudson & Dorothy his wife born decemb^r 23 bapt. Jan. 2^d.

Charles son of George Mayer & Elizabeth his wife born Febr. 16 bapt. 27.

James son of Elizabeth Hamblin widd. born March 16 bapt. 21.

1704.   1704.

Anthony s. of John Boycat & Mary his wife born may 13th bapt. 26.

James son of James Woodyard & Susan his wife born June 12 bapt. July 9th.

A son of Samuel Breun born June 13.

A daughter of John May born june 21.

Sarah daughter of Michael Daniel & Elizabeth his wife born June 30 Bapt. July 2^d.

Rebecka daughter of Stephen Bond & Margaret his wife born at ye Whitehorse in St Matthews baptized in this church July 2^d.

Sarah daughter of James Newton & Anne his wife born July 5th bapt. 9th.

Samuel son of Thomas Shuckforth born July 11th bapt. 31.

John son of Robt Dash & Mary his wife born July 19 bap^t 30th.

Hannah daughter of Edmund Luff born Septr 5.

Edward son of William Green born Septr 30 bapt. octob. 8th.

Hannah daughter of James Pinboro & Martha his wife born dec^r 10th bapt. 17th.

Sarah daughter of George Pratt & Priscilla his wife born dec^r 13
bapt. Jan. 10th.
Susan daught. of Tho. Kendal & Susan his wife born Jan. 13 bapt 20th.
Mary daughter of Thomas May & Bridgett his wife born Jan. 13
bapt. 16.
Robt son of Robt Bond & Mary his wife Feb. 10th.
Elizabeth daughter of Henry Bond & Elizabeth his wife born febr. 22
bapt. 23^d.

Geo. Raymond.

Page 102.

1705. Christenings.

William son of Peter Proctor & Elizabeth his wife born April 18
bapt. 19th.
Hawes son of Thomas Turner & Sarah his wife born Jun^e 10th
bapt. 17th.
Peter son of Peter Parter & Margaret his wife belonging to Stow-
market bapt. July 1st.
Jacob son of John May & Dorcas his wife born July ye 4th.
a daughter of Mary Findly base born July 7th.
Thomas son of John Reynolds & Martha his wife born July 21
bapt. 23.
Elizabeth daughter of Thomas Stollery & Sarah his wife born
Aug. 10th bapt. 26th.
Zachariah son of Francis Weltum & Anne his wife born Aug. 11
bapt. 12th.
Jonathan son of Elizabeth Daniel Widdow born Novr 5th bapt. 11th.
John son of John Bretton & Hannah his wife born Novr 4th
bapt. 11th.
Sarah Daughter of Richard Bretton & Sarah his wife born dec^r 15th
bapt. 16th.
Mary daughter of John Allen & Frances his wife born January 13
bapt. 20th.
Anne daughter of George Clarke & Anne his wife born & bapt.
Jan. 20th.
Elizabeth daughter of Henry Snell & Elizabeth his wife born & bapt.
Jan. 20th.
Catherine daughter of James Ratford Mary his wife born febr. 18
bapt. March 10th.

1706. 1706.

Samuel son of Robt Dash & Mary his wife born April 15th Bapt. 23^d.
Noah son of Robert Bond & Mary his wife born & bapt. April 30th.
Sarah daughter of John Dun & Elizabeth his wife born & bapt.
May 15.
Ruth daughter of Jonathan Rilye & Rebecka his wife born & bapt.
May 19.
Lettice daughter of James Newton & Anne his wife born May 22
bapt. 28.
Susan daughter of James Woodyard & Susan his wife born & bapt.
June 16.

John son of John Brazier & Hannah his wife born & bapt. June 20.
Joseph son of John May born July 30.
Mary daughter of James Pinborough & Martha his wife born
  Septemb. 13 bapt. 29th.

Geo. Raymond.

Page 103.

1706.   1706.

Mary Anne daughter of william Burton & Barbara Susanna his wife
  born Sept. 25 & baptizd at St Lawrence beïg strangers.
John son of John Brown & Rebecka his wife born octob. 9 bapt. 13.
Rebecka daughter of Charles Sadd & Rebecka his wife born octob. 28
  bapt. novemb. 10.
Sarah daughter of Thomas Bemish & Rose his wife born novemb 1st
  bapt. 10th.
Jonathan son of John Reinolds & Martha his wife born novemb 2
  bapt. 6th.
Mary Daughter of Willm Haywood & Elizabeth his wif. born
  decemb. 30 bapt. Jan. 7th.
Richard son of Richard Bretton & Sarah his wife born March 13
  bapt. 16.
Thomas son of John Boycat & Anne his wife born March 18 bapt. 23.

1707.   1707.

Jonathan son of John Hammond & Elizabeth his wife born mar. 24
  1706 bapt. April 11 1707.
Joseph son of Peter Procter & Elizabeth his wife born June 24 bapt. 27.
Mary daughter of Thomas Stollery & Sarah his wife born July 10th
  bapt. 20th.
Frances daughter of James Newton & Anne his wife born Aug. 1st
  bapt. 13th.
Mary daughter of Robert Dash born Aug. 29th bapt. Septr 7th.
Mary daughter of John Carver & Mary his wife born Septr 6 bapt. 9th.
Benjamin son of Joseph Hudson & Dorothy his wife born Septr 12
  bapt. 14th.
John son of John Allen & Frances his wife born Novemb. 9th bapt. 16.
Susanna daughter of Willm Tought & of Susanna his wife born dec^r 8
  bapt. 14.
Sarah daughter of Moses Sly & Catherin his wife born & bapt. dec^r 26.
Thomas son of Thomas Turner & Sarah his wife born dec^r 28 bapt.
  Jan. 7th.
Mary daughter of Willm Green & Anne his wife born febr. 16 bapt.
  Mar. 1st.

1708.

Samuel son of James Woodyard & Susan his wife born mar. 23 1707
  bapt. mar. 28 1708.

Geo. Raymond.

Page 104.

Robert son of Robert Bond & Mary his wife was baptized April 25.
Robert son of William Oate & Elizabeth his wife was bapt^d April 25.

Edward son of Edward Bird & Thomasin his wife was bapt^d May 16.

Anne daughter of John Pattison & Jane his wife was bapt^d June 27.

Thomas son of Richard Bretton & Sarah his wife born July 31 was bapt^d August 10th.

George son of Stephen Bond & Margaret his wife born August 5th was bapt^d 22^d.

Nathaniel son of Nathaniel Ward & Anne his wife was bapt^d Septemb^r 12.

Barbara daughter of Edward White & Johanna his wife born Octob^r 14th was bapt^d ye 22^d.

Jonathan son of Francis Weltum & Anne his wife born Octob^r 20 was bapt^d ye 24th.

Martha daughter of John Reynolds & Martha his wife born Novemb^r 28 was bapt^d dec^r 5th.

Jane daughter of John Marshall & of Mary his wife born January 23^d was bapt^d Febr. 2^d.

Elizabeth daughter of James Pimborow & Martha his wife born March 8th was bapt^d 13th.

1709.   1709.

Anne daughter of Thomas Norris & Elizabeth his wife born April 3^d was bapt^d ye 4th.

Sarah daughter of John Baddison & Sarah his wife born & bapt^d April 27.

Edmund son of James Smith & Anne his wife born May 17 was bapt^d May 23.

John son of Thomas Turner & Sarah his wife born May 26 was bapt^d 31.

Mary daughter of Henry Snell & Elizabeth his wife born April 20 was bapt^d June 12.

William son of William Rogers & Anne his wife born January 27 1708 was bapt^d June 12 1709.

William son of William Scarlet & Elizabeth his wife born August 28 was bapt^d Septemb 6th.

Martha daughter of John Allen & Frances his wife born Aug. 31 was bapt^d Septemb 11th.

Elizabeth daughter of Richard Bretton & Sarah his wife born Septemb. 2^d was bapt^d ye 18th.

William son of William Tought & Susanna his wife born Novemb. 20 was bapt ye 22^d.

Jane daughter of John Pattison & Jane his wife born decemb 19 was bapt^d ye 25.

Sarah daughter of James Woodard & Susan his wife born February 1st was bapt^d Febr. 5th.

Geo. Raymond.

Burialls.

1551.

26 mar. Joane Smyth.
27 Ap. Willm Andrewe.
8 May. Alice Blomfeld.
3 Jun. Joane Peccock.
8 Jun. Thoms Bucknam.
6 Jun. Joane Richardson.
Robte Legete.
Willm Cressye.
Alice Williams.
Margarett Norham.
James Nottingham.
Willm Stile.
Willm hyllye.
Clare Michaell.
Anne Micheldye.
Robte Pecock.

1552.
9 Mai. helene Rawson.
Elizabeth Williamson.
17 Mai. Cicilie Bushe.
7 Jun. Margery Woode.
14 Jun. James Bobbet.
20 Jun. John ffosdick.
3 July. Lettis Selsden.
25 July. John Tranice.
28 Aug. Edmond yongne.
30 Aug. Agnes Banyngs.
George Bushe.
9 Octo. John Robson.
12 Octo. Margery Robson.
13 Octo. Alice Swysco.
11 Nove. Richard Wellis.
26 Nove. Jone herest.
12 dece. Cornelius Peterson.
16 dece. John Bentley.
10 Jan. Peter Quante.
14 Jan. Elzabeth herne.
24 Ja. John Coote &
Katherine.
3 febr. Thoms Legi.
15 feb. Willm Stannard.
16 mar. Cicilie Belcham.

1553.
31 mar. John Martyn.
14 Apr. Thomas Man.

10 Sep. Margarett Grai.
20 Sep. George Belcham.
6 nove. Joan Batham.
28 Dece. Richard Bird.
3 Ja. John hanmon.
7 mar. Amy Scvtt.
22 Mar. Thoms holland.
23 mar. Katheryn Yong.

1554.
16 mar. Mergery holland.
21 July. Alice huxley.
26 Aug. Rebecca hunte.
3 Sep. Jone Robinson.
23 Sep. John hunt.
30 Sep. Paskyn Crowfed.
28 Octo. Susan houe.
3 decem. Susan Osborne.

1555.
28 Mar. Mary Peterson.
16 Apr. Willm. Plastow.
16 May. Richard Swayne.
14 July. Blanch English.

11 Aug. Alice Wood.
2 Octo. Robte Kiriche.
Philip Bucknam.
8 octo. John Cleark.
22 No. John havens.
7 Dcc. Margarett Wood.
9 Ja. John Redgrave.
29 Ja. John Bugg.
13 mar. John Smyth.
24 mar. Elzabeth Bugg uxor.

1556.
24 May. John Redgrave.
4 July. helene Witman.
17 July. Elzabeth Bugg fil.
27 July. Katherin Bushe.
2 Aug. Sara Buckenham.
13 Aug. { Robte hailes.
{ John Bache.
14 Aug. Jone hawis.
22 Aug. { Nicholas Stanley.
{ George Michell.
28 Aug. Robte hargrave.
30 Aug. { Thoms Cage.
{ Alice hart.
4 Sep. Edward Johnson.

6 Sep.	Thoms Redgrave.	7 Aug.	Richard Grenewich.
8 Sep.	Jone Woodhowse.	8 Aug.	Margarett sharpe.
9 Sep.	Richard Robinson.	17 Aug.	Emme Garad.
16 Sep.	Amy Borrough.	19 Aug.	Beatryus hãmond.
17 Sep.	Kathery Beman.	30 Aug.	Elzabeth Johnson.
18 Sep.	ffelice Archer.	1 octo.	Barnabye Johnson.
19 Sep.	Margarett Smith.	4 octo.	Agnes Newton.
22 Sep.	Gilbert Edwards.	13 octo.	Alis Doune.
30 Sep.	Willm Beman.	20 octo.	Anne Swayne.
8 Octo.	{ Margarett hailes.	29 octo.	Rose Leman.
	{ Robte Cleark.	30 octo.	James herst.
19 Octo.	Adam Daye.	1 nove	Martin frett.
	(Cornelius Kitching.	11 nove.	Thoms Sebote.
	) Willm Richman.	18 nove.	Katherin Johnson.
22 Octo.	} John Parson.	24 nov.	{ Jone hart.
	(Rowland Johnson.		{ John Gillar.
6 nove.	John Gaskyn.	22 de.	John Goodwin.
8 nov.	Elzabeth Boone.	26 de.	Willm keriche.
20 nov.	Cicilie leder.	11 Ja.	Agnes ffynkle.
26 nov.	Edyth Belle.	31 Ja.	Jone Goodwyn.
	Jone Bell.	16 feb.	Magdelene Panton.
9 Dece.	John Carlton.	27 feb.	Beatris Goodchild.
13 dece.	{ Thoms Bennett.	9 Mar.	Robte Courtnall.
	{ Willm Colman.		1558.
24 de.	{ xpian Bennett.	30 mar.	Anne Sebotte.
	{ Katheryn Eldar.	1 Apr.	Robte Gowte base.
29 de.	Willm Yonge Peterson.	23 Apr.	Mary Dereslye.
		3 mai.	Willm hatche.
10 Ja.	{ Willm Riccard.	4 mai.	Robte Burman.
	{ Leonard ffrette.	22 mai.	Willm Lattymer.
18 Ja.	Agnes Bucknam.	18 Jun.	Margarett Cage.
20 Ja.	John Grenewich als Bagmaker.	4 July.	Robte Selsdon.
		6 July.	Mathew Braser.
Page 107		17 July.	Richard Waylocke.
24 Ja.	Thomasin Sparrowe.	10 Aug.	Nicholas Coleyne.
5 feb.	Margarett Newell.	20 Aug.	Margarett Edwards.
18 feb.	Amy Orynge.		(Margarett Michell-
	1557.	27 Aug.	{ fourth.
2 Ap.	Jeffrey Bele.		(Jone Buckenham.
7 Apr.	Dorethie Anseldye.	16 Sep.	Margery Warren.
19 Apr.	Lawrence [*blank*].	25 Sep.	Agnes Peerson.
21 Apr.	Robte Cockerell.	7 octo.	Cicely Chapman.
30 Apr.	Thoms Pinswine.	8 octo.	Peter Peterson.
14 Mai.	John Yonge.	20 octo.	John Peterson.
18 July.	Willm herst.	20 octo.	Agnes Riccard.
19 July.	Peter Richardson.	8 Novē.	helene Whittman.
31 July.	John Wilson.		
1 Aug.	Margareta Yonge child of Gorge Ball.	*Page* 108.	
		18 Nove.	Robte Petersonne.
		19 Nov.	Richard Johnson.

25 Nov.	{ Robte Clifton. { Rose Judgis.	19 mai.	John Laye.
26 Nov.	henry Petersonne.	9 Jun.	George Barton.
2 decem.	Charitie Johnson.	14 Jun.	henry Newton base.
3 decem.	Rose Smythe.	20 Jun.	Jone Mills.
5 decem.	Alice Rankyn.	30 Jun.	Suzan Milles.
12 decem.	Anne Johnson.	8 July.	Thoms huntick.
14 decem.	Elzabeth hawes.	17 July.	Valentyne Sweare.
20 decem.	George Clarke.	16 Aug.	Jane hailes.
7 Janu.	Roger Lawrence.	19 Aug.	Annes Lane.
23 Janu.	John Copping.	25 sep.	Ales Abbott
5 febr.	{ Lettes Bird. { Robte ffoxe.	11 nove.	Jone Witherbye.
		11 decem.	Xpofer Oswald Gibson.
6 febr.	Agnes Mossock.	16 dece.	Alis ffosdick.
7 febr.	John Moos.	27 dece.	Jone Carter.
9 febr.	Ann Smythe.	15 Janu.	John Johnson.
13 febr.	Margery Bugg.		

Page 109.

1560.

19 febr.	{ Jone Gillar. { Margery Shortchred. { Daniell Lawrence.	17 Jan.	Thoms Woode.
		24 Jan.	Elzabeth Swayne.
26 feb.	Roger lynes.	28 Jan.	Jone Newton.
27 feb.	Prudence Collins.	23 feb.	Jone Grosse.
19 mar.	Jone Wittman.		
21 mar.	Philip Baley.		1561.
24 mar.	{ Richard Clubbe. { Thoms Rooper.	3 may.	Thoms [*blank*].
		24 may.	Dorothie Alger.
	1559.	24 Jun.	Annes Owtred.
4 Apri.	Agnes keryche.	3 July.	John Ragett.
8 Apri.	Willm Balthasar.	15 Aug.	John Denis.
25 Apri.	Edmond Gardner.	17 Aug.	John hallebred.
11 may	John Leman.	2 octo.	John Clogg.
28 may	Jane karleton.		{ John Peterson.
9 July.	Ales Sadde.	8 octo.	{ Elzabeth hone.
27 Aug.	Jone Todde.		{ Margaret Pollyn.
30 Aug.	{ Jone Coleman. { Jone Regate.	18 Jan.	Walter Sponer.
		24 Ja.	Margarett Bridgges.
14 sept.	Robte Richardson.		1562.
27 sept.	Jone & Jone lane twynes.	1 June.	Katherin Millen.
		6 Jun.	Suzan haman.
6 octo.	Dorothie kinderslye.	18 Aug.	Robte Smyth.
10 octo.	Elzabeth Vucle.	20 Aug.	Margarett Buccoke.
3 nove.	Jone Raymer.		1563.
26 dece.	Thoms Osburne.	1 febr.	Margery Stallworth.
20 Janu.	Margaret Smythe.	19 Sep.	John hailes.
12 feb.	helene Johnson.	29 Sep.	An hampton.
		30 Sep.	Annis Quante.
	1560.	31 octo.	George English.
23 Apri.	Bridgett Clogge.	29 dece.	Margery Cannon.
11 mai.	John Man.	6 Jan.	John Quante.
14 mai.	Jone Baker.	31 Jan.	Thoms Wood.

1564.
28 Mar.   John Cage.
30 Apr.   Addry hubbard.
31 May.   Nicholas Turner.
14 July. Willm Binkett.
10 Sept. Mr Madock.

1565.
24 July. hubberd Ryvers.
22 dese. Thoms. harryson.

Page 110.

Burialls.

1566.
5 Apri.   John Alderman.
16 Apri. Cornelis Gilbert.
25 Apri. Alis hallybred.
29 Jun.   John Wilkenson.
22 July. Margett Alderman.
5 Sept.   { Margery Rivers.
          { Elzabeth Clubbe.
26 febr. Agnes Colman.
16 mar.   Christian Ponyard.

156[7].
26 mar.   Robte Ponyard.
19 Apri. John ffosdick.
15 Jun.   Robte Wood.
29 Aug.   John Waple.
3 Sept.   John Smith.
4 Sept.   Margery Joyner.
21 Ja.   Walter Sponer.
28 Ja.   Margarett Briggs.
6 Feb.   Thoms lane.
24 Mar.   John Smythe.

1568.
7 May.   John Vugle.
28 May.   Jone Cage.
9 Jne.   Thoms Lambes wife.
10 Jun.   John Day & uxor.
12 Jun.   Robte Gravell.
9 Aug.   Nicholas killing-
          Worth.
27 Aug.   Jone Rivers.
1 Sep.   Edmond Cantrell.
26 octo. Steven Clyford.
28 octo. { Willm Lene.
          { Judith Stowe.
11 Jan.   Robt. Colman.
16 Mar.   Willm Bardwell.

21 Mar.   Jone Pattridge.
24 Mar.   Margaret Symonds.

1569.
1 May.   Clement Blackmore.
8 May.   Xpian Tymplak.
15 June. Ellen hempson.
20 July. John Smith.
4 octo.   Edward Batham.
5 No.   John Canon.
26 No.   Thoms Smith.
16 Ja.   Thoms Clenen.

1570.
14 Jun.   Margery Tymplak.
19 July. Agnes Cressley.

1571.
15 No.   John Warree.
18 No.   Robt Briggs.
23 Dec.   Agatha Garrett.
27 Jan.   Willm Rynes.

1572.
18 Ap.   Peter hailybred.
7 July.   Xpofer Batham.
14 July. ffather habbart.
29 July. John Bishoppe.
11 Aug.   Elzabeth Nottingham.
26 Aug.   Thoms hockett.
29 Aug.   Seuson Parneel.
15 octo. Abigaill Wade.
18 octo. Cicely Belchine.

Page 111.

Burialls 1572.

20 octo. Jone Scrivener.
27 octo. Alice Denny.
1 dece.   Willm Starling.
12 no.   Jone Alderman.
1 dece.   Lucy Jlian.
27 dece. Anne hailes.
15 feb.   Anne Bate.
18 feb.   Willm Sprate.
20 feb.   Richard Lukas.
24 feb.   Jone Grenewich.
3 mar.   Elzabeth Baker.
4 mar.   Robart Rotte.
16 mar.   hughe knitts.
19 mar.   John Goulding.
22 mar.   { Anns lyne.
          { Thoms ffatter.

1573.	
17 Ap.	Anne Estall.
4 May.	Tobias Wood.
13 May.	⎧ Thoms Waterman.
16	⎪ John Sutton.
17	⎩ Thoms Jve.
21 May.	Thoms Ashefield.
11 June.	Mary hitchbone.
14 Jun.	Nicholas Plevent *or* Peevent.
31 Jun.	xpofer Alderman.
1 July.	Thoms Liste.
5 July.	John Anthony.
27 Aug.	Jeffrey Cage.
28 Sep.	Anne Johnson.
12 Jan.	Thoms Archer.
17 Jan.	Jone Mossock.
16 fe.	Willm hall.
10 Mar.	Richard hill.
1574.	
8 May.	Amy Basse.
2 Jun.	Elzabeth Watson.
10 Jun.	Roger lynes.
14 Sep.	John Beniamyn.
30 Sep.	Lawrence Clubbe.
13 No.	Annes Cleveland.
1 dece.	Elzabeth Gleed.
1575.	
25 Apri.	Robte ffosdick.
27 Ap.	Margarett ffuller.
11 May.	John Lawrence.
22 de.	Rose hitchbone.
7 Ja.	Thoms Samon.
27 Ja.	Margaret Gardner.
2 Mar.	Nicele More.
1576.	
18 Jun.	Thoms Curtes.
24 Jun.	Thomazin Sowden.
19 Aug.	Abigall Adams.
17 Sep.	Ambros Everett.
8 No.	Garrett Johnson.
7 de.	John hart.
16 de.	Agnes Aggas.
25 fe.	Anthony Prick.
5 Mar.	Ellyn Bate.
19 Mar.	Jane hitchbone.

Page 112.

Buryalls.

1577.	
1 June.	Mawd Dammeron buried.
10 Sep.	Suzan Smyth.
9 Nove.	Bastian fflower.
17 Nove.	Annys Cheape.
23 Jan.	John Goodwich.
24 feb.	Robte heard.
9 mar.	John Croford.
24 mar.	Margarett ffosdick.
1578.	
1 mai.	Robte Sherman.
11 Jun.	Angill hart.
15 July.	John Dawbney.
19 July.	Richard Grymshawe.
4 Sep.	Willm Greene.
19 Sep.	Margery Clearke.
	Joane Raggitt.
1579.	
15 Apr.	Elzabeth Johnson.
21 Apr.	Katheryn Quick.
22 Apr.	Thoms Morfle.
29 Apr.	Abygail Beniamyn.
10 May.	Margery Osburne.
3 July.	Thoms Wake.
4 July.	Beniamyn Cole.
16 Aug.	Anna Quick.
2 Sep.	Edward Cook.
3 Sep.	Willm Goodriche.
4 Sep.	Anna Lord.
7 Sep.	Agnes Cook.
10 Sep.	John Cooke.
14 Sep.	⎧ Widd Morfle. ⎩ Steven Cooke.
15 Sep.	Suzan Wake.
16 Sep.	Rebecca Rose.
18 Sep.	Margery Wake.
19 Sep.	John Longley.
23 Sep.	Elzabeth Wak.
25 Sep.	Elzabeth Cook.
1 Octo.	Jone ffynche.
2 octo.	John Scote.
10 octo.	Ellyn latland.
18 octo.	Alis ffrier.
6 dece.	Johñ Stowe.
3 Jan.	John Greene.

	1580.
7 feb.	Peter True.
17 Apr.	Willm̃ Boycate.
23 Apr.	Martyn Brooke.
30 Jun.	Joan Garner.
26 July.	Gerthritt Coxe.
11 Aug.	Elzabeth Eastow.
14 Aug.	Suzan Estow.
1 Nove.	John Kennigale.
28 Jan.	Jone Burman.
28 feb.	Robte Greve.
2 mar.	Henry Cuff.
	1581.
5 Apr.	John Ethrige.
27 Apr.	John Garth.
1 Mai.	Arthur ffokes.
12 Jun.	helen Daye.
21 Jun.	Jusina Bus.
19 July.	Mr Wynder.
20 July.	Samuell Jenkinsons wife.
18 Aug.	David Eare.

Page 113.

26 Aug.	{ ffrancis ffreeman. { henry Perrys wife.
11 Nov.	Wulh. hubbard.
9 de.	Wulh. Swayne.
26 de.	Mathew ffoxes wife.
28 de.	James harman.
14 fe.	John Smith.
18 fe.	Steven ffoster.
16 mar.	Katheryn kennigale.
20 mar.	Robt Burman.
	1582.
22 Apr.	John Shepherd.
3 May.	Joan Palmer.
25 Jun.	Robte Stowe.
28 Jun.	John Croxall.
30 dece.	John kennigale.
25 feb.	Dorcas Bloise.
14 mar.	Jone Grene.
19 mar.	Willam Martyn.
	1583.
11 Apr.	Thoms Sturgeon.
8 May.	Richard Toplife.
5 Jun.	Anne Asheley.
16 Jun.	ffathe Sever.
13 Aug.	Jone Smith.

12 Sep.	Willm̃ Burman.
22 octo.	Margaret Cage.
	1584.
8 Apr.	John Croxall.
9 Jun.	John Johnson.
	1585.
14 Jun.	Gabriel Wake.
17 Jun.	Edward hunting.
	Robte Lylly.
22 Aug.	Joan Barcock.
24 Aug.	Margerett Sturgeon.
1 Sep.	Magdalen Burman.
4 Sep.	Alis Wilkin.
7	Anne Symson.
	{ Thoms Symson. { Jeames hill.
9	{ Elzabeth kyme. { Alis Beniamyn.
12 Sep.	Ursula Ward.
	Steven Whittle.
21 Sep.	henry kyme.
22 Sep.	Thoms Browne.
23 Se.	Xp̃ian Beniamyn.
24 Sep.	Thoms Burman.
27 Sep.	{ John Kyne. { Margarett hailes. { Rauph Beniamyn. { Sibell Burman.
29 sep.	{ Jone Burman. { Abigail Sturgen.
1 octo.	Anne Clubbe.
5 octo.	Marion Wincoll.
8 octo.	Mary Markin.
9 octo.	Jarome Beniamyn.
10 octo.	Thoms Burman.
12 octo.	Anne Cooper.

Page 114.

13 octo.	Anne Beniamyn.
16 octo.	{ Anne hailes. { George Eareman.
19 octo.	Alice London.
25 octo.	Margery Cage.
28 octo.	Walter Estall.
1 no.	Margery Cage fil.
3 no.	henry Cage.
11 no.	Edith Webe.
26 no.	Alis Croxall base.
28 no.	Elzabeth boycat.

3 dece.	Valentyne hart.	26 may	Isack Stamford.
9 dece.	Margaret Burges.	10 Jun.	Margarett Blanch-
21 dece.	Anne Estall.		flower.
8 feb.	Alis hart.	17 octo.	Margarett Mallowes.
26 fe.	John Gost.		1590.
27 feb.	Mary Christmas.	28 mar.	George Brundishe.
7 mar.	Elzabeth hart.		Ellene Grenewich.

1586.

Page 115.

10 apr.	Jone fford.	6 Jun.	Alis Cvtsmere.
19 apr.	Elzabeth Grymstone.	22 Jun.	Jone Cason.
29 apr.	Willm Cleark.	27 Jun.	Robt Wak.
30 apr.	John Blacksvll.	8 July.	John Gray.
13 Jun.	Nicholas Keyes.	11 July.	Elzabeth Williams.
19 July.	Willm Black.	13 July.	Jane Bettes.
4 sep.	Robte Cheape.	30 July.	Katheryn Gage.
7 octo.	Anne Batham.	31 July.	Jone Man.
28 octo.	Elzabeth Bramford.	30 feb.	Mary Cage.
14 Jan.	Mary Andrew.	4 no.	Gilbert leche.
25 Jan.	Willm Spalding.	5 no.	John Thaxter.
6 mar.	Bridgett Dawbney.	15 no.	Lawrence Daynes.
		13 mar.	Thoms Cuff.

1587.

25 July	Cicely Colbye.		⎧ Willm lisborne.
29 July	John Leman.	18 mar.	⎨ John ffunell.
31 July	Michael Traynam.		⎩ Steven Grosse.
30 Aug.	Beatris hart.		1591.
7 Sept.	Robt Alderman.	19 July.	Willm Rudd.
10 Sep.	Suzan Keningale.	12 Aug.	John Bates.
20 Sep.	Robte Jackeryn.	17 Aug.	⎧ Willm Archer.
			⎨ Elzabeth Blagg.

1588.

		31 octo.	Thoms Barker.
11 May	Jone hart.	13 dece.	Judith Lord.
1 July	John Alderman.	23 dec.	Thoms Osburne.
13 July	Elzabeth Prick.		⎧ John Bond.
22 July	Dorcas Aggas.		⎪ Alis Cole.
7 Sep.	Bridgett Badison.	23 dece.	⎨ James Bonne.
10 Jan.	Sara Yong.		⎪ Robt Widnall.
22 Jan.	Elzabeth fisk.		⎩ George ffannell.
2 feb.	Alis Cuff.		1592.
10 feb.	Roger Sparrowe.	30 Ap.	⎧ Dorethie Pattall.
21 feb.	John Bantock.		⎨ Debora Stidman.
28 feb.	Margarett Greene.	19 May.	Mother Archer.
12 mar.	LawrenceRichardson.	25 Aug.	Miles Riggs.
13 mar.	Margarett hill.	7 Sep.	Richard Badison.
14 mar.	Ann lost.	12 Sep.	Susan Ranson.
15 mar.	Thoms Cambold.	17 Sep.	Symond Wilkin.
	1589.	28 Sep.	⎧ Charitie Yong.
16 Apr.	⎧ MirabelBlanchflower.		⎨ Elzabeth Crashfeld.
	⎩ humfrey Barnes.	13 octo.	Richard Stamford.
14 may	Henry Crane.	14 octo.	Marian Alderman.

19 octo.	Elzabeth harman.	5 July.	Suzan hattock.
23 octo.	{ Xpian Osburne. { Katherin Wilkenson.	18 July.	henry Boise.
30 octo.	Amy Jolly.	14 Aug.	David Mixar.
5 no.	Margarett Selsdon.	30 Aug.	Dorithe Croxall.
22 no.	Jone Lylly.	4 Sep.	Abigaill Croxall.
23 no.	Annis Grenewich.	5 octo.	Willm̃ Prick.
1 Dece.	John Belcham fi.	20 octo.	{ Willm̃ Aggas. { Lettis Aggas.
4 Dece.	John Belcham pa.	2 dece.	Margarett Batham.
8 dece.	Richard Peterson. Thoms hakins.	22 dece.	Elzabeth kymbleton.
12 Jan.	Margarett Baite.	25 dece.	{ Wid. Sherman. { Willm̃ Phillipps.
22 feb.	henry Writt.		
24 feb.	Ann Wastell.		

Page 116.

Page 117.

25 feb.	Richard Ayres.
24 mar.	Elzabeth Cook. Richard Lynge.

30 dece.	Widd. Cariatt.
23 Ja.	Arch. Rogers.
30 Ja.	Elzabeth Steven.
6 Feb.	Willm̃ Mason.
16 feb.	John Morse.
22 mar.	John Cutler.

Burialls.

1593.

October the Sixe Day. { The Wife & Child of Ralph Coocke was Bureyed the Day afore said 1680.

1594.

20 feb. Alice Cole wife of Thoms Cole.

26 feb. The wife of David Goodeare.

1596.

12 may. Robt Cutler th elder a Portman.

1596.

17 July. Willm̃ Jeffrey.
4 dece. Widdy Warren. Richard Whittle.
7 dece. Cicilie Bradbrvke.
12 dece. Widd. Grimson.

1597.

5 June. Elizabeth Cole. Cicilie Channell.

1598.

15 may. { Clement Saxe. { Margarett Burrell.
15 June. Margery Wright.
24 Jun. Jone hailes.
25 Jun. Elizabeth Martyn.

1599.

Elzabeth Dubble.
Mathew Molson.
Jane Cutberd.
Jone Whitting.
27 feb. Mary Buck.
16 mar. Rose harryson base.

1600 [*sic.*]

6 Aprill. Margarett Batham.
12 May. Nicholas Osburne.
30 May Robt Gynninge.
12 July. Elzabath Barison.
1 Sep. Thoms Robartson.
6 Sep. Alis Caldime.
18 Sep. Martha Bennett.
John Lynes.
Raffe hurse.
Elzabeth Buckton.
Jone Swayne.
Ann Alderman.
Mary Margetts.
John Grenwich.
[*blank*]
Aldetone
Lawrence } p'son".
Cleark
Jane James
An Johnson.
John Parker.

Ann Martyn.
[*blank*]Dewe
Richard
Blower
John Lynge } p'son'^s.
Madlen
Anstick
Robte
Gooldes.

3 octo.   David Goodere.
5 octo.   Susan Smythe.
10 octo.   Emme Bell.
27 octo.   Pricilla kennigale.
28 octo.   Widd Batham.
6 Jan.   Peter Barren.
           Mary Stidman.
17 feb.   Reynald hailes.
10 mar.   { Anthony Bunne.
           { Willm Boycate.
[*blank*] hallybread.
           Edward lynd.
           Philip Tayler.
           Prudence Stidman.
           Rowland Buckton.
           Willm Tappe.
           Robt Mowson.
           Isack Poppes.
           [*blank*] Cone.

1599 [*sic*].

16 Aug.   Alis Scritener.
           An Coock.
           Robt Seresent.
           Willm Sudbury.

Page 118.

Burialls.

1601.

1603.

9 Jun.   Willm Purham.
18 July.   { Anne Garrett.
           { Jone Parkin.
22 July.   Anne Cage.
26 July.   { Willm Sanders.
           { Benjamyn }
           { Garrett. } of the
           { Susan   } plague.
           { Garrett. }

28 July.   { John   }
           { Garrett   } of the
           { Rachel   } plague.
           { Garrett   }
19 Aug.   John Brewer.
20 Aug.   Thoms Phillipps.
26 Aug.   Margarett Cage.
29 Aug.   Thoms Cage.
31 Aug.   { ffrancis Buller.
           { Arthur Smith.
1 Sep.   Mary Gipson.
2 Sep.   Widdy Brewer.
8 Sep.   Mathew Martyn.
18 Sep.   Thoms Buller pat.
19 Sep.   Robt Cheape.
30 Sep.   { John Cook.
           { Thoms Buller fil.
           { Widdy Cock.
           { Stephen Band.
           { Dorcas Colbye.
2 octo.   Anne ffrank.
8 octo.   John Backhowse.
18 octo.   Barbary harris.
           Richard Marks.
25 octo.   { Widdy Cheape.
           { Willm Marks.
26 octo.   Katheryn Cariatt.
27 octo.   { Willm Powlin.
           { Elzabeth Powlin.
5 nove.   { John Peryman.
           { Marian Slack.
6 nov.   Thoms. Clubbe.
11 nov.   Thoms Pops.
16 no.   Marian Phipott.
20 no.   Allen Slack.
22 no.   John Peryman Ju^r.

Page 119.

12 dece.   Pawle Peterson Ju.
5 Jan.   Elzabeth Croxall.
12 Jan.   Jone Towlson.
14 Ja.   Margarett Curtis.
30 Ja.   Rebecca Wesson.
6 feb.   Thoms Leesse.
25 feb.   George Cobball.
6 mar.   Willm Lodbrok.
21 mar.   Willm Stidman.

1604.

2 Apri.   Robte Channell.

7 Apri.	{ John Beale. / Elzabeth fforthen.
23 Ap.	Suzan Bias.
28 Ap.	Miles Riggs.
30 Apr.	{ Robte Tailor. / henry Lurkin.
2 May.	John Stephens.
4 May.	ffranc's Barker.
5 May.	{ Ann Moulson. / Giles Stidman.
6 May.	Mary hart.
9 May.	Anne Jackson.
12 May.	John Bias.
14 May.	{ ffrancis Edwards. / John Stidman.
16 May.	{ Jone Barker mat. / Thoms Barker fil.
18 May.	Elzabeth Barker.
31 May.	Robte Rowe.
3 Jun.	John Wilson.
5 Jun.	John Cage.
2 July.	Xpian ffere.
9 July.	Anne hailes.
19 July.	Mary Johnson.
24 July.	John Curtes Ju.
30 July.	John Johnson.
8 Aug.	John Curtes sen.
12 Aug.	Suzan Cobie.
14 Aug.	Suzan Parker.
20 Aug.	Anne Andrewes.
26 Aug.	Elzabeth Starling.
29 Aug.	{ John Colbye / Richard Colbye } fra.
30 Aug.	Rauff Davye.
31 Aug.	Anthony Colbye pat.
1 Sep.	{ Sara Davie. / John Lyon.
2 Sep.	{ Thoms Lyon. / Rose Marshe. / Anne Godfrey. / John Davie.
21 Sep.	Alice Wilkenson.
2 octo.	Thoms Grenewich.
9 octo.	Margery Bate.
11 octo.	Tobie Tovell.
20 octo.	Steven Acock.
31 octo.	Abigail Paul.
3 nove.	John Acock.
12 nove.	{ Richard Davie. / Alice Davie.

K

16 nov.	John Crashfeld.
3 dece.	Elzabeth wood.
5 dece.	John Philipps.

Page 120.

2 febr.	Thoms holmes.

1605.

15 Apri.	John Starling.
8 May.	Marian hart.
16 May.	Isack Cleveland.
26 May.	Willm Philippes.
29 May.	Rose hart.
3 Jun.	John Tassell.
8 Jun.	Thoms Cole.
16 Jun.	John hill.
14 July.	Richard Watters.

1605.

1606.

Page 121. 1607.

27 February. Mr William Bloys
senior one of ye Portmen
of Ipswitch was buryed.

1608.

5 Nouember Mrs Alice Bloys
widowe was buried.

1609.

May	1.	A child of Willm Stopher.
	26.	John the sonne of Widdowe Knappe.
Sep.	6.	A child of Wilder.
Sep.	11.	{ A child of Thoms Martyn hisname was John. Willm Cope & Cornelius.
Oct.	9.	A child of Garrette.
	10.	[*blank*] Veribell & Elzabeth Banbridg.
Decemr	7.	Charles sonne of Charles Wines.
	17.	Thoms Storling.
		[*blank*] daught of henry Veale.
februa.	4.	John Wilbore.
	8.	Widdow Wilbore.
Mar.	3.	Thomasine helmett.
	24.	One out of the Jaile

March	28.	hanna daught. of Nathaniell Cook.
April	4.	[blank] a child of Edward Dolton.
	25.	Mary Perham.
May	3.	Stephen Coe.
	15.	Richard Wilder.
	20.	Richard Beomond.
June	28.	[blank] Watters.
July	3.	Thoms Cutler & James Skeete.
Aug.	28.	Britt out of the Jaile.
Septe.	23.	Abraham Johnsonne.
	30.	Willm Bate.
Novemʳ	4.	Sara Bate.

Page 122.

S. Nicholas parish
in Ipswich.   Burialls.   1610, 1611, 1612, 1613.

| feb. | 5. | John sonne of John Bateman buried. |

1611.

Apri.	24.	[blank] of James hobbes.
	27.	John the sonne of John Alderman.
	28.	Samuel Estowe.
May	3.	[blank] Venwell.
		[blank] Wattʳᵃ.
		[blank] Venvell.
Sept.	10.	Willm hebden.
octobʳ	28.	Moises Cleveland.
Novemʳ	11.	[blank] harman.
februar.	2.	[blank] the wife of Thoms Topliffe.
		[blank] a prisoner.

1612.

March	27.	hester daughtʳ of Mʳ Monsie.
		[blank] a pore psonnᵉ.
	31.	John Daines.
Maij	16.	John Smithe.
	18.	{ Widd Barrell. / Simon Pointer. }
August	16.	Thomazine Evered.
Septembʳ	7.	Elizabe the Wife of James hobbes.
Nouembʳ	9.	{ [blank] the Daught of James hobbes. / [blank] Willes. }
Nouembʳ	27.	Katherine Jeffrey widdow Deceased.
Decemʳ	5.	[blank] the wife of [blank] Clearke.
	26.	widdowe Birde.
January	16.	Edmund Osburne & a prisonner.
february	6.	{ Widdowe ffortune. / Marie Osburne. }
	23.	Margaret Cornelis widowe.
	24.	[blank] the Wife of [blank] wilkin.

1613.

August	11.	ffrancis Smith.
	13.	Bridgett Beomond Widdo.
	27.	Thomas Topliffe & Joan Mansfeld Widd.
Septem^r	8.	Joane Alderman Wife of xpofer Alderman.
	10.	John the sonne of John Helman was buryed.
October	2.	Robert the sonne of John Bateman was buryed.
August	19.	Anne ye wife of Mr Thomas Cutler of Sproughton was buryed.
	27.	ffrances Hogheard servãt to John Waters was buryed.
		John Johnson was buryed.
October	21.	Richard Barker a prisoner was buryed.
	22.	Thomas Stevenson was buryed.
	25.	Hugh Edwards was buryed.
	26.	Mr Thomas Salter schoolemayster was buryed.
	28.	Henry ye sonne of Thomas and Elizabeth Jefferye was buryed.
November	4.	John Cobbold was buryed.
	8.	Robert Saywell servant to James Gravener was buryed. Hee falling into ye river was drowned therein yesterday.
December	21.	Elisabeth y^e daughter of Robert & Elisabeth Pascall was buryed.
January	15.	A childe of ffrancis & Mercy Pouncett was buryed.
	18.	Geffery Pattridge a prisoner was buryed.
	28.	Thomas Cole was buryed.
February	1.	Marye y^e daughter of Robt & Anne Browne was buryed.

Subscribed by $\left\{\begin{array}{l}\text{John Daye minister of S}^t\text{ Nicolas pish in Ipswich.}\\ \text{Edward Langley} \\ \text{Rycheard Smith}\end{array}\right\}$ Churchwardens.

Page 123.

S. Nicolas pish in Ipswich.

Burialls. 1613, 1614, 1615.

February	9.	Robert y^e sonne of John & Susan Greene was buryed.
	12.	William Sparke a prisoner was buryed.
March	9.	Mr George Woode was buryed.
	9.	Alice y^e daughter of Thomas & Alice Parker was buryed.

Anno Dni 1614.

	25.	Nicolas Watters was buryed.
Aprill	18.	The wife of Thomas Dawson was buryed.
	20.	Beniamin ye sonne Roger & Wynnifred Cutler was buryed.
	22.	Humphrey ye sonne of Humfrey & Elisabeth Weelye was buryed.

K^2

[Aprill]	27.	John Beamish a prisoner was buryed.
Maye	11.	Joane yᵉ daughter of James & Priscilla Osburne was buryed.
	15.	Joane the wife of William Evered was buryed. ·
	19.	Denys yᵉ sonne of Humfrey & Joan Meares was buryed.
	29.	Margaret Hobson widdow was buryed.
June	21.	Emme yᵉ wife of William Cornelius als Joyner was buryed.
	29.	John yᵉ sonne of John & Alice Bateman was buryed.
July	4.	John Tyler was buryed.
	7.	Christian yᵉ daughtʳ of Nicolas & Christian Watters was buryed.
	11.	George the sonne of George & Margarett Bentham was buryed.
	12.	Anne Deale was buryed.
	20.	William Evered was buryed.
	25.	Margarett Edwards widdowe was buryed.
	26.	Simon yᵉ childe of yᵉ sayd Margarett Edwards was buryed.
August	6.	Margerye yᵉ daughter of John & Alice Alderman was buryed.
	9.	John yᵉ sonne of John & Alice Alderman was buryed.
	19.	Christian yᵉ wife of Mʳ Bends minister of Burstall was buryed.
September	14.	Martha Whittle was buryed.
	27.	An infant one of yᵉ base sonnes of John Hobbs & Elisabeth Mockted was buryed.
October	25.	The childe of James & Magdalene Hayward was buryed.
November	15.	Cicelye Starling widdowe was buryed.
December	1.	The childe of Daniel & Rose Barker was buryed.
	7.	Jonathan the sonne of William & Elisabeth Stopher was buryed.
	25.	Margerye the wife of John Cornish was buryed.
	26.	Susanne yᵉ daughter of Edmund & Susanne Dalton was buryed.
January	17.	Agnes yᵉ wife of Gwalter Drane was buryed.
	22.	The childe of Jeremy & Elisabeth Sicklemer was buryed.
	23.	Beniamin yᵉ sonne of William and Hannah Panton was buryed.
February	5.	Thomas yᵉ sonne of Thomas & Elisabeth Woodgate was buryed.
	14.	Elisabeth Lines was buryed.
	20.	{ Walter Attlebrigge was buryed. Timothye yᵉ sonne of Richard & Mary Homes was buryed.
	25.	John the sonne of Thomas and Susan Man was buryed.

March	15.	Mary Gryce was buryed.
	22.	Margaret yᵉ daughter of George & Margaret Bentham was buryed.

Anno Dm̃ 1615°.

Aprill	1.	William yᵉ sonne of Walter & Bathsheba Gilbert was buryed.
	13.	Bathsheba yᵉ wife of Walter Gilbert was buryed.

Subscribed by ⎰ John Daye minister of Sᵗ Nicolas
⎱ parish in Ipswich.
⎰ Nathˡ Warde.

Page 124. S. Nicolas parish in Ipswich.

Maye	3.	Joan yᵉ daughter of Thomas & Susan Stevenson was buryed.
	6.	Anne Cooke widdowe was buryed.
June	15.	Magdalene yᵉ wife of James Hayward was buryed.
July	5.	Margarett yᵉ wife of Richard Bennett was buryed.
	6.	Katherine yᵉ daughter of John & Alice Alderman was buryed.
	26.	Katherine yᵉ daughter of Richard & Katherine Osburne was buryed.
August	4.	⎰ Henrye Pyper ⎱ were buryed. ⎱ one Hill ⎰
	5.	William Smyth was buryed.
	12.	William Gilbert was buryed.
	15.	Anne Dilworth alias Bentham widdowe was buryed.
	19.	Christopher Alderman was buryed.
	21.	Eunice yᵉ daughter of Richard & Margarett Bennet was buried.
	24.	Nicholas Crashfeild was buried.
	28.	Richard the sonne of Richard & ffrancis Dazly was buried.
September	2.	Thomasine the wife of Peter Brett was buried.
	3.	Elizabeth the wife of Joseph Weely was buried.
	5.	Suzan hãmond servant to John Wilkinson was buried.
	16.	Joseph yᵉ sonne of Humfrye & Elisabeth Weely was buryed.
	17.	Bartlemew yᵉ sonne of Thomas & Anne Bird was buryed.
	24.	John Garrood yᵉ younger yᵉ sonne of Joan Garrood widdow was buryed.
October	1.	Two children of William and Elisabeth Stofer were buryed.
	6.	Isaak yᵉ sonne of James & Judith Gravener was buryed.
	4.	John yᵉ sonne of Thomas & Alice Parker was buryed.
	21.	George Aldrich servant to Thomas Lyst was buryed.
	24.	Hellen the wife of Edward Langley was buryed.
	27.	Margarett Saerford widdow was buryed.

November	1.	{ John Harrison was buryed. { Joan the wife of Richard Church was buryed.
	11.	Abigail yᵉ daughter of Robert & Margarett Potter was buryed.
	12.	John Lynes was buryed.
Desember	16.	Ebgᵗle brovne the davter of John brovne and Elysebeth Brovne was buryed.
	19.	John Edwardes the sone of mary edwardes weddoe was beryd.
	28	Valentine Bate was buryed.
		Mʳ John Day, Minister of Sᵗ Nicholas buryed.

1616.

		Mʳ John Day minister [*incomplete.*]
		Alice Clarke widdow was buried.
July		[*blank*] Debden gent was buried.
August.		Avice the wife of Monsonn.	Richard swaine buried.
		Rahab Yelloup buryed. [Entered Oct. 26 1616.]
		Wllm̄ Lacish buryed.
		Widdow Peter buryed.
		Willm̄ Nunn buryed.
		Nicholas Hale was buryed.
Sept.	4.	Robt Potter buryed.
Sep.	7.	Joan Daines the wyfe of Richard Daines buryed.
Sep.	12.	Isacke Church the sonn of Richard Church buryed.
	13.	Alice Alderman the daughter of John Alderman buryed.
October	5.	Mʳ Maddocke of Sᵗ Peters Parresh buryed.
Octob.	10.	John Brewster a stranger was buryed.
Octo.	11.	Elihabeth the wyfe of one ffere buryed.
Octob.	12.	John Tyler Prisoner buryed.
	15.	John Day sonn of Mʳˢ Day widdow buryed.
	16.	William Hempson buryed.
	20.	{ Widdow Johnsonn was buryed. { Hester Starcke buryed the same day.

Page 125.

	26.	Richard Swaine yᵉ sonn of Richard Swaine buryed.
	30.	The Daughter of one Thomas was buryed.
Novembʳ		The child of one Blunt was buryed wᶜh was still born.
	11.	{ The daughter of Richard Hardie buryed. { The wife of Daniell Barker was buryed.
		John Garred was buryed.
	28.	Prissilla Blosse was buryed.
		Isacke the sonn of James Gravner buryed.
Decembʳ	4.	William Sanderson was buryed.
	9.	Godffre Ostler was buryed.
	13.	Mʳ William Bryden was buryed.
	15.	Catherinn Sanderson widdow buryed.
	17.	Mʳˢ Benns widdow was buryed.

| [Decemb^r] | | William Butler was buryed. |

[Decemb^r]   William Butler was buryed.
   24.   Catheren Trayford was buryed.
Januar.   21.   John Traford was buried.

Page 126.   Burialls.
1617.

August   27.   William Marit the sone of Alexander Marit deceased buried.
Septemb.   5.   Christopher Topley the sone of John Topley was buried.
Septemb.   23.   Thomas the sone of Robert Steddie was buried.
Octob.   3.   Prudence Topliffe the wife of John Topliffe Was buried.
Novemb.   10.   Robert Potter the sone of Margaret Potter was buried.
  21.   Jeremie Batteldore was buried.
  22.   Thomas Notley was buried.
  23.   Barbarie Guttridge was buried.
  26.   John Bateman was buried.
Decemb.   17.   Edward Brewster was buried.

Burialls 1617.

Januarie   17.   Elizabeth Chaffe was buried.
  18.   Bridget Jarvis was buried.
30 Janu.   Nathaniel the sone of Nathaniel & Hanah Smart was buried.
21 Febru.   { The child of Robert Allen was buried.
{ Robert fokes prisoner was buried.
March   1.   Richard Whittrigge was buried.
  10.   John Wilkinson was buried.
  15.   William Roffe was buried.
  23.   Abigail Clarke the Elder was buried.   1618.
  28.   Ane Alderman the daughter of John Alderman was buried.
April   7.   Thomas Miles the sone of Edmund Miles was buried.
  16.   { Robert Allen was buried.
{ Ane Hills was buried.
  20.   Thomas Exman son of [*blank*] Exman was buried.
  21.   { Elizabeth Stover wife of William Stover buried.
{ Nathaniel Stov^r sone of William Stov^r buried.
{ Agnes Storke the daughter of Joane Storke.
May   4.   Marie the daughter of John Dearinge buried.
[*blank*] Simons was buried.
  15.   [*blank*] Warns was buried.
[*blank*] the wife of Hellman buried.
Tobias Spinks was buried.
Edmund Basse was buried.
Decemb.   Susana the wife of John Cooper was buried.

1619.
Septemb.   15.   Jane Steddie the daughter of Robert Steddie was buried.

| Novemb. | 18. | Ane Cutler the daughter of Mr Thomas Cutler was buried. |

Novemb. 18. Ane Cutler the daughter of Mr Thomas Cutler was buried.

26. [*blank*] Cutler the daughter of Mr Thomas Cutler. was buried.

1620.

June 8. William Blunt was buried.

August 3. Richard Selsden was buried.

Octob. 16. Robert paine was buried And the child of Mr Benjamin Cutler.

23. [*blank*] the sone of [*blank*] Benet widow was buried.

December 26. Winifred Cutler the daughter of Mr Roger Cutler was buryed.

Año Dñi 1621.

Aprill 9. [*blank*] Copping daughter of Rich^r Copping & Elizabeth his wiffe was buryed.

Aprill 13. Lidia Hebden the daughter of William Hebden was buried.

May 11. Deborah Hebden the daughter of Willm Hebden was buried.

June 11. Joseph Savage the sone of Joseph Savage was buried.

15. Susana Hebden the daughter of Willm Hebden was buried.

17. Thomas Renengale buried.

24. Joseph Savage was buried.

Julie 13. [*blank*] Neale.

15. [*blank*] Sicklemore the daughter of Jeremie Sickle-more was buried.

Septemb. 7. [*blank*] Church.

Novemb 3. Alice Cutler the daughter of Mr Benjamin Cutler was buried.

15. Elizabeth Stopher the daughter of William Stopher was buried.

18. Alice Crashfield widdowe was buried.

Page 127.   Anõ Dm̃ 1621.   S^{cti} Nicolai parochiã.

Janu. 9. Elizabeth Coppinge the wife of Mr Richard Coppinge was buried.

Mar. 12. m [*blank*] Noble the wife of William Noble was buried.

20. Christian Chadderton the wife of [*blank*] Chadderton was buried.

Mar. 9. [*blank*] Wilkinson the wife of Christopher Wilkinson was buried.

Año Dñi 1622.

April 13. ¹ Lidia Hebden the daughter of [*blank*] Hebden buried

May 11. ¹ Deborah Hebden the daughter of [*blank*] Hebden buried.

¹ Repetition of same entries in 1621.

April	28.	{ Margaret Bates Widow was buried. { Hañah panton the Wife of William panton.
May	22.	Margaret Brett.
June	4.	Susaña Cooper the wife of John Cooper buried.
Septemb.	7.	Adam Luke singleman bur.
Novemb.	2.	Sara Smith daughter of Thomas Smith buried.
	29.	Thomas Cutler the sone of Mr Benjamin Cutler.
Decemb.	17.	Alexander Thomas was buried.
Januar.	29.	John Brixton was buried.
March	2.	Rose Baldwin the wife of William Baldwin.

Año Domini 1623.

May	26.	Francis puplet the sone of Mr Richard puplet buried.
June	6.	Robert Wade buried the sone of Richard Wade.
Novemb.	6.	Margaret Nawler buried.
æt. 4 months	27.	John Steggoll buried w fallinge into ye fire was burnt to death in his mother's absence his forehead w^n hee was taken out beeinge as red as a cole.
		William Baldwin was buried.

Año Dñi 1624.

April	7.	The widow Floy buried.
May	17.	Rose Groome widow was buried.
	18.	Mrs Winifred Cutler the Wife of Mr Roger Cutler buried.
	27.	Marie Blosse the daughter of Mr Thomas Blosse was buried.
June	12.	Marie Stocke the maid of Thomas Hardie.
Julie	21.	Abigail Male the daughter of Willm male.
	22.	marie Cooper was buried.
August	25.	Nathan bonifant the sone of Nathan Bonifant was buried.
	26.	William Litbe was buried.
Septemb^r	10.	Winifred the wife of Richard Swaine buried.
	18.	Susaña maidenhead buried out of ye countrie prison.
	20.	Andrew Cuñisbie was buried.
	23.	Chrian Smith ye daughter of Nicholas Smith.
October		Hañah panton.
Novemb^r	14.	John Boicatt was buried.
	16.	Edmund lord was buried.
March	10	Bridget Wade.
	13.	Thomas List.
	20.	Abraham Wathwait sexton of ye parish was bur.
	22.	Randoll Crew sone of Mr Crew of London merchant.

Año 1625.

March	27.	Robert Faireweather was buried.
April	3.	[*blank*] Longlie daughter of [*blank*] Langlie bur.
Julie	25.	Humfrey Wealie was buried.

Septemb.	15.	{ Marie Huggins the daughter of Daniel Huggins. { Sara List the daughter of Thomas List.
Septemb.	18.	[*blank*] Bias was buried.
October	6.	Nathaniel Puplet sone of Mr Richard puplet buried.
	20.	Hañah male daughter of Willñi male buried.
November	7.	Mr Robert Cutler was buried.
	20.	Cutbert Browne was buried.
	21.	a child of Robert Fishe.
	22.	Margaret Fishe the wife of Robert Fishe was bur.
December	5.	Elizabeth Reccard.
	6.	Samuel Battle.
Januar.	5.	Elizabeth Wilkinson daughter of Christopher Wilkinson.
	20.	A child of Parishes was buried.
	21.	A child of Berries.
Febr.	22.	A child of Paines.
	27.	A child of Willñi Longlies was buried.
March	15.	Bridget Wade the wife of Richard Wade was bur.

Año Dñi 1626.

March	29.	Robert Ladish was buried.
Aprill	17.	Hañah Smart the Wife of Nathaniel Smart Minister.
May	2.	Mathias Martin sone of Mathias Martin was bur.
June	12.	John Simons was buried.
	15.	Marie Wade the daughter of Richard Wade.
	17.	[*blank*] Hawkins the Wife of Caleb Hawkins was bur.
July	17.	John Waters son of Thomas Waters bur.
	28.	William Lambe was bur.
	30.	Marie Bates daughter of Valentine Bates.
August	9.	Thomas Rice buried.
	24.	Marie Martin daughter of Mathias Martin.
Septemb.	2.	Rebeckah Jude daughter of Daniel Jude bur.
	5.	Abigail Cope daughter of Samuel Cope.
Octob.	2.	Ane the wife of John Firmin buried.
	16.	Ane Salter was buried.
	19.	John Bucknam buried.
Novembr	21.	Henrie Paschal was buried.
Januar.	28.	Thomas Melendor was buried & Willñi the son.

Page 128.

Januar.	30.	Marie the wife of Thomas Allein was buried.
Februar.	16.	Elizabeth daughter of Robert Bordman.
	27.	A child of Steven Johnsons bur.

Año Dñi 1627.

Mar.	28.	Marie the daughter of Jacob Wathwait.
	29.	Edmund Colechester apprentice to Robert Bordman bur.
April	8.	Thomas Johnson sone.
	18.	{ Thomas Hardie the sone of Thomas Hardie bur. { Willñi Nichols the sone of Willñi Nichols.

May	2.	William Topliffe hurt by souldie[rs] was buried.
	7. {	Francis Cocks carver was buried.
		Joane Hayward wid. was buried.
	14.	Margerie Cocks wife of Francis Cocks was buried.

June 2. Margerie Acton widow was ⎧ June 20. John
buried. ⎩ Wilkinson soñe of
27. [*blank*] Huggen widow was ⎫ Christopher Wilkin-
buried. ⎭ son.

October	2.	Mr William Brydon was buried.
Novem[r]	20.	Samuel soñe of Nathaniel Smart was buried.
Decemb[r]	7.	Eñe Wilbey daughter of Nicholas Wilbore was buried slaine by a brick fallinge down the chymney.
	21.	Richard Perkin was buried.
	30.	Thomas Haiward was buried.
Januar.	2.	A child of Mr Benjamin Cutler's was buried.
	23.	William Stover was buried.
	29. {	Elizabeth Molendor widow was buried.
		Hañah Smart daughter of Nathaniel Smart was buried.

Año Dm̃ 1628.

April	17.	[*blank*] Pembertou was buried.
May	3.	Marie Price wife of Thomas Price was buried.
	7.	Triphena Skeet widow was buried.
	16.	Thomas onge was buried.
	17.	John List was buried.
	22.	Susana Stanifer wife of John Stanifer was buried.
June	2.	Katherine Holliway wife of John Holliway buried.
	3.	Isake servaunt of Alexander mariat tailo[r] was buried.
Novemb[r]	20.	The wife of John Lowe was buried.
Decemb[r]	8.	Gervase Jackson was buried.
	26.	Edmund Cutler sone of Mr Benjam Cutler buried.
Januar.		Marie Glover.
		Marie Blumfield wife of William Blumfield was bur.
Mar.		Elizabeth Friet wife of Gregorie Friet was bur.

Año Dñi 1629.

Aug.	23.	Margaret Buick wife of Robert Buick was buried.
	27.	Jeremie Barber was buried.
Septemb[r]	4.	Benjamin moulson sone of Thomas moulson buried.
	12.	A child of Mr Blumfields buried.
Octob[r]	1.	Thomas de la Hay buried And ye Wife of Downinge.
	6.	Edmund Clarke was buried.
	10.	Dorothie Edgar was buried.
	19.	Elizabeth Gray wife of Robert Gray was buried.
	22.	Lydia Spause wife of Thomas Spause was bur.
Novemb.	13.	Agnes Hutchison daughter of martin Hutchison was buried.
	27.	Rose Barber widow | dyinge suddainlie | was buried.
	28.	The Wife of John Weeks was buried.
Decemb.	6.	James Gravener was buried.

| Februar. | 27. | Marie Paine was buried and $\left\{\begin{array}{c}\text{Olive \&}\\\text{Elizabeth}\end{array}\right\}$ Barb^r. |

Februar.   27.   Marie Paine was buried and { Olive & Elizabeth } Barb^r.

March   3.   William Steward was buried.

     20.   John Lakeland sone of Theophilus Lakeland was buried.

Año Dñi 1630.

May   7.   John Goodwin was buried.

     21.   Sarah Loe y^e daught^r of John Lowe.

June   1.   Michael Warde was buried.

Julie   19.   A child of Mr Catchpoles was buried.

August   1.   { The wife of Simon Thursbie the younger was buried. Sarah Blumfield buried.

     20.   Ithiel Smart sone of Nathaniel Smart minister was buried.

     26.   Sara Allen buried.

     27.   Samuel Cope was buried & a prisoner out of ye countrie Jaile.

Septemb.   3.   A child of John pulfords.

October   13.   Elizabeth Sicklemore widow was buried.

     14.   William Exman was buried.

     21.   Martha Petit was buried.

Novemb.   4.   William Patridge was buried. The wife of Richard Norris.

Decemb^r 16.   Henrie Norman sone of Henrie Norman was buried.

     23.   [*blank*] Duke was buried.

     31.   A child of Nathaniel Smarts minister was buried.

Januar.   26.   Marie Bates the Wife of Valentine Bates was buried.

Febr.   11.   Margerie Goldson was buried and John Clarke.

     15.   Robert Warne was buried & [*blank*] Norris.

March   11.   Marie Rivers daughter of John Rivers was buried.

     19.   A child of Henrie Brames w^c died by drinckinge poison.

Page 129.   # Burialls.

Año Dñi 1631.

April   16.   George Baker died at ye halfe moone was buried.

May   6.   A child of Mr Benjamin Cutlers buried.

     8.   Marie Lakeland daughter of Theophilus Lakeland was buried.

     15.   Marie Tailor daughter of John Tailor was buried.

     16.   Robert manhood was buried.

     22.   William Scabie was buried.

June   4.   Joan Leigh was buried.

     5.   { Sarah Wealie daughter of Joseph Wealie was bur. John Gates was buried.

     17.   { Christopher Alderman buried. John morgan prisoner buried.

     28.   Alice Lucas buried.

     20.   William Skeet was buried.

Julie	3.	William Wilkinson was buried.
	7.	William Akelie was interred.
	15.	Samuel Coleman was buried.
	21.	A child of Mr John Lames was buried.
	26.	Audrie spicer wife of Anthonie spicer buried.
	27.	The wife of Samuel Rich was buried.
August	4.	Edward Coppin buried at St Laurence.
	12.	marie Nawler wid was buried.
	13.	Marie Greenewich wife of Steven Greenewich was bur.
	10.	John Reeve was buried. August 29 Jane Brame.
Septembr	15.	John Allein was buried.
mathew	20.	Widow Reeve was buried.
Octobr	11.	{ Mrs Alice Cutler widow was buried.
		{ Rose Cornelius was buried and mathew moulson.
	12.	Añe Browne widow was buried.
	13.	Dionie Downinge was buried.
	26.	Elizabeth faireweather was buried.
	27.	Sarah Benet daughter of John Benet was buried.
Novembr	10.	Hañah Acton was buried.
	11.	William Cornelius was buried.
Decembr	1.	Marie Clemens wid. was buried.
	3.	[blank] Cutbert a prisoner buried out of ye jaile.
	7.	John Foxelie was buried.
Februarie	9.	Ellice Constance was buried.
	18.	Lydia Cutbert daughter of Richard Cutbert was buried.
	28.	Francis Pouncet was buried.
March	15.	Marie wicks buried.
	19.	Susaña Hunt was buried.

Año Domini 1632.

March	31.	William Edgar was buried.
April	7.	James Croine was buried.
	22.	Bartholmew Brooke was buried & Samuell Harris.
May	31.	Bridgit the wife of John Leigh was buried.
	+	+ Mr Roger Cutler.
feb.	23.	John Prince [smudged, intended for erasure] was buryed.
	24.	[blank] Stedd was buryed.
feb.	28.	Mr Nathanell Smart minister buryed.
mrch	13.	John prince was buryed.
Novemb. 30th.		+ Roger Cutler portman buryed.

Anno Domini 1633.

Thomas [sic].
Thomas [sic].
William Pantame buryed.
Thomas Maye Buryed.
George Bret   } both buryed together.
Robert Sparow }

July.   Widdow Whitinge burjed.

Jul.		Widdow Alderman burjed.
		A child still borne burjed.
		Robert Cooper son of Robert Cooper burjed.
Aug.	26.	John Browne the son of John Browne burjed.
Sept.	3.	John Bedome burjed.

Page 130

9 Oct.		Two Infants burjed.
Novemb.	21.	Randall the wife [*blank*] was buried.
Nov.	25.	Thomas Moulson buried.
Novem.	29.	[*blank*] moulson the widdow of thomas Moulson buried.
Decemb.	2.	Elizabeth Blomefeild burjed.
Decemb.	5.	William Writ [*blank*] buried.
Jan.	2.	Thomas Hutchinson buried.
Jan.	21.	Robert Bewike buried.
Feb.	2.	Tho. Stygen buried.
March	16.	An Infant burjed.
March	23.	[*blank*] Sansome buried.

1634.

Aprill	21.	John Whelye burjed.
Maij	15.	Thomas Wilkinson burjed.
Maij	30.	Nicholas Wilbore burjed.
June	1.	Joane Cutbert the wife of Ri^d Cutbert burjed.
June	25.	John Burman the son of Robert Burman burjed.
July	11.	Mr John Lee prisoner buried.
Julye	19.	Mary Crane daught^r of ye widdow Crane burjed.
Septemb.	26.	Dorothje Blosse daughter of Thomas Blosse burjed.
Octob.	2.	Elizabeth Martyn the wife of Thomas Martin burjed.
Octob.	4.	John Stanifer the sone of John stanife buried.
Octob.	14.	{ Anne Proctor the wife of John proctor burjed. Abigail Wixe daughter of John and Margery burjed 14th.
November	2.	Anne Som̃ers the wife of John Sum̃ers burjed.
Decemb.	16.	[*blank*] Franklin ye wife of Isaake Franklin burjed.
Decemb.	19.	M^{rs} [*blank*] Fowler widdow burjed.
Decem.	28.	John Wixe son of John and Margery Wixe burjed.
Decemb.	31.	The Widdow Daoje burjed.
Januar.	31.	a poore girle in ye Fryars burjed.
Jan.	20.	Thomas Price burjed.
Feb.		Joane Vintner burjed.

Page 131.

Burialls 1635.

Aprill	25.	Elizabeth Copping daughter of Richard Copping and Elizabeth his Wiffe was Buryed the 25th of Aprill.
May	30.	Margery Martin wife of Mathyas Martin buried.
June	28.	Tabitha Bridges was buryed.
July	6.	John ye sonne of Nicholas Wilbore was buryed.
	20.	Widdow Parkin was buryed.

[July]	22.	Anne Barker was buryed.
	30.	Elizabeth daughter of Francis Lewen was buryed.
August	13.	Thomas y⁰ sonne of Valentine Bate was buryed.

[July] 22. Anne Barker was buryed.

30. Elizabeth daughter of Francis Lewen was buryed.

August 13. Thomas yᵉ sonne of Valentine Bate was buryed.

2c. John Francis was buryed.

20. Alice yᵉ daughter of Francis Lewen was buryed.

Septemb. 10. The wife of James Stone was buryed.

13. Edward Johnson was buryed.

15. Susan yᵉ daughter of Sarah Eton was buryed.

30. Susan yᵉ daughter of Thomas Cooper was buryed.

Octob. 19. Joane yᵉ daughter of Henry Norman was buryed.

Decemb. 9. Anne yᵉ daughter of William Kevington minister & of Anne his wife was buryed.

12. Nicholas Kircke was buryed.

31. Elizabeth daughter of Thomas Allen & of Elizabeth his wife.

William yᵉ sonne of Nicholas Bishop & of Francis his wife.

January 14. Helena daughter of Robert Darnell & of Elizabeth his wife.

26. Robert sonne of William Barrow & of Jane his wife.

February 2. The widdow Purham was buryed.

4. Allen sonne of Mᵣ Gabriell Catchpole & of Elizabeth his wife.

17. The wife of John Watson.

March 3. Margaret daughter of Mᵣ John Cresse & of Anne his wife.

7. Nicholas Loft was buryed.

13. Joseph yᵉ sonne of Henry Brame & of Parnell his wife.

Buryalls.
Anno Domini 1636.

Aprill 17. Katherine yᵉ wife of John Bucknam.

June 2. Joshua harris.

24. Alice Parker widow.

July 11. Margaret the Wyfe of Robt seamon.

26. Johannah the Wyfe of Olifer Barbor.

26. Mary the Wyfe of Jeames Ladbrooke.

31. Nicholas Archer.

Aug. 9. Isax the son of Jeames Osburne.

10. William the sonn of Edmund Garwood.

13. Edward the sonn of Edmund Garwood.

Sepᵣ 3. Anna the Wyfe of Ellexsander marrit.

15. Tamisen the Widow of Geroge pᵏis out the gaile.

20. Margert the wyfe of John Wright.

Octobᵣ 7. John Manward.

27. Robᵗ Gurling prisoner in yᵉ gaile.

Page 132.

Decᵉ 17th. [*blank*] Curtis sonn of Thomas Curts was buried.

Januarye 12. Priscilla Sorrell wife of Thomas Sorrell was buried.

Januarye the 12. Alice the daughter of Thomas Pounsett was buried.
The sonn of Wm Tranham was buryed Aprill the 6th 1637.

A child of Stumifere buried the 27th of March 1637.

Tobie the sonn of Tobie Browne was buried the 22 of ffeb. 1636.

1637.   John Stannifer was buried the 21th of Aprill 1637.

Mary the daughter of Alice Lakeland was buryed June 18th 1637.

Elizabeth Neale widdow was buryed June the 25 1637.

July	24.	Thomas Smyth the Son of Mr Robert Smyth and Katherin his wife.
July	21.	The wife of Abraham Alberrie was buryed 1637.
Agust	5.	Parnell Brame the wife of Henry Brame 1637.
Agust	7.	ffrances Hewling widdow.
Agust	7.	William Scott was buryed 1637.
August	27.	Thomas the Son of Thomas Sudjck & Mary his wife.
August	20.	John the Son of John Pascall & Margret his wife.
Septemb.	13.	Xtopher Wilkinson the Son of Xtopher Wilkinson & Elizabeth his wife.
October	7.	John the Son Benjamin Cutler and Joane his wife was buryed.
Octob.	11.	Stevin the Sonne of John Reyner & Elizabeth his wife.
Novemb.	5.	Henry the Son of henry Syir & Beatrix his wife was buryed.
Novemb.	8.	Robt Smythier the Son of John Smythier & Elizabeth his wife buryed.
Novemb.	15.	Sarah Church the daughter of Sarah Church widdow was buryed.
Decemb.	17.	Matthias Martin was buryed.
Decemb.	29.	Joseph Wylie was buryed.
January	2.	John the son Dorcas Gower widdow was Buryed.
January	12.	Margret Tod was Buryed.
January	22.	William the Sonne of Robt ffoxe and Beatrix his wife.
ffeb.	3.	Elizabeth the daughter of Tobith Browne and Sarah his wife.
ffeb.	13.	Abigal Seman the daughter of Abigall Seman widdowe.
March	12.	Richard Eliott was buryed.
March	22.	Henry Skinner the Son of Henry Skinner & Susan his wife.

1638 Burialls.

March	27.	Dorcas Manwood the daughter of widdowe Manwood buryed.
May	11.	Richard Bidam the sonne of widowe Bidam was buryed.
May	23.	William the sonne of Thomas Wilshin and Anne his wife buryed.

June	5.	Thomas Martin was buried.
July	28.	Edward the sonne of Edward Vaile was buryed.
July	30.	Emme wilbore widowe was Buryed.
August	2.	John the sonne of Edward Gnat was buryed.
August	7.	Elizabeth the daughter of Robt Yellop & Joanne his wife buryed.
August	27.	Elizabeth the base borne daughter of Marget Branson.
August	27.	Widowe Archer was buryed.
August	29.	Edmund the sonne of Edmund Brooke was buryed.
Septemb.	5.	Margaret the wife of Edward Vaile was buryed.
Septemb.	15.	Edmund the Sonne of Widow Wilbore was buryed.
Septemb.	22.	Mr Richard Copping was buryed.
Septemb.	24.	Elizabeth the daughter of William Barrow & Jane his wife.
Septemb.	25.	Samuel the Son of Samuel Dixon was Buryed.
Septemb.	29.	Marget the wife of Thomas layman was buryed.
Septemb.	29.	Thomas the sonne of John Bantock & Ann his wif.
Septemb.	29.	Robert Ling was buryed.
October	15.	Thomas Layman was Buryed.

Subscribed by { Alexr Rainold Minister of St Nicholas psh in Ipswich.
Thomas wyther } Churchwarddines.
Adrian Shawe }

Page 133.

October	16.	The widdow Eatons sonne was buryed.
October	18.	Martha the wife of John Burnish was buryed.
October	23.	Anne the daughter of John Burnish.
October	26.	ffrances the daughter of John Pascall was buryed.
October	29.	John Watson was buryed.
October	29.	John Manship was buryed.
October	31.	James Marshell was buryed.
Novemb.	5.	William the sonne of James Marshall was buryed.
Novemb.	8.	William Asty was buryed.
Novemb.	20.	Amaris Stebben }
Novemb.	20.	Thomas Rocket } wer buryed.
Novemb.	20.	Penelope the daughter of Edward Gnatts.
Decemb.	8.	Elizabeth the daughter of William Brett & Anne his wife.
Decemb.	16.	James the sonne of Symon webber & Anne his wife.
Decemb.	23.	Robert Yellop was buryed.
Decemb.	31.	Mary Mose a vagrant was buryed.
Janury	18.	Philip the son of William hemson was buryed.
ffeb.	1.	Elizabeth the wife of Henry ffidgett was buryed.
ffeb.	3.	heliner the daughter of Timothie Reeue.
ffeb.	10.	Andrew wright also a childe unbaptized.
ffeb.	12.	widdow Onge was buryed.
ffeb.	12.	The Goodie wright.
ffeb.	15.	Elizabeth the daughter of Timothie Recue.
ffeb.	17.	Elizabeth the daughter of John Reyner.

L

ffeb.	20.	The widow Scoffield was buryed.
ffeb.	23.	Margret the daughter of John wright.
March	1.	The daughter of Goodman Mallet.
March	13.	George the son of George Allen.
March	14.	The childe of goodman hagges.
March	22.	The wife of Goodman ffrost.

Burialls 1639.

March	25.	Robert the son of Robert Hempson was buryed.
March	27.	Peter Brett was buryed.
Aprill	3.	Elizabeth ShingleWod was buryed.
Aprill	7.	William the son of William Micklefield was buryed.
Aprill	8.	Dorcas the wife of Robert ffiske was buryed.
Aprill	19.	Lettice hardie widdow was buryed.
Aprill	19.	Alice the wife of Gilbert Lewis was buryed.
Aprill	25.	Marie the wife of Francis Smyth was buryed.
May	10.	Anne Margets was buryed.
June	12.	Martha hawkins widow was buryed.
June	17.	Sarah Parkhurst was buryed.
June	26.	Goody Pulford was buryed.
July	1.	Mary Cowper was buryed.
July	1.	Henry Rivers was buryed.
July	7.	Dorothy Bragge was buryed.
July	7.	Susan Wantwhait was buryed.
July	10.	the sonne of widow Skeat was buryed.
July	14.	Elizabeth the wife of Jeremy honnex.
July	23.	Timothy Reeue was buryed.
August	17.	Anne Goodrick was buryed.
October	4.	The wife of Thomas Cowp.
October	5.	The wife of goodman Punsett.
October	31.	hannah the daughter of John Denton was buryed.
Novemb.	25.	Thomas Moulson was buryed.
ffeb.	3.	Richard Smyth was buryed.
ffeb.	13.	Thomas Lewell buryed.
March	11.	Richard hust buryed.
March	20.	John Godfrey buryed.

Burialls 1640.

| Aprill | 2. | Steven Tovell was buryed. |

Subscribed by { Alex^r Rainold Minister of St Nicholas.
the m^k ⩘ of John Sorrell Churchwarden.

Page 134.

May	2.	Anne the wife of John Boggas was buryed.
May	5.	Robert Woodhouse was buryed.
May	10.	Judith Gravener was buryed.
June	1.	Nathaniel Pye was buryed.
June	10.	the wife of Robt webbe was buryed.

July	13.	Elizabeth the wife of James Reyner.

July   13.   Elizabeth the wife of James Reyner.
August   18.   A child of Jeffery Estie was buryed.
August   22.   Elizabeth the wife of Jeffery Estie was buryed.
August   25.   the widdowe Estie was buryed.
August   31.   The wife of John Browne was buryed.
August   31.   Elizabeth wife of Christopher wilkinson was buryed.
Septemb.   2.   George Bucknam was buryed.
October   23.   Joanne Coe was buryed.
Decemb.   10.   Marie Smyth widow was buryed.
March the 6th.   Henry Rayner potter was buryed.
March the 9th.   Elizabeth the daughter of John Earman was buryed.
March   24th.   John the sonn of Rose Ward was buried.
Aprill the 13th 1641.   the wife of Richard Hust was buried 1641.
Thomas Hardie & Hannath his wife weare buried the 18th of Aprill 1641.
The widowe Pye was buried the 7th of May 1641.

1642.

Aprill   12.   Christopher Story buried.
May   4.   Richard Nightingale child buried.
M   5.   Isaak the son of Isaak Bough buried.
M   6.   Hanna the wife of Edward Syre buried.
   12.   Liddia Miles widdow buried.
June   1.   Abraham Osbourne bur.
   7.   The wife of Henry Norman bur.
   9.   John Suñers the elder bur.
June   11.   The wife of Addam Mallet bur.
Septemb.   27.   Christopher Wilkinson . . . . N.S.
Octob.   7.   { Mr John Alderman bur.
             { The wife of Mr Phillips portman.
   16.   Daniel Dalton churchwarden buried.
   30.   Elizabeth Wilkinson daughter to Christopher deceased.
Nouem.   17.   Jacob wontwoot was buried.
Novem.   John Smith buried.

Page 135.   **1643.**

ffeb.   8.   Jeames Huleinge was buried.
may   23.   the widdow Ward buried.

1644.

ffeb.   11.   Susanna the daughter of the widdow Wantwot was buried.
ffeb.   20.   the widow watson was buried.
March   10.   goodwife Ixarsie was buried.

1645.

January the 26.   John Cutteler the sunne of Roger Cutteler was buried 1645.
1646.   John Elsden was buried maye.
May   27.   Margaret the wyfe of George Bentham was buryed.

L²

1653 [*sic.*]

december the 9.		the wife of william ledes was buriede.
decem.	23.	Mary story wed was buryed the wife of Christopher Story.
January	6.	John freman was Buryed.
febr.	6.	Martha the daughter of John sickelmor & of martha his wife was buried.
March	6.	Mr John lee presoner was buried.
March	16.	Wid belle was buried.
mar.	19.	william thurston was buried.
mar.	24.	Mara willder the wife of Richard willder was buried.

Page 136.   ## Buryalls Ano 1654.

Aprill the viijth.	Richard Wade Widdower Was buryed.
Aprill the viijth.	Wiłłm Lester sone of Wiłłm Lester & Dorcas was buryed.
Aprill the xijth.	Wiłłm the sone of Wiłłm Barrowe Was buryed.
Aprill the xiijth.	·Richard Downinge Was buryed.
Aprill the xvth.	Nathaneel Church was buryed.
April the 23.	Beniemen sonne of bassalcel brame & Ellen his wife buried.
May the 19.	Thomas Mathes was bvried.
July 27.	wod Smeth was buried.
August 19.	Alce the Wiffe of [*blank*] haggrafe buryed.
Septem̄ 13.	Ralphe Bloyes was buryed.
Septem̄ 15.	[*blank*] Withe Sone of Tho. Withe buryed.
Noucm̄ 12.	Sêphen Sone of Stephen dyer Was bryed.
Dese. 05.	James Sone of James Canting buryed.
Dese. 15.	Darckos brame buryed out of the ffowndacion.

1655.

March	27.	Adam Mallett buryd.
Aprill	2.	Anne ffrences was buyrd.
Aprill	8.	Susan wife of Tho. Baker was Buried.
Aprill	21.	Mary daughter of Michell Osborne Burid.
May	1^t.	[*blank*] Elletts child buried.
May	11th.	The wife of James Clifford buried.
May	23.	the wif of tomas bellemoer buried.
Septemb.	1th.	John son of John Sicklemore Esqr buried.
Sept.	9th.	Thom. Parrett buried.
Sept.	14.	ye wife of John Vsferell bũd.
Novemb.	10th.	Abigaell wife of Cłm Barber buřd.
Novemb.	ye fe. [? five].	[*blank*] wife of Willm Lister buried.
Novemb̃	26.	Ric° Annis buried.
Decemb̃	6th.	Barnes child buried.
January	25.	y^u wife of John Browne buried.

1656.

July	1th.	ye wife of Willm Boycott buried.
July	12th.	Henry ffigett buried.

Augus	21.	John son of John Coe buried.
August	24.	Margarett yᵉ wife of Joseph Lyntso būd.
Sept.	25.	Stephen sonn of Edmond Brooke buried.
Sept.	?8.	yᵉ wife of John Alderman the lder buried.
Octob.	10th.	Martha dawghter of Ricᵒ Clopton buried.
Octob.	16th.	Margarett Clopton buried.
Novemb.	23.	Tobias Browne buried.

Page 137.

Novemᵬ	24.	Simon Webb buried out foundacon.
Decemᵬ	22.	wife of christopher Longly.
Decemᵬ	22.	Clm Barber buried.
Decemᵬ	22.	yᵉ child of Rico Burroughes.
January	3ᵈ.	yᵉ wife of Henry Molson bu.
January	12.	yᵉ wife of Edward Shinglewood bu.
ffeᵬ	9th.	Philip sonn of John Sickelmore.
March	2ᵈ.	Thomas sonn of Anne Smith wid. bu.

1657.

March	31.	William Waters bu.
Aprill	14.	Willm son of Willm Longly bu.
July	10.	Hannah daughter of Thomas with bu.
July	29.	daughter of Michaell Casban bu.
August	14.	The wife of John hubbord bu.
Septem.	8.	Mary the wife of Joseph Hudson bu.
Septem.	12.	Widow Dedham bu.
Septem.	14.	Robbart sonne of Robbart May bu.
Septem.	15.	Widow Mosse bu.
Septem.	22.	Mary daughter of { Jerʰ *over* / John *erased* } Cole bu.
Septem.	23.	Widow Hadwick bu.
Septem.	26.	Isaac sonne of Jeremiah Cole bu.
Septem.	29.	Mary daughter of Robbart May bu.
Octob.	14.	widow Ottoway bu.
Octob.	14.	Nicolas [*blank*] the locksmith bu.
Octob.	23.	Thomas Cole bu.
Nouem.	2.	John Browne bu.
Decem.	2.	Goodman Mackarell bu.
Decem.	3.	The wife of Edmund Brooke bu.
Jan.	24.	Michael sonne of [*blank*] Carter bu.
Jan.	27.	Susan daughter of Roger younge bu.
feb.	10.	Mʳ Alderman widow bu.
feb.	12.	The wife of [*blank*] Carter bu.
feb.	15.	Thomas Badeston bu.

1658.

March	28.	Goody Badeson bu.
Aprell	5.	John Carter bu.
June	15.	Edward Snill buried.
June	17.	the widd Dixon buried.
June	26.	yᵉ wife of John Canham buried.

June	28.	widd Randall buried.
August	13.	Hannah Mann Daughter of Edw. Mann Esqr bu.
August	16.	ye wife of Tho Daniell bur.
August	20.	ye child of John hubbard bur.
August	26.	ye child of Isaac Buffe bur.
Septemb.	8th.	John Sorrell bur.
Sept.	14.	ye wife of John Ridnall bur.
Sept.	15.	Susan Daughter of Tho : Cooper bur.
October	10th.	Elizabeth Daughter of William Kird bur.
Novemb.	29.	John Gladwine bur.
January	28.	ye child of John Mixster bur.
ffeb.	5.	John Sonn of Henry Buckenham bur.
ffeb.	25.	widd. Dodson bur.
March	11th.	John Lucus bur.
March y^e	24th.	William Shaw bur.

Page 138.   1659.

Aprill	14th.	[*blank*] sonn of Jeremy Cole bur.
May	15th.	Elizabeth Whitinge buried.
June	11th.	Benjamin Wiseman buried.
June	30th.	[*blank*] Dawghter William Leedes.
July	13th.	The Wife of Robert Maye Buryed.
July	17th.	[*blank*] Poyse Buryed.
November 11th.		The Wife of [*blank*] Gennery Buryed.
November 15th.		Mary Daughter of William Mondy Buryed.
January	20th.	James Hulinge Buryed.
January	30th.	The Wife of Bassell Braham Buryed.
ffebruary	07th.	Mary the Wife of James Applewhite Buryed.

Buryalls Anno Domini 1660.

September 17th.		Richard Coe buryed.
December^r 18th.		The wife of Richard Pippin buryed.
March	22th.	Mary wife of Thomas Strong buried.

Burialls Anno Dni 1661.

July	7th.	John Wilder Buryed.
Novem.	9th.	John Baker Burryed.
Novem.	9th.	Elizabeth Nuttall Buryed.
ffeb.	13th.	the Wife of George Page Buryed.
ffeb.	23th.	the wife of Nathaniell Church Buryed.
ffeb.	24.	Widdow Taylor Buryed.
March	23.	Symon Thursbie Buryed.

Burialls 1662.

Aprill	1st.	Widdow Beamont Buryed : John Garwood buried April 13th.
Apr.	12th.	the Wife of Edmond Brooke Buryed.
Apr.	16th.	Edmond Brooke Buryed.
Apr.	27th.	the Wife of George Gosnold gent. Buryed.
May	26th.	Mary Dixon Buryed.

July	24th.	John Tillison Buryed.
Julij	27th.	M[r] Gabriell Catchpole Buryed.
Aug[t]	1st.	The Wife of John Church Buryed.
Aug.	23.	the Widdowe Wealy Buryed.
Sept.	20.	the Widdowe Billamore Buryed.
Sept.	29th.	John Buckenham Buryed.
Octob.	13th.	the wife of Thomas Brooke buryed.
Octob.	23th.	Mary daughter of Edward Mann Esq. buryed.
Novemb	17th.	the Widd Buckenham buryed.
Decemb	8.	John Pricke buryed.
Jan.	2[d].	Robte Moulson buryed.
ffeb[r]	10th.	Isaacke Bough Buryed.
March	2[d].	The wife of Symon Burryed.
March	12th.	Alice Sherwood burryed.

Page 139. Anno 1663.

June	26°.	Widdowe Skeele Buryed.
July	19°.	Thomas Ottaway buryed.
Sept.	9°.	Widdow Strutt Burryed.
Sept.	9°.	George Robinson Burryed.
Sept.	25°.	[blank] Mullinder Buryed.
October	5°.	John Rivers Buryed.
October	11°.	William Barrow Burryed.
Novemb	14°.	Mary wife of W[m] Coop Buryed.
Novemb.	30°.	Anne Persivall Buryed.
Sept.	10°.	Mary wife of William Cole burryed.
Sept.	10°.	Widdowe Cage burryed.
January	14°.	[blank] the Wife of [blank] Hayward Burryed.

Anno 1664.

Apr.	12°.	George Hogger Burryed.
Aprill	22.	Mary the wife of Edward Catchpole.
	22.	Steephen Son of Steephen Dyer.
May	18th.	mary the wife of John Breett.
June	18th.	Benjamen Cutler Gent.
June	23th.	Robert Townes.
Nouember	5th.	Elyas Tharston.
Nouember	16th.	william Thorne.
December	27th.	william ffarman.
December	28th.	mary the wife Joa Tavner.
Jañ	9th.	Rosse ffiske.
March	19th.	Susan the wife of John laarence.

Anno 1665.

Aprill	16th.	Thomas Barns.
Aprill	21th.	Thomas Noris.
May	15th.	Elizebeth the wife of William Sayer.
May	24.	John naraway.
May	30.	Iare the wife of John webber.
June	8th.	Thomas Stornge.
		The same day Daniel Tharsbie.

| June | 19. | Thomas Cooper. |
| June | 27. | the wife of Jacob wanthworth. |

Page 140.

July	5th.	the widdow Reaevs.
July	9th.	william Cooke.
July	12th.	Henry wright.
July	14th.	M^rs [*blank*] Skinner.
July	25.	Thomas Billimar.
Augs.	4.	Alice wife of William Skeete.
Augs.	14.	Anderew Creamer.
Augs.	16.	Debora the wife of Robt Cooke.
Augs.	17.	Richard Pippine.
		the same Thomas Smyth And Thomas Otteway.
Aust	18.	Edmund Garwood senior.
Augs.	29.	Sarah wife of Will Boycatte.
Sept.	4th.	Elizcbeth daughter of Steephen Dyer.
Sept.	6th.	Thomas Pounsett.
Sept.	7th.	Ann daughter of wid. Creamer.
Sept.	8th.	Edward son of Ed. Sterlinge.
September y^e	13th.	Josuah Sonn of Robert Wade buried Plag.
Septćber y^e	18th.	Mary Street buried of the Plage.
Septćber y^e	20th.	Steuen Dier buried of the Plage.
Septćber y^e	22th.	John Dier senior buried of the Plage.
Septćber y^e	23th.	Elizabeth Richison buried of the Plage.
Septćber y^e	27th.	Timothy Wade buried of the Plage.
Septćber y^e	29th.	Goodwife Wade buried of the Plage.
Septćber y^e	30th.	the Widdow Richisonn buried of ye Plage.
October y^e	first.	a child of Gorge Greene: Pl: buried.
Octo.	4th.	Goodwife Risdle buried of ye P.
Octo.	5th.	Goodwife Bond buried Cleere.
Octo.	7th.	Gorge Green buried of the P.
Octo.	7th.	Robert Wade buried of the P.
Octo.	8th.	Edmond Garwoods Sonn b: of ye P.
Octo.	11th.	Goodwife Reed & har Daughter buried of ye Plage.
Octo.	12th.	the Widdow Dier buried of the Plage.
Octo.	16th.	Mary Garwood: b: P: Octo. 18th Henner buck-
		nams daut.
Octo.	24th.	Edmond Garwood b: P.
Octo.	25th.	Widdow Huke buried Cleere.
Octo.	29th.	Jacob wantwiths child buried.
Octo.	30th.	a child of John Hugwells buried Cleere.
Nouember y^e	first.	a child of Joh. Bostons buried C.
Noućber y^e	3th.	Goodwife Brooke buried Cleere.
Noućber y^e	3th.	widdow harwick: b: P.
Noueber	5th.	a child of Goodman Kings buried C.
Noub.	6th.	Barne Durant buried.
Noueƀ	10th.	Widdow ffiggitt buried.
Noueƀ	12th.	Hennery Buckenham b: P: Goodwife Milksope
		likinge P.

Noueb	12th.	John Hunt: b: of the Plage.

Page 141.

Nouember	17th.	Frances Willkinsonn buried Cleer.
No.	22th.	on browne from yᵉ Joyle: b: C.
December yᵉ	18th.	Widdow larthor: b.
Decē	26th.	doctor Robbinsonn: b.
January	7th.	Widdow Boybes [? Boyles]: b: P.
Janu.	14th.	yᵉ wife of Jeames Cooe: b.
ffebuary yᵉ	15th.	Jeames Houlder: buried.

1666.

May the	2th.	Rose wife of Thomas Whithead buried of the Plage.
Maij	14th.	Widdow Smyth: buried: Cleere.
Maij	18th.	a child of Thomas Steddies buried.
June	21th.	yᵉ wife of Gorge Warring buried.
June	26th.	bloses child buried.
Ju.	27th.	Robert Curke buried.
July	8.	a child of ffrancis Turners buried.
July	9th.	Timothy Carters wife buried.
July	14th.	Steeven Mudds wife buried of the Plage.
July	24th.	Edmond Veales wife buried: C.
July	27th.	Steeven Mudd: b: P.
July	30th.	John Walers wife: b: C.
July	30th.	Edmond Hulings Sonn Richard: b: P.
August	13th.	Jeames Canten's daughter lidda: b: P.
Au.	14th.	Edward Huling: b: P.
Au.	19th.	a child of Jeames Cantens: b: P.
Au.	23.	Jeames Canten: b: P.
October	18th.	Robert Ceebles wife: b: C.
January	26th.	John Creesels wife: b: C.
ffebuary	3th.	the wife of Weekly: b.
ffebuary	8th.	Jeames Mills: buried Cleer.

[*For some more burials in* 1666, *see page* 156.]

[1667].

Maij yᵉ	. . .	Chese the wife of Mʳ Richard Cloping: b: Cleere.
June	20th.	Thirkels Daughter b.
Octo.	first.	Richard Trulove buried.
Octo.	4th.	Mʳ Stockdons Child b.
Octo.	7th.	a daught of mʳ Stockdons buried.
March	12th.	Cristofer Sonn of Mʳ Melton esquire.
March	18th.	yᵉ wife of John Lawrance: b.

1668.

June	9th.	Alice The wife of Edward Martinn buried.
June	23th.	Mary Osborne: b.
August	21th.	Mʳ John Sparrow b.
Octo.	31th.	Samuel Ward buried.
Nouember	7th.	Timothy Mowdie Sonn of William Mowdie b.
Deceber	6th.	John Creesell buried.

Decĕb	10th.	Ann Daughter of Mr Williã Green : b.
Decem^b	23th.	Mary davter Geo. Raymond be.
Jane	16.	John Sonn of Jeremy Colle was be.
Jane	22th.	Margret wife of Izak Allbrov was be.
Faber	22th.	the wedow Wilkinson was be.

Page 142. 1669 an. do.

Aprel the	8th.	the wedow barrow was bv.
July the	27th.	eaff wife of Jacob wathwet was bv.
July the	29th.	Mary wife of Willyam movde was bv.
Sept$^{ber}_{em}$ the	20th.	george warin was bvryed.
October the	15th.	Mr Jeremi Cole was bvryed.
October the	26^t.	John Burch servant to Edward Martin bvried.
Novem. the	14th.	the wife of Branson was bvryed.
Decem. the	11th.	Willyam Coppar was bvryed.
Decem. the	14th.	Edward Coats was bvryed.
Decem. the	29th.	John Melton gent. was bvryed.
Feuery the	9th.	the wife of John Pillgrim Buryed.
1669.		the wife of Peter Stronge was buryed Jany 30th 1669.

1670. Burialls Anno Dom. 1670.

Aprill	24th.	Mary Wife of William Bath of St Peters was buried here.
May	28th.	Thomas Stevens was buryed.
	30th.	John Paskall the yonger was buryed.
June	11th.	John Lawrence was buryed.
August	13th.	Ann the wife of Ambros ffrost was buryed.
	22th.	Thomas Deeplake was buryed.

1670.

October 17th. Mrs Abigall Muninge widiwhoe had tooe housbonds both Ministers her first housbond was that Reverand & holy man of God Mr Nathonile Smart whoe was Minister of this pish of St Nicolas fiveten yeares & dyed here in his Ministery whose p^{r}sious ashes lyes Interred close to the Entrance into the vestery in the Choncell in whose grave rests the boddy of this holy Matrion waiting til her Redeemer Comes whoe was buryed october 17th 1670.

Novem.	12th.	a base Child of Ann Cowper was buryed.
December	20th.	Ann wife to Edward Cooke was bvryed.
	29th.	Mrs Susanna Mann daughter of Edw. Mann Esqr of Mrs Martha Mann his wife was Buryed.
Januery	8th.	[*blank*] son of Thomas Donill & [*blank*] his wife buryed.
March	10th.	Elizabeth wife af John Rye was Buryed.
	20th.	Thomas Sonn of Thomas Bloss was Buried.
1671.		
March	29th.	Thomas Sonn of Thomas Goulding & [*blank*] his wife Buried.
Aprill	7.	ffrances Cooke was buryed.

Anno Dom. 1671.

May	6th.	Mr Georg Raymer of St Peters pish was Buryed.
May	7th.	Margery Eldsden & a child of Arnold Tillyson was buried.
June	29.	Symond Smith was Buryed.
		the same day A Son Peter Strous was buryed.
Jull y^e	2.	Margeritte Longly the daughter William Longly was Buryed of St Stephens pish.
July	14°.	Mary Daughter of Edward Man Esq° was buried in St Nickolas Parrish Church.
August	8°.	Temothie Carter was Buried in St Nickolas Church yeard.
November	26.	Christo^r Wilcoke was Buried.
Jan^r the	31.	Richard trueloue was Buried.

[*There is apparently only one entry in* 1672, *see page* 156,
"*Out of the Kings ospetell*," *&c.*]

Page 143. **Bearels 1673 [*sic*].**

Aprill y^e	2th.	John Cannom was beared.
May y^e	19.	the wife of John Branten was buried.
May y^e	29.	the wife of Peeter Colle was buried.
June y^e	2.	Edward Veale was buried.
July y^e	6.	then Jararniah the sonne of John Barber was buried.
July y^e	18.	the wife of William Boicett was buried.
August y^e	15.	the wife of Edward Catchpole was buried.
September y^e	5.	John Church was buried.
September y^e	23.	Christifer Collin was buried.
September y^e	25.	Thomas Townes was buried.
September y^e	30.	ye wife of Gabrell Catchpole was buried.
October ye	6.	then James Cole was buried in ye chancell.
October y^e	10.	the wife of Henerry Locwode was buried.
October y^e	26.	the wife of Thomas Coock was buried.
Nouember y^e	17.	the wife of Thomas Wilshen was buried.
December y^e	28.	the wife of Robert Thorpe was buried.
January y^e	23.	Robert Thorpe was then buried.
February y^e	22.	George Pascall was then buried.
February y^e	26.	the wife of John Simans was buried.
February y^e	27.	the wife of William Lemmon was buried.
March y^e	4.	ye wife of Thomas Goage was buried in the church.
March y^e	5.	then was William Sudbery buried.
March y^e	8.	then was the widdow Stone buried.
March y^e	11.	then Robert Sceatrie a Surgin was buried.

1674. **Buriels.** 1674.

Edward the sonne of Mr Man was buried in ye chancel Aprill ye 9.

Aprill the	9.	then was Jarimiah ffocer was buried.
Aprill the	30.	then was John Pascall buried.
May the	27.	then ye widdow Matthe was buried.
July the	30.	then was William Lake buried.
Sept.	25.	The Widd. Church was Buried.

Octo.   1.   Elizabeth Thridgall was buried.
Octo.   14.   then was wiliam moiDet buried.
October 31.   the wif of m^r edward man esqier was buried in the chansel of St Nickolas.

Page 144.

Burialls Anno 1666 [*sic*] of Seamen out of the Kings hospittall at Cussum house that weer buryed in the pish of St Nicolas in Ipsw^{ch}.

1666.

June	8th.	William Allport.
	8th.	Edward Young.
	8th.	Marmyduke Gowthrop.
	8th.	Walter Choplin.
	11th.	Nicolas Bennitt.
	10th.	James Hare.
	10th.	Michaell Stenslye.
	13th.	Hughe Blonwell.
	14th.	George Chapplemon
	14th.	John Lamboth.
	15th.	Peter Thompton.
	16th.	Henery Karye.
	16th.	Henery Curtice.
	16th.	Robt ffoster.
	18th.	Thomas Porter.
	20.	John Marthall.
	28.	Edw. Mafslye.
	29.	John Harris.
July	30th.	Edw. Keen.
Aug.	2.	William Elgate.
	2.	William Mulline.
	5th.	John Rutter.
	5th.	Richard Boston.

6th.	Georg Cory.
6th.	John Tyler.
7th.	Mathew [*blank*].
7th.	William Edwords.
8th.	Thomas Osborne.

August the 05th. {	John Ruter [*repetition*].
Aug. 5.	Richard Baston [*repetition*].
Aug. 6th.	Georg Cary [*repetition*].
	John Tyler [*repetition*].
7th.	Mathew Sugg [*repetition*].
7th.	Willim Edwards. [*repetition*].
August the 08th. {	Tho. Osbonne [*repetition*].

Out of the kings ospetell ther was buerd In St Neclos Robert Will [*sic*] the 8th Janvery 1672 [*sic*].

[1674 *resumed.*]

Jenevary ye 8th 74.   the wiffe of John balderson buried.
Jenw.   27.   the wid gales was bered.
ffeb.   9th   74.   Jacob wantwith bered.
16 ffeb.   John whitine was bered.
ffeb.   the   24.   the wife of phillipe willames bered.

March the 24th 1674.   Anne ye wife of Phillipe Write buried.

Page 145.   [1675].

March   the   25th.   the wife of John Pilgram was buried.
Aprill   the   12th.   Anne Creemer widd. was buried.
Aprill   the   30th.   George Heady was buried.
May   the   11.   Charles bines of woluerston was buried.
May   the   26.   marey dauter of petter Cooke was buried.
May   the   28.   Margrett skinner was bearred.

June	the	2.	James haward was buried.
June	the	2.	Ann Kitson of worlingworth bur.
Jun	the	6.	Ann the wife of thomas Lee was buried.
Jun	the	7.	margery barrow widoe of ffokenham buṝ.
Jun	the	26.	Iaske ffoster was buried.
Jun	the	28.	John ffoker was buried.
Jun	the	30.	Ann Duater of phillipe wright was buried.
Julye	the	6.	thomising Duater of nʳ [? mʳ] Melton burried.
July	the	7.	Edmund Luffe was burried.
July	the	10.	suann the wife of basell huett was burred.
July		19.	suann collinge widdoe was burred.
July		22.	Elen Argent was burred.
Nouemb.		18.	Elezebeth Tayler was burred.
Desemb. the		7.	marrey wif. of John Duce was burred.
January the		21.	marrey pascall widoe was burred.
ffeb.		24.	ffrancies woller was barred.
ffeb.		27.	marrey Davies widdoe was barred.
March the		10.	Ann smith widoe was burred in the Church.

1676. Burialls Anno 1676.

Aprill	17th.	Elizabeth the daughter of Tho. Cooke.
Aprill	25th.	Gabriel Catchpole.
May	2th.	Abigail the wife of Willm Hadducke.
June	3th.	Alis the wife of John Skinner.
June	3th.	Sarah the wife of Richard Hawyard.
October	6th.	Jacob Wantwith.
October	11th.	Margaret Cannum widdow.
December	3th.	Sarah ffox widdow.
Decemḃ	29th.	Mary the Wife of George Browne.
January	1th.	John Pillgrom̄.
January	7th.	Em Arrenton widdow.
January	11th.	Margaret the wife of Thomas Cushion.
March	16th.	John Stone.
ffeb.	6th.	Mathew Hasted of the Tower pish.

1677. Burials Anno 1677.

March	29th.	Georg Browne Buried.
Aprill	18.	Aydery Cook Buried.
Aprill	29.	Lettice the daughter of Richard Newton and Lettice his wife was Buried.
July	7.	Mary Goodwin widd was Buried.
July	9.	John Bret was Buried.

Page 146.

July	14.	Susan wantwith widd. was Buried.
Aug. 15	1677.	Sarah the wife of William Muttly was Buried.
Aug. 24	1677.	Edward Martin was Buried.
Sept.	17.	Mary Cole daughter of Jeremiah Cole & Jane his wife.
October	4.	John Kinge was Buried.
October	9.	Peter Cole was Buried.

Novem.	9.	Henry sonne of Henry and Elizabeth Genry was burrd.
ffeb.	10th.	Henry Cole was bureyd.
March the	4th.	Ann Paise was bureyd.

1678. Burials.

April	14th.	Elizabeth the wife of John saman was buried.
April	18th.	Richard Bushup was buried.
Jun	11.	david Richason was buried.
August	6.	Simond ffovlle was buried in wolling.
August	17.	Richard Richason was burred.
August	18.	Mary Daniell was burred.
August	23.	Robart wales was burred.
August	29.	Elizabeth the sister of henry tash was burred.
Septem.	10.	Elizabeth the wife of James Clarke.
	17.	Henry Pasy was Burred.
	18.	Henry son of Henry Truloue & Elizabeth.
	20.	Rose the wife of thomas Brown.
	23.	Mary the wife of John Hollson.
Novem.	16.	Sameul sonn of Philip write.
desember	6.	William Green was buried.
Janery	7.	Gamaliel Hawyard was burred.
	19.	Edward Luess was burred.
	26.	Elizabeth the wife of John Sparrow burred.
febuary	3.	Edward York was burred.
march	9th.	Cristeffer Abell was bured.

$$1679. \qquad \text{the } 8^{\text{day}} \text{ of October}$$

Sarah Coleman the daughter of Will was borne   burred.

April the	7.	Elizabeth dafter of Mr Richarb Clopten.
May the	12.	William svrry was burried.
May the	20.	Pressilla Abell weedow was burred.
June	18.	Elizabeth the wife of henry Genry burred.
September	8.	Ann fernes wedow was burred.
September	25.	Elizabeth smith wedow was burred.
October	12.	Mary the wife of thomas wabb was burred.
desember	23.	Margret the wife John Mansuh burred.
febauary	15.	Susan the wife of Robart Geldersleue burred.
	17.	James daniel burred.
	19.	Ann the wife of John truloue burred.
	20.	tomason billemer wedow burred.
	20.	Margret Cullam burred.
	25.	Mathe the wif. of Phillip willanns burred.
March	3.	Martha the wife of Edward Green was burred.
	5.	Phillipe williams was burred.

Burials Ano dome 1680.

Aprill the	7.	Edward mann Esquir was burred.
May	15.	Elizabeth the wife of John Mixer was burred.
June	14.	Elizabeth Green wedow was burred.
	15.	brigget daniell wedow was burred.

June   the   21th.   ffrancies Brame Wase buried.
Nouem.   the   2.   the widdow melford was Buried.
September the   Martha wife of John Cooke was buried.

Octob.   the   22.   John Crouder was buried.
    Martha wife of Thomas blasby.
Decemb.   the   John Son of Thomas Steedy was buried 1680.
Decemb.   the   Thomas Hardy Was buried.
January   the   Thomas Stroggen was buried.
January   the   Dorathy Petit wife of Guiles Petit was buried.
January   the   29.   Elizabeth Canttin was buried.
Febeuary the   9.   of [*sic*] Thomas Cook was buried.
Febeuary the   13.   Jeffery Easty was buried.
Febeuary the   28.   John the Son of John Girling was buried.

    1681.

March   the   31.   Thomas Tricker was buried.
Aprill   the   5.   Mary Daughter of Edward Cooke was buried.
10 Aprile.   William Son of William Skeet was buried.
    Ann the Daughter of Edward Cook was buried the same
        Day.

    1681.

May   30th.   Thomas Sallows who was a Stranger was buried
        1681.
Nouember   Elizabeth Catchpole widdow was buried the
        13th of Nouember.
Nouember the 29th.   Mary wife of Michal Palmer was buried.
December the 25th.   Thomas Danil was buried.
December the 26th.   Jeremiah Trigge seruant to John Norton was
        buried.
William Munchester Scruant to Samuell Feueer was buried the same
    day.
Elizebeth yᵉ wife Of ffrancis Lea was Interred in yᵉ pish Church yard
    Of Sᵗ Nickolas Jan. yᵉ 12th Day.

    1681.

ffeb. the 10th 1681.   Timothy Daniell was Interred.

    1682.

Abigall the wife of Richard Thurston was buried the 24th day of
    Aprill 1682.
May   the   2ᵈ 1682.   Edward ffrost was Intered.
May the 11th 1682.   Susan yᵉ wife of Jefry Easta was Interd.
May   the   3ᵈ 1682.   Oliver hews was Intered.
August the first 1682.   John hardy was Intered.
Susan yᵉ Wife of ffrancis Turner was Intered March yᵉ 20th 168¾.

Burialls in 1682.

June   yᵉ   16.   Elizebeth the daughter of Jo. girling.
July   yᵉ   24th.   John Cushing Son of Jo. Cushing.

Steven gray in September.

Sept.	y^e	26th.	Priscelea ye wife of Edward Lute.
Sept.			John Jenings.
October	y^e	16th.	Susan Sparling was Intered.
October	y^e	24th.	Thomas Baker was Intered.
October	y^e	29th.	Mary the wife of Tho. Baker was Intered.

Sarah Daughter of Steven Danzey was Intered Nov. ye 23^d.

Janvery	y^e	9th 1682.	Elizebeth Topply Was Intered.
Janvery	y^e	29th.	Edward Tillot was interred.
ffeb.	the	13th.	Elizebeth the wife of Bazell Huet Was Intered.
ffeb.	y^e	14th.	Nickolas Son of Nickolas Smalladg was Intered.
ffeb.	y^e	19th.	hanah Searls Davghter of Henry Searls was Intered.
ffeb.	y^e	24th.	Mary the Davghter of Robt Allin was Intered.

Henry Son of Peyton Ventross Esq^e And of Margret his
wife was Intered in the psh. Church of St Nickolas feb.
ye 27th 168⅔.

Page 149.   Burialls In Aprill 1683.

Roberd Reedeve was Interd Aprill the 21.

Margret the daughter of peyton ventross esqi^r and Margret
his wiff. was Interd May the 4 1683.

Maregret Branson the wiffe of William Branson was
entered [*sic*] the 12th of Sept. 1683.

Oct.   15th 1683.   John Marshall was entered 1683.

October 20th 1683.   Martha Sharp was entered.

Judith Browne was Interrd August 18 1683.

Mary hall was entered october 24th 1683.

Leonard Tillot was Intered december 9th 1683.

John the Sone of Phillip Baddesun was Intered Jan. the 27
1683.

Robert Elsden Son of Robert Elsden was Intered 1684
Apr. the 28 1684.

John Danell was Intered Aperill th 27.

Martha pipin was Intered may the 28 1684.

Mary Daniell was Intered July the 8 1684.

Robert woodes was Intered August the 23.

Susan Greene was Intered may the 2 1684.

William turner Son of francis Turner was Intered Jully
the 15 1684.

John Gurling Son of Richard Gurling of S^t mary Stock
was Intered July the 16 1684.

Mary Clarke of S^t mary key was Intered July the 31 1684.

Elizabeth Baker was Intered August the 19 1684.

Elizabeth Allen Daughter of John Allen of London was
Intered August th^e 22 1684.

frences the Daughter of William Trusum was Intered
September the 6 1684.

Esther Stone wid. was Intered Sept. the 14.

Abigail hawys the wife of William hawys of the parrish of
S^t peter was Intered October the 1.

John the Sune of John Blasby of the parrish of St Stephens
was Intered october the 21.

John Denton of the parrish of S^t mary key was Intered
October the 29 1684.

Arnold tillisun was Intered octo. the 30 1684.

John Russell of the parrish of S^t matthews was Intered
September the 21 1684.

Mary hewit was intered January the 8.

thomas hercocke was Intered January the 12.

Elenor Browne of the Pairish of S^t margrets was Intered
January the 16 1684.

Page 150.

Sarah Arrington was Intered January the 25.

Sarah Sly was Intered January the 30 1684.

Robert Culler was Intered march the 28 1685.

John mixter was Intered may the 3.

mary Alburrough was Intered may the 8.

John Waller of St Stephenes parish was Intered June the 13.

Susanna morrine was Intered august the 7.

Susan Jenner the wife of Henery Jencrer of S^t peeteres
parrish was Intered august the 9.   august the 24.
Thomas Whith was Intered.

Samewell wabe presinor was Intered September the 16.

Sarah foster was Intered sept. the 18.

Ann haward wid. of St Peeteres was Intered october the 4 1685.

ffrā Gildersleue ye Wife of ffrancī Gildersleue was Intered
october ye 8th 1685.

Mary Seamons the Daughter of Robert Seamons was Intered
the 14 of october.

John the Son John Cushing was Intered october the 15.

Sarah the Daughter of Edward Cooke was Intered october
the 15.

Elenor the daughter of Elenor Smart wid. was Intered
December the 20 1685.

Ann the Wife Thomas Aldis was Intered December the 31 1685.

Edward Dowelling was interred Jan. the 12.

Peeter Baker was Intered feb. the 16 1685.

the wife of thomas Aldham was was Intered march the 21 1685.

Susan the daughter of Susan Cole presenor was Intered Aprill the 14
1686.

Wid. walles was Intered aprill the 15.

thomas blos was Intered may the 2.

The wife of willaim Sier of St Stephens parish was Intered may the 27.

Elizabeth Davghter of Eleaser Elonet was Intered Jully ye 2^d 1686.

Thomas the Hardey was Intered august ye 25th 1686.

An hazell Davghter of John hazell and An his wife was Intered
August ye 24th 1686.

M

Mary the Davghter of Samvell ffoster was Intered Nov. ye 11th 1686.
November ye 17th.   Thomas Peck was Intered.

Geo. Raymond.

Page 151.

Elizebeth Eade was Intered Setember ye 22th.
Elizebeth ye Wife of george hill was Intered ye 14th day of
December 1686.
Lidia Lewis Wido Was Intered Jan. ye 12th 1686.
John Duce of the pish of St Peters Was Intered in St Nicholas
Church yard One the 13th of Jan. 1686.
ffrancis the Son of Peyton Ventriss Esqr And of Margaret
his wife was Intered the 21th of Janvary 1686.
Martha Warne Wido was Intered the Second Day of feb.
1686.
John kersey Son of John kersey and Lidia his wife was
Intered feb. ye 3^d 1686.
James shalya a frenchman was Intered feb ye 4th 168⁶⁄₇.
Thomas the Sone of Thomas Steadey and Elizebeth his wife
was Intered feb. ye 11th 1686 Aged Six months.
Deborah Birch Late of Woolverston was Intered in the pish
of St Nicholas feb. ye 12th 1686.
An Blazeby was Intered March ye 24th 1686.
Mary Langly was Intered march ye 25 1687.

Burialls 1687.

Sarah the Davghter of Mr George Raymond Minister and Elizebeth
his wife was Intered Aprill ye 11th 1687.
Thomas Aldune was Intered Aprill ye 14th 1687.
Jonathan Skiner was Intered Aprill ye 30th 1687.
William Skeet was Intered Maye ye 9th 1687.
William Syer of St Stephens was Interred June ye 11th 1687.
Hannah the Daughter of George Raymond Cler: & Elizebeth his wife
was Interred May 23^d 1687.
Sam^{ll} Langley was Intered Avgst 15th 1687.
John ye Son of Robert Reader & Elizebeth his wife was Interred
Avgust the 25th 1687.
Samvell Son of Phillep Wright & Mary his wife was Interred Avgust
the 30th 1687.
Sarah the Davghter of Tho. garwood and Sarah his wife was Intered
Sep^t ye 12th 1687.
Willm Daniell was Intered Sept. ye 9th 1687.

Page 152.   ## Burialls Anno 1687.

ffrancis the Son of ffrancis Gildersleve And Elizebeth his wife was
Intered Sept. ye 16th.
Precilia Manester of St Helens was Intered October ye fourth In y^e
Church-yard of ye pish of St Nicholas.
Robert the Son of Robert King and Ann his wife was Interred October
ye 10th 1687.

Thomas the Sone of Thomas Newton gente and Sarah his wife was Interred October ye 29th 1687.

Lidia the wife of Samuell Lews of St Steuens parish was intered in St Nicholas churchyard the 28 of nouember 1687.

Mary the wife of Richd. Girling of Stock by Ipswich was interred in S^t nicholas churchyard the 2^d of December 1687.

Elizabeth wife of Henry Lockwood was interred the 19th of December 1687.

Samuell the Son of the Aforesd Samuell Lews & of Lidia his Deceased wife was interred also the 10th of December 168-.

Mary the wife of William Cooper was interred the 30th of December 1687.

John the 1 son of John Leas & of Bridget his wife was interred the seauenth Day of January 1687.

Jane the wife of Francis Cany of the Parish of S^t mary Elmes was interred the 27th of January 1687.

William Cooper widdower was interred the 28th of January 1687.

Ann the wife of George Bumsteed was interred the Eight of february.

Thomas Son of Alexander Sinch was interred the nineteenth of february 168-.

Martha Reeve out of the foundation was interred the Second of march 1687.

William Mutly the Elder widdower out of the foundation was bu ye 9th march.

1688.

Mary the Daughter of Philip Baddeson was interred the Second of Aprile.

Jean Moulson widdow out of the foundation was interred the twentieth of April.

John the Son of James Wheatly was interred the three & twenty of Aprile 1688.

Elizabeth Daughter of John Canton of St Steuens Parish was buried the fifteen of Jun. 1688.

Mary wife of Samuell foster was Buried the twentieth two of Jun. 1688.

Thomas Son of John Browne was Buried the Eight Day of July 1688.

John Truelove was Buried the Eleauenth Day of July 1688.

Eliazer Elonet was Buried the twentieight of July 1688.

Richard Sayer was Buried the thirty one of August 1688.

Mr John Sparrow widdower was buried the Eighteenth of September 1688.

[*blank*] Moulson widdow was Buried the twenty fourth of Octob. 1688.

Samuell Son of Samuell Havves of St Peters Parish was buried the 28th of Octob.

Ambros Frost Senior was buried the thirty one of October 1688.

Elizabeth the wife of Joseph Esticke was buried the 14th of Nouember.

Samuell Son of Samuell Woledg was buried the twenty eight of Nouember.

Michall Palmer Junior was buried the twentifiue of January 1688.

M^2

Mr Francis Harison Singleman was buried in the Chancell the 2^d of february.

Sary Daughter of Philip Baddeson was buried the twenty two of february.

Rebecca Daughter of John Carsey was buried the third of march 1688.

Geo. Raymond.

Page 153.   1689.   Burialls.

Rose Bough widdow was buried the tenth of march 168$\frac{8}{9}$.

1689. Dorithy Whitting was buried the 28th of March 1689.

Marg^t Ede widdow was buried the 7th of Aprill 1689.

Dugly Hill y^o Son of Dugly Hill was bury the 12 of May 1689.

George Allen Sexton of this Parish St Nico. was interred May y^e 30th 1689.

Margret y^e wife of Dugly Hill was bury June ye 12th 1689.

Mr Richard Clopping was bury^d in ye Chansell of this Church of St Nicho. June ye ninth 1689.

Mary ye daught. of John Cushing and Eliz^b his Wife was bury^d June 16th.

Henry ye Son of John Milsupe brought out of St Mary Tower p. and was buryed in St Nicho^s June 20th.

Ann Cooper widdow brought out of St Peters was buryed July y^c 7th 1689.

Elizabath ye Daught. of Henry Riches & Mary his wife July ye 9th 1689.

Jeremiah The Son of Jeremiah Esty July 21th of St Hellen^s 1689.

Mr Tho: Goo^{r}ges of St Hellen was buried in St Nichal^s Church July 27th.

Mary daught^r of Robert Cooke was Buryed July 30th.

ﬀ dennie D Proy a prisner out of ye Goale one of the Priorts July 31th.

ﬀ Allense Sallo:^{mon} a prisnor out of ye Goale one of y^c Priorts Augt 3th.

ﬀ Isaac Sone of Willm Lockwood of St Perters p. August 4th day.

[*blank*] a prisnor out of ye Goale was buryed Augt 9th day.

Henry ye Son of Willm Trusson was bury August ye 11th day 1689.

ﬀ [*blank*] a prisnor out of ye Goale was burried Augt 20.

Ann: Milsupe: Lat wife of John Milsupe of St Mary Tower parish was buried in this Church-yeard August 21th day 1689.

Richard ye son of ye widdow Lac^{k}lly was buried Sept. 1th.

ﬀ [*blank*] a prisnor out of y^c Goale was burid Sept. ye 2th.

Tho. Ropper out of y^c Goale was buried Sept. ye 4th.

Mary ye daughter of Tho: Hewett Ju^n was buried Sept. ye 22th.

Ann Martine widow was Buried Septemb^r ye 24 day 1689.

Mr Beni^{tt} Benett ffreme man was Buried October y^o 9th day 1689.

Robert Grome : a prisnor was Buried october ye 14th ⎰ 1689.
Isaac Till : a prisnor was Buried october ye 14 ⎱

Samuell Game a prisnor was buried octob. y^c 15.

Jeames Wethers : Gent : Lat of St Hiallens octob. ye 20.

Roger [*blank*] a prisnor was buried october y^o 26th.

Judith ye daughter of William Truson was buried octob. y^o 27.

Michall Pamer lett of y^c foundasion was buried nouemb. 8.

Thomas Son of John Blaseby of St Steuens p^{sh} was burd N° 4.

Mr Philup Neuill out of ye Goale was Buried Nouemb 9th 1689.

Susan y^o daug^t of Jeffery Easty of St Hellen : Nouemb. 14 day.

Robert y^o son of John Blasby of St Steuens Nouemb. 19th 1689.

Marg^t y^e daug^t of And^w ffindly was buried Decemb 5th 1689.

John y^c son of George Hill was buried decemb 19 1689.

Matha y^e daught. of Goodm Cook was buried decemb. 28 1689.

John Daniell was buried January y^e 5th 168$\frac{9}{90}$.

Richard Canton Lat of St Steuens was buried Jan^o 10th.

Ann : lat wife of Joh. Hastell was buired Jan^o 14 day 16$\frac{8 n}{0 0}$.

[*blank*] son of Goodman Stronge January 16th.

Geo. Raymond.

Page 154.   1689.   Burialls.

George Gossnall lat of St Marye Kee was buried in the Chancell of this Church ffebruary y^e 7 1689.

march		Johnathan Sparkes was buried feb. 27 1689.
Mar.	11th.	A child of Nic^o Cannyby & Margett his wife out of St Mary kee.
April 1690.	2^d.	ye widow warters was buried 1690.
Mar.	31. ⎰ 31. ⎱	Mary wife of Georg Warden in St Clements was buried.
Ap.	12.	William Brand of Wolton was buried.
	13.	A Child of Charles Harleys was buried.
	20.	John Godbull was buried.
	29.	Mistris Mary Wieth widdow was Buried.
May y^o	3.	Thomas Son of Mr. Tho. Newton of Ste^{n}en^{e}s Parish was Buried.
Jun. y^e	23.	Mary the Daughter of Jeffery Easty was Buried being of S^t helenee Parish.
July y^o	30th.	Elizabeth Daughter of Thomas Cushin of St Lawrance was Buried.
Augst y^c	22.	Jone The wife of William Roleson was Buried.
		A child was buried out of St Peters Parish.
Sept. y^c	4.	Elizabeth Culyer was Buried.
	8.	A child of William Trusson was buried.

Octob.	9.	A child Base Borne of The Body of Eliz. Crouder was Buried.
	16.	[*blank*] Cooke widdow was Buried.
	21.	A Child of Thomas Huit Juner was Buried.
	27.	A child of Mary Daniel widdow was Buried.
Nouemb. yᵉ	2.	Mary Daugh. of the same widdow Daniel was Buried.
	3.	John son of the same widdow Daniel was Buried.
	11.	Elizabeth the wife of John cushing was Buried.
Decemb.	22.	Daughter of Elizab. Bungey base borne was buried.
January yᵉ	2ᵈ.	Hannah Finch of Sᵗ Stephens Parish was Buried.
	yᵉ 16.	Judith the wife of Thomas Bret was Buried.
feb. yᵉ	15.	a child of Christopher Chamberlain was Buried.
	yᵉ 26.	Mary James was Buried.
March yᵒ	1.	[*blank*] Son of Thomas Garwood was Buried.

1691.

April yᵉ	2.	Isaac yᵉ child of Goodn Lockwood in Sᵗ Peter pˢ.
April	10th.	Sʳ Payten Venterhouse one of there Magtˢ Judges was interred in a volt in yᵉ East end of yᵒ Canchell next yᵉ vestery.
Aprill	26.	Margret yᵉ daught of Will Wood was Buried.
May	23.	Mʳˢ Ann Wyth was buried in yᵉ Ile of yᵉ Chancell.
	24.	Elizb. yᵉ daught. of Tho. Breet buried.
June yᵉ	7th.	William Rogers Senoʳ of this parish was Buried ⎫ A still borne Child of Timothy Wade the same day ⎬
	11th.	Mary The Wife of Timothy Wade of Sᵗ Steuens pish.
	23th.	Mary the Wife of Tho. Hewett Sen.
July	7.	A child of John Milsope of Sᵗ Mathews pish.
	22.	John yᵉ son of Tho. Martin lat of Sᵗ Hellians pish.
August	14.	Madam Venterhouse sener wido was Intered in yᵉ volt in yᵉ Chanᶜ.
	16.	Robert Seamons of Sᵗ Peters Pish was Buried.
	20.	A child of Rob Whalls in Sᵗ Margretts was Buried.
	21.	Mary Wright Singˡ was Buried.

Geo. Raymond.

Page 155.   1691.   Burialls.

Augˢᵗ	23.	A Child of Goodman Lewis of Sᵗ Hellians buried.
Sept.	13.	Elizb yᵉ wife James Townsing of Sᵗ Peters Pish.
	21.	Margret yᵉ wife of William Chinery was Buried.
	25.	John yᵉ son of John Slead & Elzb his Wife.
	29.	Goody Hall wido and Elzb Easty wido.
Oct.	3th.	Edward yᵉ son of Edward Alderid.
Noᵉ	5.	Mary Shephard widow was buried.
	20.	Thomas yᵉ son of John Hazell was buried.
	15.	John a Child of Tho. Garwood was buried.
Decemb.	20.	John Baker of Sᵗ Mary Elmes pish buried.
Janᵒ	10.	Ann yᵉ daugᵗ of Edw. Alderid & Mercy his wife bur.
Feb.	1.	A Child of Will Rogers was buried.
	4.	Tho. Miells a singell Man was buried.

[Feb.]	10.	John Rollerson single was buried.
	28.	a Child of Bazzell Huetts was buried.
March	3.	Walter Baker a single man was Buried.
	24.	A Child of Abiā Blisingham senē was Buried.
1692.		
	28.	Mary A Child of Base daught of Mary Brame buried.
Aprill	8.	ffrancis Turner of this pish was buried.
	13.	Tho. yᵉ son of yᵉ wido Semonˢ of Sᵗ Peters was buried. The same day was buried an Infant was found dead in a mash in Sᵗ Mary Stok parish.
	25.	Mary Bolton single of Henly was buried.
May	10.	Benjamin yᵉ son of Joeseph Catlen was buried.
	17.	Petter Barett A french man was buried.
	28.	Judith a child of William Trusson was buried.
June	5.	John Barber was buried.
	23.	Sarah yᵉ wife of Tho. Chriswell buried.
July	13.	Elizab. Leakless single woman buried.
Augᵗ	10.	Mary Luffe wido. was buried.
Sept.	23.	Thomas yᵉ son of Roƀ Cook buried.
Oct.	12.	John yᵉ son of Roƀ Reader was Buried.
	20.	Isable daugᵗ of mʳ Georg Raymond buried.
No.	1.	Mʳˢ Joane Raymond wido. was Buried.
	24.	William Wood was Buried.
		Joeseph Estwick was Buried.
		John Partridge a stranger Buried.

⎱ 24th
⎰ nouemƀ.

Geo. Raymond.

Page 156. **1692. Burialls.**

Decemƀ	11th.	William May was Buried.
	18.	John son of Simond Wilkerson was buried.
Jan°	9th.	Joane yᵉ wife George Armestronge.
	10.	a Soulger and child of yᵉ said Geo. Armestronc.
feb.	6.	Eliz. daugᵗ of Roƀ king was buried.
	23.	Samuell Boseting was buried.
Mar.	22th.	Sʳ Chistophere Melton of Rushmore was buried in the Church of this parish Sᵗ Nicholas Ipswich.
1693.		1693.
March	26.	William Sounds was Buried.
Apr.	17th.	Deborah Deadham Singˡ woman was Buried.
	30.	ffrañ Thridfeell was Buried.
May	7th.	Mary daugᵗ of John Mouson was Buried.
	8.	a child of John Whitley a stranger was Buried.
	25.	Ann Baker wido was Buried and the same day witħ a Child of william Coeman.
June	10.	Tho: a Child of Tho: Billemore was buried.
	17.	Sarah Purkis Widow of Munkesealy [*Monks Eleigh*] was buried.
July	11.	Mary Alexsander singlewoman of Sᵗ Peters.
	28.	A Child of Roƀ Rollerson Stile borne was Buried.

Aug.	6th.	Robert Elsden of this Parish was Buried.
	11.	ffrãc a daugᵗ of Henry Jennerys of Sᵗ Peters was Bu.
	20.	Abra son of Abraham Blislingham Junʳ was Bur.
Sepᵗ	3.	John Son of Tho. Smyth of Great Yarmouth in Norffolke was Buried Sepᵗ yᵉ third.
	9.	Sarah daugᵗ of Phill Church was buried.
Oct.	29.	Elizᵬ wife of John Slaed was Buried.
No.	3.	Tho. Clerke of yᵉ kee pish. } were Susan wife of Tho. Aldus of Sᵗ Law̃. } buried.
No.	17.	Edward Alderidge was buried.
	19.	Goody Elsdens wido. was buried.
+	27.	then The bell ded Ringe for Tho. Bayle a prisner.
	29.	A child of Sam̃ Baths of Sᵗ Clements was Buried.
Decemb.	3th.	mary daughᵗ of John Haywood of Sᵗ Peters buried.
	12.	Hannah daugh. of Bazell Braine was Buried.
	19th.	Susan Pricke wido. of Sᵗ Lawrence pish was Buried.
	17.	Mary daughᵗ of yᵉ wido. Semons of St. Peters was Buried.
Janᵒ	24.	Susan Rollerson singlewoman was Buried.
feb.	28th.	Elizᵬ Allin wido. of Sᵗ Mary at yᵉ Ellms was Buri.

1694.

Apr.	9th.	Sarah daught. of Tho. Toply was buried.
June	10.	Mary yᵉ wife of John Deefore A french man was buried.
July	1.	Margrett wife John Hayward of Sᵗ Petters pish was buried.
	3.	Roger son of Roᵬ Cook was buried.
	13.	William Pege was Buried.

Geo. Raymond.

Page 157.   ## Burialls 1694.

Julij	23th.	Ann yᵉ wife of Tho. Breet was Buried.
	24.	Mʳˢ Elizabeth Wyeth was buried in yᵉ Iyle of Chancell of Sᵗ Nicholas.
Augᵗ	20.	John Cooper Searuet to John Mixer was buri.
Octo.	5.	Nathaniel Church was buried.
Oct.	18.	Ailce daugᵗ of Tho. Toply was buried.
	20.	A child of base Stile borne of Abigal Hafferd.
	29.	Willi. a child of Willi Coeman.
No.	3.	Mʳˢ Elizabeth Haruey widow was intered yᵉ Ile of yᵉ Chanchell.
No.	7.	William Roulleson was Buried.
Dec.	2.	Isaac ffoster of Sᵗ Peters pish was Buried.
	3.	Joeseph Sauurge a Child was Buried.
	5.	Mathew Calode a child was Buried.
	6.	Dinah Sayer widow was Buried.
	23.	Catherine yᵉ wife of Docter Theophilus Paʳson in North Ile of yᵉ Church.
	30.	Richard Holborrough singlman was Buried.

Jan°	17.	Susan wife of Mathies Eads was buried.
	18.	Mary wife of Rich Pullurne of Sᵗ Peters.
	20.	Richard Holborough Gentlem of Presston near Lanham was Buried.
feb.	7.	Dugly Hill was buried.
	24.	Henry Sly was Buried.
	26.	Paul sonn of Paul Louevine.
March yᵉ	17.	Margrett wife of Simond Wilkersonn was Bur.
	20.	John Milsupe of Sᵗ Mathies pish was buried.

1695.

Aprill	5.	Abgiall filint widow was Buried.
	12.	Mishell daugᵗ of Jeames Leene A frenchman.
	15.	Rebaca daugʰ of Alexsader Weller.
	28.	The [*blank*] Breet widow was buried Apr. yᵉ 28 day.
April	29.	Sarah daugʰᵗ of John Slade was buried.
May	16.	Elizabeth wife of Benjamin Hall.
May	19.	Sarah Garwood wife of Thomas Garwood.
May	21.	Mʳ Robᵗ Smith one of yᵉ portmen of Ipsw.

Geo. Raymond.

Page 158.   Burials 1695.

May	30.	William Hadduck of Sᵗ Peters was buried.
June	14.	Elizabeth a child of Georg Hill of Sᵗ Mary at the Elmes.
June	27.	Bridget wife of John Lees.
July	3.	James Smith of Sᵗ Margaretts pish.
July	6th.	Elizabeth daughter of John May & Dorcas his wife.
July	23.	Martha Wantworth widd.
Aug.	6.	Sara daughter of William Rogers.
Aug.	11.	John the Son of John Lees.
Octob.	1.	Henry Son of John Blazeby of Sᵗ Margerets.
Octob.	10.	Mʳ John Richardson of Sᵗ peterˢ.
Octob.	13.	Thomas Blaseby.
Novemb.	1ˢᵗ.	Edw. Dowling of Sᵗ Peters.
decemb.	3ᵈ.	George Son of George Coe from Sᵗ Stephens.
decemb.	20.	Ann Huke.
decemb	21.	Margaret daughter of John Cogan french.
Jan.	20.	Abraham son of Witt Coeman.
Jan.	31.	John son of William Danel.
febʳ	2.	Thomas Lucas from Sᵗ Peters.
febr.	12.	Susan wife of Thomas Adams.
febr.	28.	Thomas son of Tho. Criswell.
March	10.	Mary daught. of Thomas Hewit.
March	21.	Peter Pillot a frenchman.

Burials 1696.

March	29.	Anthonina Melsup an Infant from yᵉ Tower.
April	3.	John Mowson.
April	30.	Elizabeth daughter of Robt Realer.[1]

[1] ? Reader, see *sub* 28 June.

May	17.	Sarah a child of Benj : Skeet.
May	22.	Vrsula Balden.
June	3th.	Catherine Dowling widow.
June	8th.	Abel-Anthony son of Mr Duluc Gubaber.[1]
June	11th.	Jane daughter of George Hill.
Ju^e	17.	Samuel Haves frõ St Peters.
June	19.	Lydia Packard wid.
June	24.	George Luffe an infant.
June	28.	Eliz. wife of Robt Reader.
July	1st.	Eliz. wife of Jeffery Estwick of St. Hellens.

Geo. Raymond.

Page 159.

July	28.	Elizabeth wife of Thomas Ballard.
Aug.	27.	Mary wife of John Harper frõ St Mary Key.
Sept.	21.	Willm son of Willm Osborn.
Sept.	28.	Henry Searles.
Octob.	17.	Daniell Patree.
Octob.	18th.	Elizabeth Lakeland Widow.
Jan.	22.	{ Mary Hogger frõ St Mathews. / Elizabeth daughter of John Cushion.
Jan.	31.	Mary daughter of Robt Reader.
Febr.	3^d.	Margery Floyd from St Clements.
Febr.	13.	Sarah daught. of William Green.
Febr.	14.	George son of George Hill.
Febr.	15.	Bridget Peak widd from St Lawrence.
Febr.	25.	John Peak from St Lawrence.

1697.

April	25th.	Marey ye wife of James Bird.
May	16.	Daniel son of Thomas Creswell.
May	14.	David Syer from St Mary Key.
May	19.	Robert Reader.
June	2^d.	David Morgan.
June	7th.	Anthony Dulac Gallabure from Nowbourn.
June	17th.	Mary daughter of William Trusson.
July	28.	Ann daughter of Abraham Chenery.
August	8th.	John Cushion from St Mathews.
Septemb.	16.	Abigail Denton widd from St Mary Key.
Sept.	16.	Willm son of will^m Rogers.
Sept.	19.	John Seamon from ye Goal.
Sept.	28.	Isaack son of Stephen Bond.
Nov^r	22.	Amy Blaseby widd.
Jan.	4th.	Alice Melsup widd from ye Tower.
Jan.	11th.	Rose Moulsin widd.
Jan.	9th.	Mary wife of David Morgan.
Jan.	27.	Thomas son of Thomas Porter.
Jan.	30.	Hannah Baker from St Margets.
Jan.	31.	Nathaniel son of Basil Hewit.

[1] Or Gulaber, see 1697, June 7.

Mar.	8th.	Martha Searles widd.
Mar.	14.	Samuel Bennet.
Mar.	15.	Philip Wright.
Mar.	22.	William Harris.

1698.

Mar. 29th 1698.		Walter Sickleprice.
April	5th.	Ann Breet.

Geo. Raymond.

Page 160.

April	5th.	Michael son of Michael Daniel.
April	14.	John Salmon.
April	24.	Elizabeth Walledge an infant.
May	6th.	Mary Smith.
May	15th.	Lettice wife of Richd. Newton Gent.
May	15th.	James Simpson from St Peters p^{sh}.
May	16th.	Isaack Lewes.
May	20.	Sarah Rogers.
June	7th.	Susan Richardson widd from S^t mary Key.
June	19.	Samuel son of Francis Welton.
July	17.	Judith wife of Willm Cole.
July	22.	George son of George Raymond Cler :
July	23.	Elizabeth daughter of Thomas Ballard.
July	26.	Margaret Hill.
Septemb.	20.	Elizabeth Rose from St Mary Elms.
		Sarah daughter of Benjamin Skeet.
Nouemb.	29.	Margeret Barber br^t from Layham.
dec^r	4th.	John son of John Smyth.
dec^r	5th.	mary Daniel Widd beried by the parish.
Jan.	16.	Hannah daughter of Tho. Hewet.
Jan.	29.	Mary daughter of James Bird from St M. at Elms.
febr.	6.	Rose Harper a child from S^t mary Key.
Mar.	5th.	John Melsup a child from St Mathews.

1699.   1699.

mar.	28.	James Newton an infant.
April	5.	Charles Money an infant.
Apr.	23.	Eliz. Culyer from St Mary Key.
May	1st.	Mary Howard an Infant.
May	4th.	Margaret Coeman an Infant.
May	8th.	Edmond son of Edmond Luff an infant.
May	17.	George Carrew a base borne child.
Nov.	26.	Finie daughter to Thomas Creswell.
July	3^d.	Mrs Sarah Clopton a maiden from St Peters.
July	4th.	Thomas Wilkenson.
Sept^r	11.	Elizabeth Tillerson widd.
Sept^r	28.	Daniel Sands an infant.
Octob.	29.	Hannah Smith sol.
Nov^r	7.	William Chinnery from S^t peters.
Decemb^r	17.	Roger son of Roger Sands.

Jan.	15.	Elizabeth wife of Jacob Hidson gent from St Mary Tower.
febr.	11.	Esther Dulack a child from London.

Page 161.   Geo. Raymond.

Mar.	19.	Phœbe Tillerson buried by ye parish.

1700.

Mar.	25.	Mary pegg widd buried by y^c parish.
Mar.	31.	mary Daniel a child.
Apr.	14.	John Dew town sergeant.
May	8th.	Mary Dains widd from St Margarets.
Apr.	25.	Basil son of Basil Hewet from St Margarets.
July	25.	William Holding an infant from the Tower.
Aug.	30.	Nathaniel Hawys Gent^n from S^t peters.
Octob.	7th.	Elizabeth Johnson.
Octob.	16.	James Weekly.
Nov^r	26.	Sarah Smith an infant from the Tower.
Dec^r	1st.	John Shephard.
dec^r	6th.	Isaack Elbrough.
dec^r	20.	Mary Hill.
dec^r	26.	{ [*Elizabeth Salmon widd. erased, see second entry following.*] William Lockwood an infant from St Mary Elms.
Jan.	1st.	Elizabeth Salmon widd.
febr.	1st.	Thomas Stead from St Mary Key Jan. 31.
febr.	16.	Ann Dew widd.
Mar.	19.	Robert Bird an infant from S^t mary at Elms.

1701.   1701.

April	6th.	Edward Daniel an infant.
May	1st.	Susan Trapnel wid. frō St Lawrence.
May	27.	Ann Melsup an infant from St Mathew.
May	28.	Robt Allen from St Mary Elms.
June	18th.	Elizabeth wife of Thomas Stollery.
June	21.	Ann Sands from St Margarets.
July	17.	Rose Froggit & Thomas her son.
July	22.	Francis son of William Coeman.
July	25.	Elizabeth daughter of John May.
Aug.	11th.	Mary Melsup widd. from St Mathews.
Aug.	25.	John Daniel an Infant.
Sept^r	8.	Alexander Weller.
Sept^r	21.	Susan May Widd.
Octob.	2^d.	Anna Baker from ye Foundation.

Geo. Raymond.

Page 162.

Octob.	19.	Thomas son of Thomas Cole.
dec^r	19.	Benjamin son of John May.
Jan.	14.	William Boycat Junr.
Jan.	28.	Martha Jannings widd.

Jan.	28.	Priscilla Stead widd. from St Mary Key.
Febr.	9th.	John Melsup from St Mary Tower.

1702.		1702.
May	22.	John Beaumond from St Peters.
May	31.	William Cole.
June	9th.	Hañah Hawes from St Lawrence.
June	30th.	Elizabeth Boycat an infant.
June	31.	Jeffery Easty from St Hellens.
July	12.	Henry Alderige an infant.
July	13.	William Rogers an infant.
Aug.	11th.	Deborah y^u wife of David Seydy from S^t peters.
Aug.	20th.	Anne ye wife of James Smyth from St Mary Tower.
Aug.	24.	Sarah Baker Spinst.
Aug.	28.	Hannah Baker Widd.
Sept.	13.	Thomas Milles an Infant.
Octob.	25.	Dorothy Syer an Infant.
Nov^r	4th.	Margaret Syer an Infant.
Nov^r	5th.	John Smyth a bricklayer.
Nov^r	16.	Mary Hudson an infant daughter of Jos. Hudson.
Nov^r	22.	Jacob son of Michael Daniel an Infant.
Dec^r	6.	Ann Gorbold widd. from ye Goal.
Dec^r	10.	Benjamin son of John May an Infant.
Dec^r	28.	Jean ye wife of Willm Rogers.
Jan.	17.	James Bird from St Mary at Elms.
Jan.	20.	Rachel late wife of Willm Coeman.
Jan.	26.	Sarah daughter of Willm Coeman.
Jan.	27.	Henry Son of Thomas Stollery.
Feb^r	4th.	Henry & Elizabeth son & daughter of William Creeting both buried in one grave frō St Lawr.
Febr.	16.	William son of Thomas May.
Feb^r	21.	Margaret Martin.
Mar.	9.	Thomas son of Thomas Creswell.
Mar.	7th.	Samuel Wallage.
Mar.	15.	Richard Porter esquire.
Mar.	14.	John Francis.

Geo. Raymond.

Page 163.

Burials 1703.

April	4th.	Margaret wife of William Boycatt.
April	7th.	Elizabeth Clench widd.
April	15th.	A child of William Lockwood frō St Mary Elms.
May	9th.	John Brown from St Mary Key.
May	16th.	Zachariah Wilton an infant.
May	21.	Ann Proctor an infant frō St Mary Key.
May	29.	Ann Trapnall from St Lawrence.
May	30.	Sarah Blichenden.
June	4.	Samuel Denton from St Mary Key.
June	17.	Basil Hewit from St Mary Elms.
Aug.	16.	Elizabeth daughter of Thomas May.

Aug.	22.	Penelope Cabine.
Sept^r	12.	Alice Osborne.
Sept^r	30.	Jane Ponder from St Mary Elms.
Octob.	19.	Francis Bird from St Peters.
Octob.	27.	Sarah Sharp wife of Peter Sharp.
Octob.	31.	Nathaniel son of John May an Infant.
Dec^r	5.	George Hill.
Dec^r	27.	Mary Daniell.
Feb^r	1st.	Bridget Shrive widd.
Febr.	20.	Mary Baker from St Peters.
Mar.	19.	Alice Kersee from St Peters.

1704.   1704.

March	28.	Elizabeth a base child of Susan Richerson.
May	1st.	Richard a base son of Susan Richerson.
May	2^d.	Dorcas Smith widd.
May	5th.	Abigail Clarke from St Mary Key.
May	21.	Charles son of George Mayer.
May	26.	Mary wife of John Boycatt.
June	2^d.	Anne wife of Jonathan Riley.
June	7th.	Robt. Reader from St Mary Tower.
June	16.	John Hall.
July	1st.	A child of John May.
August	6.	Thomasin Lockwood from St Peters.
Sept^r	1.	Edward Cooke from St Peters.
Sept^r	13.	Prudence Harecock from Stutton.
Sept^r	22.	Elizabeth wife of George Mayer.
Sept^r	29.	Sarah wife of Daniel Creswell from St M. Elms.
Octob.	22.	John son of Robt. Dash.
Octob.	25.	Philip Baddesun.
Decemb.	3.	Anthony son of John Boycat.

Geo. Raymond M^r.

Page 164.

1704.   .   Mary Smith widd Jan. 3.

Jan.	14.	Margaret Bond widd from St Mary Key.
	21.	John son of Henry Snell.
Jan.	23.	{ Samuel son of Robt. Smith. { Susan Gildersleeve. { Mary Skeet widd.
Feb^r	13.	Robert son of Robt. Bond.
March	11th.	Rebecca Lockwood from St Peters.

1705.   1705.

April	6th.	Mary daughter of John Boycat.
Apr.	15.	James Stebbing from St Peters.
Apr.	19.	Frances Gee a stranger.
Apr.	24.	Susan wife of John Bundock.
Apr.	30.	Deborah Church widd.
May	29.	Thomas Wilson.

June	10.	Jonah son of John Thorne from St Clemẽts.
June	15.	Sarah daughter of Michael Daniel.
July	15.	Elizabeth daughter of Wiłłi Osborn from St Stephens.
July	30.	Elizabeth Covel.
Aug.	2.	Robert Ventris Clerke from Hopford [? Copford] in Essex certifyd ye letts by Mr Slinger.
Aug.	28.	Michael Daniel.
Sept^r	14.	Abigail Hardy Widd. from Bently.
Sept^r	10.	Mary Danks Widd.
Sep^{tr}	24.	John Haward from St Peters.
Sept^r	30.	Alice Lockwood from St Peters.
Octob.	15.	Susan wife of Thomas Kendal.
Octob.	28.	Elizabeth daghter of Thomas Stollery.
Octob.	29.	Susan daughter of Thomas Kendall.
dec^r	12.	Elizabeth daughter of Christian Brown.
dec^r	27.	Mary Findly a base infant.
Febr.	15.	Lady Margaret ventris from Hopford [? Copford] in Essex certified by letter by Mr Slinger.
Febr.	25.	John Alderidge.
Febr.	27.	Jacob son of John May.
Mar.	15.	Willm Coleman.
Mar.	21.	Abraham Chinery from St Peters.

1706.   1706.

Mar.	28.	Susan Richerson Widd.
April	9.	Sarah Skinner from St Stephens.
April	23.	Henry Knights.

                                            Geo. Raymond.

Page 165.

June	3.	Rebecka daughter of Stephen Bond from St Mathews.
June	11.	Deborah Sidey.
June	16.	Thomas Topley.
July	2.	John son of John Brazier.
July	14.	Mary Daniel widd.
July	15.	Lettice Newton an infant.
July	21.	Samuel Dash an infant.
July	31.	Thomas Osborn from St Stephens.
Sept^r	3.	Anne Browning.
Sept^r	15.	Sarah Rosse from St Mary Elms.
Sept^r	16.	Jonathan Daniel an Infant.
Octob.	9.	Mary Church Widd.
Octob.	20.	Mary Golden Widd from St M. Elms.
Octob.	23.	Sarah wife of Tho. Creswell.
Nov^r	10.	Catharine Radford an Infant.
Nov^r	14.	Mr John Ventris.
dec^r	13.	Joseph Humphery.
Jan.	14.	Anne Hayward from St Mary Key.
febr.	26.	Mary Skeet an infant from St Clements.
febr.	28.	Henry Trvelove an infant from St Larence.

Mar.	5.	Rebecha Woolnough.
Mar.	7.	William Morris from S^t mathews.
Mar.	14.	Eliz. wife of William Morris from St Math.

1707.		1707.
Aprill	15.	Thomas Boycatt an Infant 1707.
May	15.	John Manning from St Mary Elms 1707.
June	2^d.	Rebecka Lockwood from St Peters.
June	3^d.	John Colbe from ye Gaol.
June	29.	Robert Bloum from ye Goal.
July	1st.	Joseph son of John May.
July	18.	Alice Toply Widd.
July	27.	John Brown an Infant.
July	31.	Mary Haywood Widd.
Aug.	10.	Edward Lewes from St Peters.
Aug.	19.	Willm Barber from ye Goal.
Sept^r	9.	Willm Cole.
Sept^r	11.	Mary Cook Widd.
Nov^r	2.	James Smith from St Lawrence.
Nov^r	12.	Phillip Ead from ye Goal.
Jan.	25.	Elizabeth Rose an ffant from St Mary Elms.
Febr.	5.	Elizabeth Sanders widd from St Lawrence.
Febr.	13.	Mary May from St Mary Tower.
Mar.	7.	William Proctor an Infant.

Geo. Raymond M^r.

Page 166.   Burialls 1708.

April	27.	Thomas Toply from St Mary Elmes.
May	8.	John Reeve from ye Goal.
June	10.	Elizabeth Fenning from St Mary Elms.
July	26.	Elizabeth Beamont.
July	30.	Hannah Palmer widd.
Aug.	3^d.	Margaret Jennings.
Aug.	27.	John Boyse gent.
Sept^r	3.	John Canting from St Stephens.
Sept^r	3.	John Allen son of John Allen.
Sept^r	12.	Thomas Balls.
Octob.	2.	Sarah Knights widd.
Octob.	4.	Francis Canny from St Mary Elms.
Octob.	31.	Mary Creeting an Infant from St Lawrence.
Nov^r	15.	Richard Girling from Stoke.
Nov^r	20.	Francis Hildyard Cler.
Dec^r	2^d.	John Starlin from ye Goal.
Dec^r	12.	Anne Reader Widd.
Dec^r	12.	Thomas Hewit.
Dec^r	27.	Elenor Leweing.
Jan.	2.	Susan Tillerson Widd.
Febr.	6.	John Bret from ye goal.
Mar.	2^d.	Anne Lock.

1709.		1709.
April	1 τ .	Robert Newton Son of Richard Newton.
April	17.	George Son of George Pratt.
April	24.	Andrew Findly.
May	6.	Christian Truelove from St Law.
May	15.	Mary Butterfeild from St M. Elms.
June	9.	Stephen Willowby Hawis a base child from St Peters.
Aug.	4.	Anne Green.
Aug.	9.	Margaret Lockwood an Infant.
Septemb^r	8.	Elizabeth Scarlet.
Sept^r	16.	Phœbe Hawes Widd From St Peters.
Sept^r	23.	Francis Cushine from St Lawrence.
Sept^r	26.	Thomas Hewit.
Sept^r	28.	Phillip Butterfeild.
Sept^r	29.	Susan Blichenden.
Octob.	21.	Robert Bond an Infant.
October	27.	Ann Clarke.
Nov^r	10.	Penelope Canadie widd.
Nov^r	23.	William Tought an Infant.
Nov^r	30.	John Whitehead.
Dec^r	1st.	Alice wife of Thomas Rendall.

Page 167. Geo. Raymond.

January	27.	Henry Creeting from St Lawrence.
Febr.	5.	Martha Allen an Infant.
Mar.	19.	Anne ye wife of Thomas Toply.

1710.   1710.

April	20.	Nathaniel Creak from St Mary Stoke.

Pages 168, 169. *nil.*

Page 170.

Ministers of St. Nicholas.

Mr John Daye	1612.	Mr Alexander Reignolds	1637.
Mr Jonathan Clarke	1616.	Mr Nat Smart junior	1642.
Mr Nathaniel Smart	1617.	Mr Will Clarke	1646.
Mr Richard Raymond	1633.	Mr Roger Young	1653.
Mr William Kerington	1635.		

Oct^r	17.	Joane of Henry Norman bapt.
Oct.	19.	Joane of Henry Normã was buried.
Oct.	25.	John Beck & Prudence Belk were married.
Oct.	28.	Thomas of Thomas Sudgricke & Mary his wife Buried ? wyeir ?

Mr Roberts	1664.	Mr Willm Reeve	1725.
Mr Elseden	1666.	Mr Robert Hudson	1755.
Mr Thomas Holborough	1670.	Mr J^s Coyte	1785.
M^{cr} George Raymand			
June the first	1684.		

Finis Registri Book.

N

INDEX LOCORUM.

Compiled by SIDNEY J. MADGE, Esq., F.R.H.S.

INDEX NOMINUM.

Compiled by SIDNEY J. MADGE, Esq., F.R.H.S.

O

P

R

CORRECTIONS.

Page 93, first line, tenth word, *for* " **Ann**, *read* " And."
Index.—Boult, Fayth, 72 ; Robert, 72.

THE REGISTERS

OF

NICHOLAS, IPSWICH,

CO. SUFFOLK.

Issued to Subscribers by

THE PARISH REGISTER SOCIETY.

1897.

REGISTERS PRINTED.

1. BANSTEAD, - - - - SURREY.
2. WORCESTER, ST. ALBANS, - WORCESTERSHIRE.
3. BEER HACKETT, - - - DORSET.
4. NORTH LUFFENHAM, - - RUTLAND.
5. MONK FRYSTON, - - - YORKSHIRE.
6. STRATFORD-ON-AVON, - - WARWICKSHIRE.
7. IPSWICH, ST. NICHOLAS, - SUFFOLK.

PROSPECTIVE WORK.

1. TOTTERNHOE, - - - BEDFORDSHIRE.
2. UPTON, - - - - BERKSHIRE.
3. SWETTENHAM, - - - CHESHIRE.
4. UPTON OR OVERCHURCH, - CHESHIRE.
5. REPTON, - - - - DERBYSHIRE.
6. PLYMTREE, - - - - DEVONSHIRE.
7. LYDLINCH, - - - - DORSET.
8. SARNESFIELD, - - - HEREFORDSHIRE.
9. CHISLEHURST, - - - KENT.
10. DODDINGTON, - - - LINCOLNSHIRE.
11. WILLESDEN, - - - MIDDLESEX.
12. MOULTON, - - - NORTHAMPTONSHIRE.
13. LEIGH, - - - - STAFFORDSHIRE.
14. IPSWICH, ST. MATTHEW, - SUFFOLK.
15. WEYBRIDGE, - - - SURREY.
16. EAST GRINSTEAD, - - SUSSEX.
17. WESTBOURNE, - - - SUSSEX.
18. BAMPTON, - - - - WESTMORLAND.
19. MADDINGTON, - - - WILTSHIRE.
20. KIRK ELLA, - - - - YORKSHIRE.

AND OTHERS.

UNDER THE PATRONAGE OF HER MAJESTY THE QUEEN.

Vol. I., complete, with Index in cloth, £1 5s.

THIRD SERIES, Quarterly, Price 2s. 6d.

ANNUAL SUBSCRIPTION, 10s. 6d., post free.

Miscellanea Genealogica

et Heraldica.

Illustrated with Facsimiles of Grants of Arms and Old Charters in Colours, Armorial Book Plates, Seals, Autographs, etc.

EDITED BY

JOSEPH JACKSON HOWARD, LL.D., F.S.A.

Second Series, enlarged and improved. Vols. I., II., III., IV. and V., complete, with Indexes, etc., in cloth, £1 5s. each, or £5 10s. the set ; the Volume contains Numbers for Two Years. Indexes, etc., to each Volume, separately, price 5s. Cases, 2s. Back Numbers of this Series, Price 1s. each.

New Series of the above, consisting of Vols. I., II., III., and IV., with Indexes, price £1 1s. each, in cloth, or £4 the set. Comprising Memoranda relating to more than 1000 Families, Illustrated with upward of 500 Armorial Bookplates, Engravings of Arms, Autographs, Seals, etc. The back Numbers of this Series are on Sale, price 8d. each.

LONDON :

MITCHELL & HUGHES, 140, Wardour Street, W.